ASTRONOMY
A PRACTICAL GUIDE

Above This false colour image of Neptune was one of the first taken by Voyager in the approach to the planet.

ASTRONOMY
A PRACTICAL GUIDE

Brian Jones

Eagle
Editions

A QUANTUM BOOK

Published by Eagle Editions Ltd
11 Heathfield
Royston
Hertfordshire SG8 5BW

This edition printed 2004

ISBN 1-86160-897-7

QUMROM

This book is produced by
Quantum Publishing
6 Blundell Street
London N7 9BH

Manufactured in Hong Kong by
Regent Publishing Services Ltd.
Printed in Singapore by
Star Standard Industries (Pte) Ltd.

CONTENTS

THE SKIES ABOVE US

THE CELESTIAL SPHERE

LOOKING THROUGH LENSES

OBSERVING OUR NEIGHBOURS

STAR SEARCH

TAKING A TRIP THROUGH THE UNIVERSE

Astronomy is a pursuit of the imagination. To look up at the stars on a clear dark night is to take yourself away from Earth and to visit the objects you see. Astronomy is an interest sometimes decried because you are unable to touch what you see. To many people, a thing becomes interesting only through the sense of touch. This is fine for some things, but how often does an art lover actually touch the Mona Lisa, a conservationist take a walk through the steamy rainforests of the Amazon or a lover of classical music visit Vienna? Of course these things do happen, but for the vast majority the enjoyment of looking and listening from afar is enough. To dismiss astronomy for these reasons is to admit a lack of imagination.

Astronomers have it lucky! The universe is a celestial art gallery and a limitless physical and chemical laboratory. It has tracked and charted the paths of human history. In many ways it has defined our destinies, and there is much in astronomy to keep even the historian happy. The exploration of the solar system by automatic probes has resulted in breathtaking images of the other members of our cosmic neighbourhood, images that cannot fail to stir a sense of wonder in those who see them. The future of the human race lies in the stars, the destination for those who will, some day, break the bonds of Earth. The stars are also our roots. The material that fed the nebula from which the Sun, the planets and life on Earth evolved was created in vast cosmic factories – stars that exploded to release the heavy elements. And, who knows? – those elements may have been used in building life on other planets in the universe.

Yes, astronomy is for those who are willing to be imaginative. Next time you are out under the stars, leave your physical form here on Earth and let your imagination take you out beyond the confines of our pitifully small planet. Let it take you out past the cratered and pitted Moon, our planet's faithful attendant for billions of years; out beyond Mars, the Red Planet, the catalyst for so many science fiction novels; out beyond gigantic Jupiter, its dense atmosphere playing host to winds that whip round the planet at terrifying speed; past beautiful Saturn, enigmatic Uranus, dim Neptune and puzzling Pluto; past the cloud of embryonic comets that surround the solar system, waiting for the gravitational command of a passing star before they sweep sunward; out past the nearest stars, through the realm of the nebulae and star clusters, and beyond. Leave the Milky Way Galaxy behind as you approach and pass the Magellanic Clouds, the huge Andromeda Galaxy and the Triangulum Spiral,

Above The rich starfields of Cygnus offer much to the amateur astronomer. Straddling the northern Milky Way, this area of sky contains many interesting objects, including double and variable stars, star clusters and nebulae. Some of these objects are easy prey for amateur telescopes; others demand a somewhat higher degree of observational prowess.

congregations of billions of stars that dizzy the mind. Leave this Local Group of galaxies behind and visit other systems: galaxy clusters with seemingly infinite numbers of stars, and tiny dwarf galaxies, whose glow is so feeble that Earth-based telescopes have yet to capture and analyse it.

Finally, after a journey that would take a light ray almost 20 billion years, you will reach the edge of what astronomers call the observable universe. Yet the power of thought allows us to see beyond. We can conjure up images that

Right The dark mass of the Horsehead Nebula in Orion, first detected on a photograph taken a century ago, is seen silhouetted against the brighter nebula IC 434. This is just one of countless celestial spectacles that invite the attentions of the backyard astronomer.

make even the weird and wonderful objects catalogued, studied and sometimes understood by astronomers seem dull by comparison: images of objects that lie beyond the distant quasars and that have yet to enter our realm of experience. Until we see them, if indeed they exist, they will remain in our theories, our speculations, our hypotheses and our imagination.

The universe is indeed a beautiful place. It is our home. Using this book as a guide, go out there and look at it, see it and enjoy it for yourself.

THE SOLAR SYSTEM

The Earth is one of nine major planets orbiting the Sun. Along with the planets the solar system contains numerous smaller bodies, including minor planets, comets, meteoroids and copious amounts of interplanetary dust.

The planetary members of the solar system are split into two distinct groups, each with its own basic characteristics. The four inner planets (Mercury, Venus, Earth and Mars) are all relatively small, rocky in composition and clustered together close to the Sun. These are the terrestrial planets (from the Latin *terra*, meaning 'earth'), a name indicating that they resemble the Earth in composition. In contrast, the next four planets out from the Sun (Jupiter, Saturn, Uranus and Neptune) all have large diameters, gaseous compositions and orbits that are quite well spread out. These are the gaseous, or Jovian planets, so called because of their resemblance to Jupiter.

The formation of the solar system

The present-day layout of the solar system offers a number of clues as to how the Sun and its family came into being. From observational evidence gleaned by astronomers we have pieced together a theory as to the formation of the solar system that we believe to be correct, at least in general terms.

The solar system formed from a rotating cloud comprising gas and particles of dust and ice. This cloud is referred to as the solar nebula. Through the effect of gravity, the material in the solar nebula congregated towards the central region, resulting in an increase in density, temperature and pressure and the formation of a 'protostar'.

At the same time, the rotation of the irregular cloud caused it to flatten out into a disc. It was from the central region of this disc that the Sun was formed, the outer parts eventually forming the planets. This theory ties in quite well with observation, which shows us that the planetary orbits are more or less in the same plane.

It was from the heavier elements, that the four inner planets were formed. The outer, gaseous planets formed primarily from the much lighter elements, mainly hydrogen and helium, that existed nearer the outer edges of the cloud. Any hydrogen and helium that may have been present in the cloud's inner regions were driven away by the heat from the young Sun, resulting in a scarcity of these elements in the four inner planets.

Particles within the solar nebula began to collide with each other. This resulted in their sticking together and accumulating into small objects with diameters of the order of a few tens of kilometres. These so-called planetesimals then began to bump into each other and, by a similar process, built up into still larger bodies known as protoplanets. Eventually the four inner planets we see today formed as more and more planetesimals collided with the protoplanets. These objects were rocky worlds, rich in the heavier elements such as iron, silicon, aluminium and so on.

At this time these bodies consisted of gas and molten rock, primarily through the heat generated by the constant impact of the sizable planetesimals. This had the effect of causing all the heavier materials to sink towards the central regions of the newly formed planets, leaving lighter, less dense material nearer their surfaces. We see the legacy of this process today in the form of the iron-rich cores and rocky outer regions of the terrestrial planets, their thick early atmospheres dispersed by the hot, young sun..

The outer planets formed in a similar way with the building up of planetesimals. An initial rocky core collected the gas that abounded in the outer regions of the solar nebula. The end results were huge gaseous planets with atmospheres rich in hydrogen, enveloping rocky cores

Above A Viking orbiter photograph of Mars, one of the four terrestrial planets. These are small rocky worlds that were formed from the heavy elements present in the inner regions of the solar nebula.

Right The comparative sizes of the Sun and planets, the smaller terrestrial planets contrasting greatly with the huge gas giants.

TABLE OF PLANETARY DATA

Planet	Diameter (km)	Mean distance from Sun (km)	Sidereal period ('year')	Axial rotation period (equatorial)
Mercury	4,878	58,000,000	87.97 d	58d 15h 30m
Venus	12,104	108,000,000	224.7 d	243d 24m 29s
Earth	12,756	149,600,000	365.265 d	23h 56m 4.07s
Mars	6,787	227,900,000	686.98 d	24h 37m 26s
Jupiter	142,800	778,300,000	11.86 y	9h 50m 33s
Saturn	120,000	1,427,000,000	29.46 y	10h 39m 22s
Uranus	50,800	2,870,000,000	84.01 y	17h 14 m
Neptune	49,500	4,497,000,000	164.79 y	18h 26m
Pluto	2,300	5,900,000,000	248 y	6d 9h 17m

	Axial tilt	Inclination of orbit to ecliptic	Mean density (gm/cm^3)	Number of Satellites
Mercury	0°	7° 00′ 26″	5.42	0
Venus	178°18′	3° 23′ 40″	5.25	0
Earth	23° 24′	-	5.52	1
Mars	25° 12′	1° 51′ 9″	3.94	2
Jupiter	3° 06′	1° 18′ 29″	1.31	16
Saturn	26° 42′	2° 29′	0.69	21
Uranus	97° 54′	0° 48′ 26″	1.3	15
Neptune	29° 36′	1° 46′ 27′	1.66	3
Pluto	94°	17° 9′ 3″	1.8	1

comparable in size to the terrestrial planets.

In the meantime, things were happening to the protostar at the centre of the nebula. Here, the temperatures and pressures at its core increased until nuclear reactions were initiated. The Sun as we know it then came into being. This turning-on of the Sun occurred at the same time as the Earth itself was finally formed. The newborn Sun shed its outermost layers into surrounding space, the material ejected sweeping through the interplanetary medium and clearing it of much of the remaining debris, leaving the solar system much as it is now. Many of the remaining larger particles impacted onto the surfaces of the newly formed planets, modelling the rugged, crater-strewn surfaces that exist today.

	Mass (Earth = 1)	Magnitude at brightest	Escape velocity (km/sec)
Mercury	0.056	-1.9	4.3
Venus	0.815	-4.4	10.3
Earth	-	-	11.2
Mars	0.107	-2.8	5.0
Jupiter	317.83	-2.6	61
Saturn	95.16	-0.3	35.6
Uranus	14.50	+5.6	21.2
Neptune	17.20	+7.7	23.6
Pluto	0.003	+13.6	1

THE SUN

Containing around 98 per cent of the total mass of the solar system, the Sun dominates our region of space. As well as making life on our planet possible, the light and heat from our parent star greatly influence the other objects in our neighbourhood. Yet, bright as the Sun appears to us, it ranks as just an average star when compared to many of the other stars scattered throughout the Galaxy. The Sun has a diameter of 1,392,000 km (865,000 miles) and, classed as a yellow dwarf, it is a typical main-sequence star (see p.38).

The temperature of the visible surface of the Sun is of the order of 6,000°C (11,000°F). This region of the Sun is called the photosphere, a name that means 'sphere of light', and it is from here that all the Sun's light and heat are emitted. Yet the prodigious amounts of energy that leave the Sun are created deep within its globe. Down at the core, the temperature and pressure are so high that nuclear reactions are taking place. A temperature of over 15 million°C (27 million°F) combines with a pressure of around 340,000 million atmospheres to sustain a reaction known as hydrogen burning, in which four hydrogen nuclei are fused together to form one nucleus of helium. In the process, a tiny amount of mass is converted to energy and carried to the surface, where it escapes as light and heat. This mass loss is equal to 0.7 per cent of the total amount of hydrogen used in the reaction – amounting to 4 million tonnes per second!

Close examination of the photosphere shows it to have a mottled appearance. This so-called granulation is a result of the eruption of energy at the solar surface. The turbulence set up by energy erupting from within the Sun creates bright granules that measure around 1,000 km (625 miles) across. A darker boundary is seen to surround each granule. Observation has shown that the bright areas are regions where hot gases are emerging, only to cool by some 300°C (540°F) and spill down through the darker boundaries.

Other features visible on the photosphere are sunspots, depressions in the photosphere that appear as dark patches when seen against the brighter and hotter background. Sunspots come in a wide variety of sizes, although typically they are several tens of thousands of kilometres across.

The average lifetime of a typical sunspot is a few days and its temperature is around 4,000°C (7,000°F). Sunspots have a dark central region known as the umbra, which is surrounded by a lighter region, the penumbra. Although sunspots can appear on the solar disc at any time, there is a definite cycle of sunspot activity. This cycle was first noted in 1843 by the German astronomer Heinrich Schwabe, who pointed out that sunspot activity reached a maximum once every 11 years. During the early part of a cycle sunspots appear some 30° north or south of the solar equator. As the cycle progresses they develop nearer and nearer the equator.

Sunspots

Sunspots are associated with intense magnetic fields and these give rise to a number of phenomena that occur near the spots. Faculae are highly luminous areas above which are seen regions where sunspots are about to form. Some of the most spectacular sunspot-related features, however, are prominences, huge columns of gas that appear above sunspots. Prominences are of two types. Eruptive

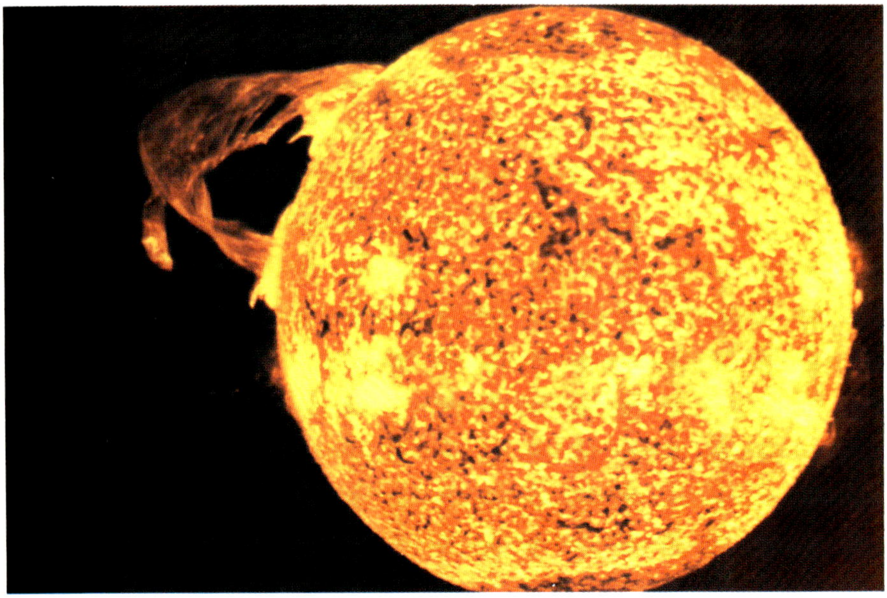

Left Skylab astronauts recorded this giant prominence as it erupted from the Sun over a period of two hours on 19 December 1973. The material within the prominence is clearly seen to be confined in a 'braided' formation by the magnetic field. This prominence was one of the largest seen in a decade. The temperature of the gas within it was generally about 20,000 °C (36,000 °F), but reached 70,000 °C (125,000 °F) in places.

Above A cross-sectional view of the sun. In the hot central core occur the nuclear reactions that create the Sun's energy. This energy, produced through the conversion of hydrogen into helium, travels part of the way to the surface in the form of radiation. It is then carried up to the photosphere by convection, the rising of hot gas. At the surface the energy escapes as light and heat. Many different types of feature are visible on or above the photosphere, including prominences, an example of which is seen here. Above the photosphere is the chromosphere, a layer of hydrogen, rarefied glowing red and thousands of kilometres thick. (In reality the chromosphere cannot be seen since the dazzling white photosphere shines through it.) The extremely tenuous corona, which has no definite boundary, extends above the chromosphere into the depths of the solar system.

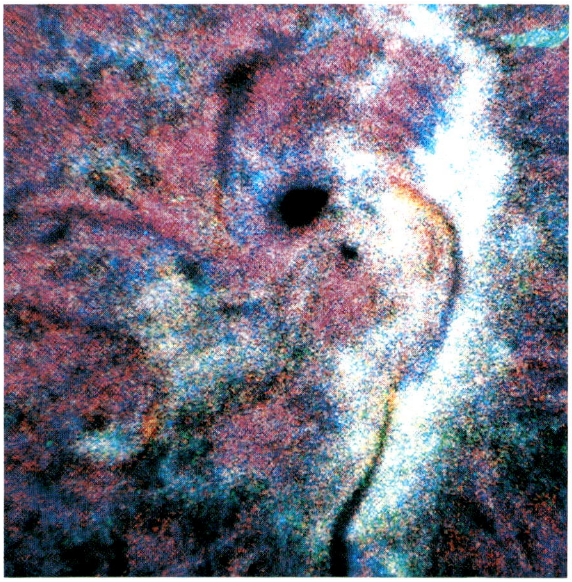

Above In this false-colour image of a sunspot region, the sunspots can be seen as black patches. The white areas are gas in the chromosphere, situated just above the sunspots and trapped by the magnetic field.

prominences are the result of material being lifted away from the Sun at colossal speeds of up to 1,000 km (600 miles) per second. Their form can change from minute to minute. Quiescent prominences, on the other hand, are relatively stable and have been known to hang above the solar surface for periods of up to several months.

Flares are the most active of solar phenomena. These arise within complex sunspot groups as bright filaments of hot gas, the temperatures of which can soar to several millions of degrees within a very short time. Flares can give rise to vast increases in the amount of charged particles emanating from the Sun, resulting in a sometimes dramatic increase in the frequency and intensity of auroral displays in the Earth's atmosphere.

Above the photosphere lies the chromosphere. This is a relatively cool region through which solar energy passes on its way from the Sun. It is in this region that the flares described above are seen. Above the chromosphere is the corona, the outermost region of the Sun's atmosphere. The corona reaches out from just above the chromosphere to a distance of several million kilometres. It is within the inner regions of the corona that prominences appear. Its outer regions stretch out until it becomes the stream of energized particles called the solar wind.

MERCURY AND VENUS

Mercury

Orbiting the Sun once every 87.97 days, at a mean distance of 58 million km (36 million miles), Mercury is the innermost planet. It is similar in size to the Moon, with a diameter of only 4,878 km (3,031 miles). It is also similar to the Moon in appearance. The Mariner 10 mission, launched in November 1973, made several flybys, revealing a surface covered in craters, mountains, ridges and valleys. There were fewer of the dark plains that dominate the lunar surface, however, the largest of those on Mercury being named the Caloris Basin.

Early observers believed that Mercury had a captured, or synchronous, rotation period, with one hemisphere permanently facing the Sun. However, radar measurements carried out in the early 1960s showed that the true axial rotation period was 58.65 days. This means that the planet spins exactly three times during two revolutions of the Sun. All parts of Mercury's surface therefore receive sunlight at some time or another. The result of this so-called spin orbit coupling is that the Mercurian solar day (sunrise to sunrise) is 176 Earth days long, or two Mercurian years.

One curious aspect of the relationship between Mercury's axial rotation period, its year, and the Earth's year is that the same hemisphere is presented to Earth every time the planet is best placed for observation. It is this that led early observers to believe that Mercury had a captured rotation.

The Mercurian atmosphere is so rarefied that it betters the best vacuum capable of being produced in a laboratory on Earth. A major reason is the fact that Mercury's escape velocity is only 4.3 km (2.67 miles) per second. Mariner 10 instruments detected traces of hydrogen and helium, probably originating from the Sun, near the Mercurian surface. Spectroscopic observations made from Earth in 1985 led to the discovery of sodium, which appears to be the most abundant component of the atmosphere. The temperature on Mercury can reach some 425 °C (800 °F) on the equator at noon, although this can drop to -180 °C (-292 °F) just before sunrise. The virtual lack of an insulating atmosphere is a major contributor to this vast range in surface temperature.

Above This photographic mosaic of Mercury's southern hemisphere is made up of over 200 separate images taken by Mariner 10 in 1975. It shows the planet's heavily cratered surface. (The indentation at the top of the picture represents an area for which no data was returned by the spacecraft.)

Below Part of the Venera 14 spacecraft can be seen in the foreground of this image of the Venusian surface taken in 1982. Reddish-brown rocks can be seen stretching away to the horizon, above which is a conspicuously orange sky.

Venus

Venus is the second planet out from the Sun, which it orbits every 225 days at a mean distance of 108 million km (67 million miles). It is the planet which can come closest to the Earth and the brightest object in our sky apart from the Sun and Moon. The reason for its brilliance is the fact that it is covered in dense white clouds, which reflect 79 per cent of the sunlight received by the planet. There are no features on the visible disc that are permanent enough for accurate measurements of the rotation period to be made. However, in 1961, radar signals were bounced from the surface of the planet. Those received back from the approaching side were of a higher frequency than those on the receding side, owing

Left Ultraviolet image of the Venusian cloud tops, taken by Mariner 10 as it passed the planet in February 1974. The blue areas do not represent the visible appearance of Venus but result from processing techniques designed to reveal ultraviolet features. Swirls of cloud at top and bottom highlight the planet's polar regions.

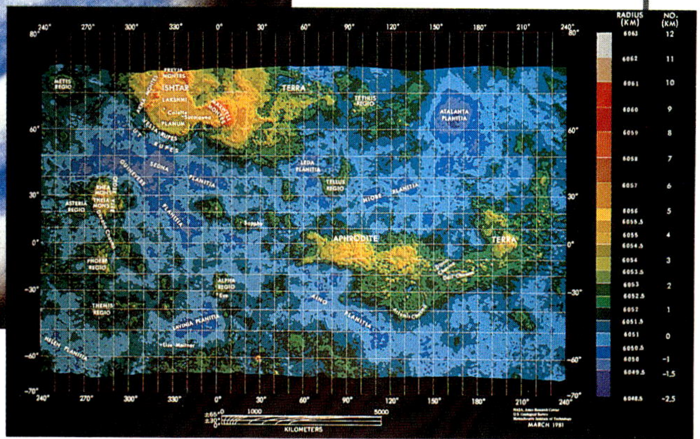

Above Topographic map of Venus compiled from Pioneer-Venus radar measurements. The two main highland areas, Ishtar and Aphrodite, are clearly visible. So are two suspected shield volcanoes, Rhea and Theia Mons.

to the Doppler effect. These observations, coupled with subsequent measurements, have led to the determination of an axial rotation period of 243.02 days. Remarkably, the rotation is retrograde (opposite to the direction of orbital movement).

The principal constituent of the Venusian atmosphere is carbon dioxide, although traces of many other materials have been found, including hydrogen sulphide, carbon monoxide, water vapour, sulphur dioxide, argon, krypton and xenon. The atmosphere extends to a height of around 250 km (150 miles) above the Venusian surface, although 90 per cent of it is concentrated within 28 km (17 miles) of the surface. The result is a surface pressure of around 90 times that on the Earth. The temperature is well over 400 °C (750 °F). This extreme temperature is due to a runaway greenhouse effect: the heat received from the Sun at the surface is trapped by carbon dioxide and is unable to escape back into space.

All our knowledge of the Venusian surface has come from Soviet and American space probes. Radar mapping has shown us that most of the Venusian surface consists of rolling plains, although there are several highland regions. These include the two areas Aphrodite Terra, which straddle the equator, and Ishtar Terra in the north. The latter contains several mountains, including Maxwell Montes, the highest mountains on Venus, situated at the eastern end of Ishtar and rising to around 11 km (7 miles) above the mean surface of Venus. Near Maxwell Montes is Cleopatra Patera, an impact crater 1.5 km (1 mile) deep, 100 km (60 miles) in diameter, which has a smaller crater 1 km ($^1/_2$ mile) deep and 55 km (35 miles) in diameter at its centre. Ishtar itself is about the size of Australia and has an average height of almost 3 km (2 miles). Aphrodite is comparable in size to Africa.

Another highland region is Beta Regio, which contains Rhea Mons and Theia Mons, two large and possibly active shield volcanoes, 4 km (2$^1/_2$ miles) high. Another feature of note is Diana Chasma, a huge valley comparable in size to the Valles Marineris system on Mars. Diana Chasma is the deepest fracture on Venus, with a depth of around 2 km (1$^1/_4$ miles) and a width of nearly 300 km (180 miles).

THE EARTH

The Earth is the third planet out from the Sun. It is very unlike Venus, with its covering of corrosive cloud and inferno-like surface conditions, and the fourth planet Mars, with its barren, desert landscape and tenuous atmosphere. Earth's nitrogen-rich atmosphere plays host to constantly changing weather patterns. It enshrouds a world covered primarily by seas and oceans with a variety of land masses, some ice-covered, others basking in tropical temperatures. It is a world ideally suited to the needs of mankind, its dominant species.

Plate tectonics

Even a casual look at a map of the Earth will reveal some interesting facts. It can be seen that the continents of Africa and South America would, if not for the intervention of the Atlantic Ocean, fit together like a huge jigsaw. The same applies to North America and Europe. This was noticed earlier this century by the German meteorologist and geophysicist Alfred Lothar Wegener. He was of the opinion that an original supercontinent, which he called Pangaea, broke up some 200 million years ago and began to drift apart. This theory has since been refined. It is now thought that the original land mass first of all broke into two pieces, a northern Laurasia and a southern Gondwanaland. Laurasia then divided into North America, Asia (except India) and Europe, while Gondwanaland became Africa, South America, India, Australia and Antarctica.

The idea of drifting continents was initially scorned, but current research has verified it. The problem with the original idea was that nobody knew just what was pushing these huge land masses across the Earth's surface. However, the discovery of volcanoes on the floor of the oceans solved the problem. The new material that is being ejected from inside the Earth along such formations as the Mid-Atlantic Ridge causes the ocean floor to expand and spread out, with the result that the continents on either side are moving apart at the rate of several centimetres (about an inch) per year. This so-called seafloor spreading has been linked with continental drift to formulate 'plate tectonics'.

Examination of seismic activity has led to the realization that the Earth's crust and upper, solid mantle is a region called the lithosphere, which is divided into a number of major and minor plates. Continents and ocean floors are of much lighter material and are simply carried around by the plates; the plates float on a layer of liquid, lower mantle rock called the asthenosphere. Beneath this layer extends the planet's molten outer core.

Currents within the Earth's mantle result in the expulsion of material through joint lines between plates. These joint lines are the ocean ridges, the effect of this upwelling of material being to force the two adjoining plates away from each other. Where plates collide, one can be dragged down below the other, resulting in the formation of an oceanic trench. The deepest known example is the Mariana Trench in the north-west Pacific Ocean, which has a maximum depth of over 11,000 m (36,000 ft). Mountain ranges can also be formed, such as the Himalayas, which have arisen through the collision of the Indian and Asian plates.

Air and water

The Earth's atmosphere differs greatly from those of its two neighbouring planets. Both the Venusian and Martian atmospheres are composed almost entirely of carbon dioxide, while the Earth's atmosphere contains very little. The dominant material in our atmosphere is nitrogen, which constitutes 77 per cent of the total atmospheric content. This is coupled with around 21 per cent oxygen, a gas which is almost nonexistent on either Venus or Mars. Why is our atmosphere so different? The answer lies with the abundance of life that populates the Earth's surface. Life has existed in one form or another on our planet for over three billion years, and the mechanisms of life, including processes such as photosynthesis, are mainly responsible for the atmosphere we have today. Our planet also has an abundance of water. This covers over 70 per cent of the Earth's surface, and has a total area of around 363 million sq. km (140 million sq. miles). Again, this is in stark contrast to either Mars or Venus, both of which are extremely arid and inhospitable worlds.

Right This photograph of Earth was taken by Apollo 15 astronauts and shows the continent of South America at centre and western Africa at upper right. The largest of the terrestrial planets, Earth is widely acknowledged to be the most beautiful planet of the Sun's family. A visiting space traveller would be struck by the dominance of water, which is exceedingly rare elsewhere in the solar system, yet covers three-quarters of our globe and controls the circulation of the atmosphere. Water makes possible the existence of life, which has created the oxygen rich atmosphere that is also unique to the Earth.

THE EARTH'S COMPANION

The Moon is the Earth's only natural satellite - but perhaps it should be regarded as a companion planet, for the mass of the Earth is just 81 times that of the Moon. When we look at other planet and satellite systems we find that the planet is always hundreds or thousands of times more massive than the satellites that orbit it (with the exception of Pluto and Charon). The ratio between the masses of the Earth and the Moon are, in comparison, so close that the system can be regarded as a double planet.

The Moon has a diameter of 3,476 km (2,172 miles), over a quarter that of the Earth. Its axial rotation period and period of revolution around the Earth are equal at 27.3 days, which results in the Moon keeping the same face turned toward the Earth. However, the distance between the Earth and Moon varies from 356,410 km (222,756 miles) at perigee, or closest approach, to 406,697 km (254,186 miles) at apogee, its farthest point.

Thr formation of the Moon

There are several different theories as to the origin of the Moon. These include the fission theory, which states that a piece of the young, rapidly spinning Earth was ejected, eventually forming the Moon. A similar idea is that the Moon formed from a number of smaller pieces that broke away from our planet. Early supporters of these ideas pointed out that the mean density of the Moon is similar to the density of the Earth's outer layers, from which the Moon would have been ejected.

Alternatively, the moon could have formed elsewhere in the solar system and been captured by the gravitational attraction of the Earth. Or it could have formed with the Earth, in the same region of space but from a gathering of debris orbiting our planet early in its history.

The final theory, and the one most recently suggested, is the collision-ejection theory, which states that a sizable object, perhaps comparable in diameter to Mars, collided with the Earth and ejected debris into space, from which the Moon formed.

Most of the above ideas have been rejected, primarily thanks to examination of Moon rocks brought back by the Apollo astronauts 20 years ago. For example, the fission theory has been discounted because notable differences have been found between lunar and terrestrial rocks.

The most popular idea today seems to be the collision-ejection theory. According to this idea, both the Earth and the impacting body had solidified sufficiently to have formed central metallic cores, around which were thick mantles of rock. The chaos and general crowding that existed in the early history of the solar system resulted in the two objects colliding with each other, the smaller object disintegrating on impact. Its core was absorbed by the Earth's. The remaining debris went into orbit around the Earth, and eventually collected to form the Moon. This would explain the similarities in density between the Earth's outer layers and the Moon as a whole, as well as accounting for the chemical composition of the Earth and Moon and the tilt of the lunar orbit relative to our equator.

The lunar surface

Even with the naked eye the main types of lunar terrain can be distinguished. The large, dark maria constitute around 15 per cent of the total lunar surface area. Most of the remaining 85 per cent is heavily cratered highland terrain. Closer examination with binoculars or a telescope will show many other features, notable among which are mountain ranges and valleys.

The features most commonly associated with the Moon are the craters, of which many tens of thousands have been revealed by Earth-based observation and by spacecraft in lunar orbit. Practically all the craters were formed from meteoritic impacts that occurred long ago.

Many of the youngest craters can be seen to lie at the centres of huge ray systems that stretch out over the lunar surface. These rays were formed as material was ejected during the impact that created the crater. Many craters also have central mountainous peaks, created as a result of the impact.

The dark plains came into being as the result of lava flows that filled the low-lying areas of the lunar surface 3.5 billion years ago. The comparative lack of cratering on the maria indicates that these areas were formed relatively recently in the Moon's history and after the main period of meteoritic bombardment.

Right The Moon's diameter of 3,476 km makes it over a quarter of the size of Earth (diameter 12,756 km), a fact that has led astronomers to regard the Earth and Moon as a double planet rather than a planet and satellite. With the notable exception of Pluto and Charon, all the other planetary members of the solar system have satellites that are considerably smaller.

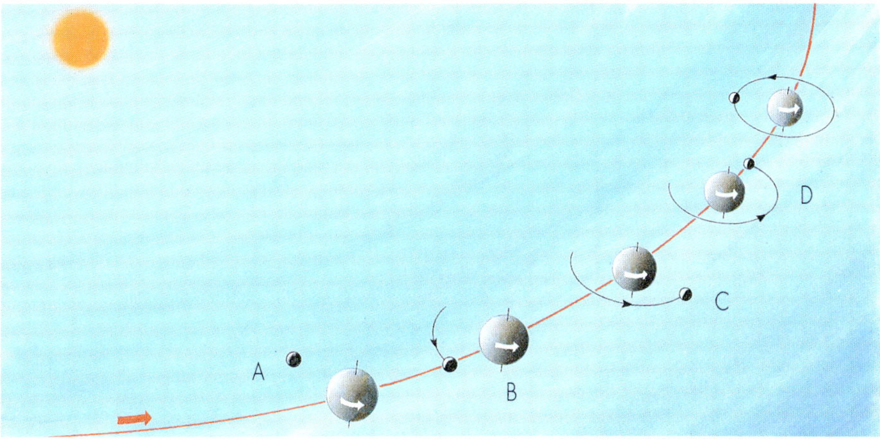

Above Lunar phases are caused by the relative positions of the Sun and Moon in the sky. New Moon occurs when the Moon is between the Sun and Earth and its sunlit half is turned away from us (A). As the Moon moves around the Earth, more of its illuminated half is presented to us, giving first quarter (B), full Moon (C) and last quarter (D). The Moon then passes between the Sun and Earth again and another new Moon occurs.

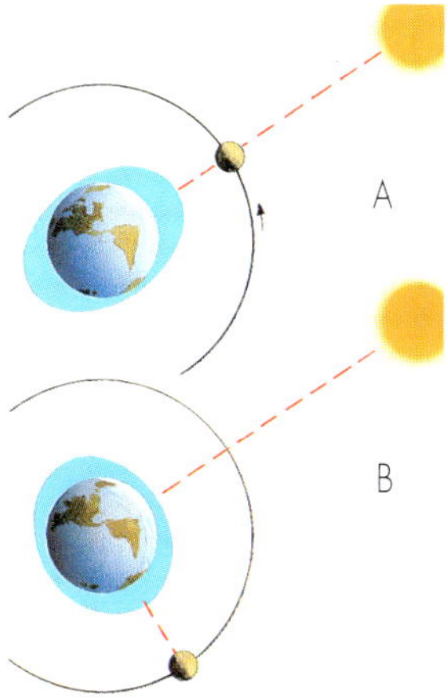

Above The gravitational force of the Moon is the main cause of tides in the Earth's oceans, although the effects of the Sun are also important. If the Sun and Moon are aligned as seen from Earth (A), their combined pull produces the strongest (spring) tides. However, when the Sun and Moon are at right angles to each other in the sky and pulling in different directions, the weakest (neap) tides take place.

Left The new Moon, seen as it sets in this wide-field photograph. The dark side of the Moon is turned towards us, and the crescent is the thin sliver of the illuminated side that we can just see. The dark side is not always wholly dark, however: at new Moon it can often be seen gleaming faintly in reflected Earthshine. This phenomenon is called 'the old moon in the new Moon's arms'.

MARS–THE RED PLANET

Mars, named after the Roman god of war, is also often referred to as the Red Planet. Its conspicuous red colour is the result of huge deserts of reddish dust scattered across the Martian surface. This dust can sometimes be raised high into the tenuous atmosphere by winds that sweep across the landscape. Sometimes these dust clouds hide vast areas of the planet from view.

Mars is the outermost of the terrestrial planets, orbiting the Sun once every 687 days at a mean distance of 228 million km (141.6 million miles). The orbit of Mars is somewhat eccentric, and the distance between Mars and the Sun varies from 206.7 million km (128.4 million miles) at its closest to 249.1 million km (154.9 million miles) at its farthest.

The Martian axial rotation period is 24h 37m 26s, just over 41 minutes longer than Earth's. The axial tilt of Mars is 25° 12' relative to the plane of its orbit around the Sun. This is similar to the Earth's axial tilt of 23° 24', resulting in Martian seasons similar to those on Earth. However, they are of much longer duration, owing to the fact that Mars takes almost twice as long to travel around the Sun.

Below This Viking Orbiter view of Mars shows both of the Martian polar caps. Craters and valleys can also be clearly discerned.

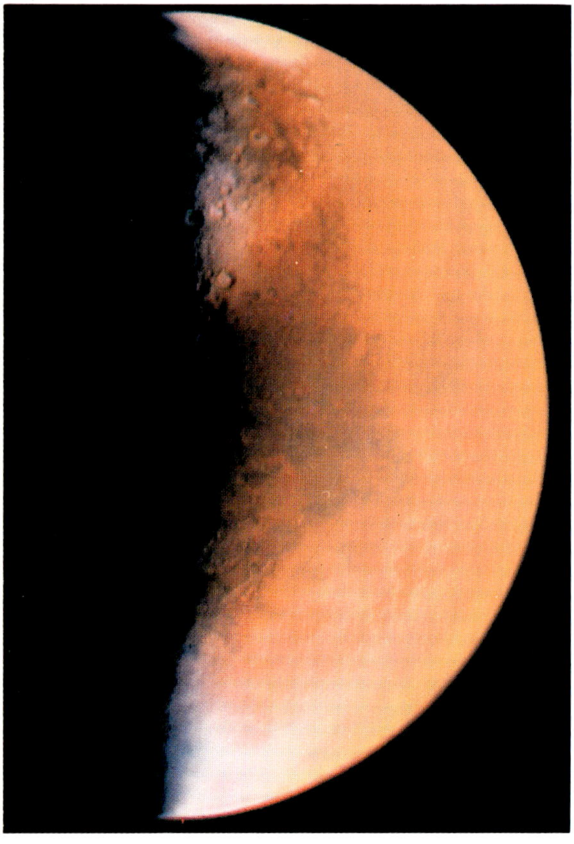

Above Water ice on the Martian surface is vaporized by the morning sunshine to form mist, as in this picture of Noctis Labyrinthus, a network of canyons.

Above A view of Chryse Planitia taken 15 minutes before sunset by the Viking 1 Lander. Surface detail is highlighted by the slanting rays of the setting Sun.

Many astronomers have been fascinated by Mars. In 1877 the Italian Giovanni Schiaparelli reported observing a number of linear features crossing the Martian surface. He referred to them as *canali*, an Italian expression meaning natural channels. However, the word soon became wrongly translated as 'canals', which are anything but natural! It was not long before the idea of an intelligent Martian civilization took hold, and astronomers, notably the American Percival

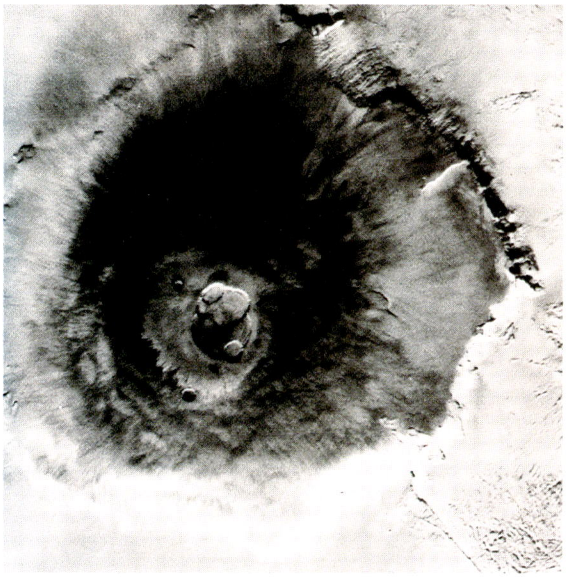

Above This Viking Orbiter photograph shows the huge shield volcano Olympus Mons, which towers 25 km (15 miles) high. Its base diameter is over 600 km (370 miles), and the caldera is 80 km (50 miles) across.

Lowell, began to report the existence of many more Martian canals. However, modern research, carried out with the benefit of space probes, has disproved the canals‘, existence.

Exploration of Mars by space probe

The first successful probes to Mars were in the American Mariner series. Mariner 4 flew past Mars in July 1965, sending back various data, including 21 pictures of the Martian terrain. Notable by their absence were Lowell's canals, although the pictures did show numerous other features, including craters. Other successful flybys were made by Mariners 6 and 7 in 1969. In November 1971 Mariner 9 went into orbit around Mars and during the following 11 months sent back well over 7,000 images before contact was lost.

The next major step forward was the successful deployment of the two Viking landers onto the surface in 1976. Each Viking mission comprised a pair of spacecraft, an orbiter and a lander. Viking 1 touched down in Chryse Planitia, a rocky area some 22° north of the Martian equator. Viking 2 set down in Utopia Planitia, around 48° north of the equator and almost on the opposite side of the planet.

The pictures received from the Viking landers showed that the sky had a reddish tint, caused by fine dust suspended in the atmosphere. The atmospheric pressure was found to be less than 1 per cent of that at the Earth's surface. The atmosphere itself consists of 95 per cent carbon dioxide, 2.7 per cent nitrogen and 1.6 per cent argon. Oxygen, carbon monoxide and water vapour make up the remainder.

The temperature at the Martian surface varies markedly throughout the day. At the equator in summer it ranges from a high of 26 °C (79 °F) in the early afternoons to -111 °C (-168 °F) before sunrise.

Martian features

Space probes have revealed a landscape containing many prominent features. Notable examples are the impressive group of shield volcanoes on the huge bulge of the Tharsis region. The largest of these is Olympus Mons, in appearance the most stunning volcano in the solar system.

Other spectacular features are the Valles Marineris, an extensive network of valleys stretching away from the area to the east of Tharsis. Named after the Mariner 9 spacecraft that discovered them, they straddle some 4,000 km (2,500 miles) of the Martian terrain and run roughly parallel to the equator.

The Mariner 9 spacecraft revealed a number of features that strongly resembled dried-up river beds. Although liquid water cannot exist on Mars today, it may have done so in the past. Where that water is today remains something of a mystery. It is known that the northern polar ice cap contains water ice covered by frozen carbon dioxide. This covering disappears with the onset of Martian summer, leaving large quantities of water ice behind. The Martian surface itself may also conceal water, locked away in the form of permafrost.

Below Mars has two moons, Phobos and Deimos, both discovered in 1877. This Viking Orbiter image shows Phobos, the larger of the two and the closer to Mars. The crater visible at the left is Stickney. The impact that produced this crater, 10 km (6.25 mile) in diameter, is also thought to have given rise to the grooves that extend from it right around Phobos.

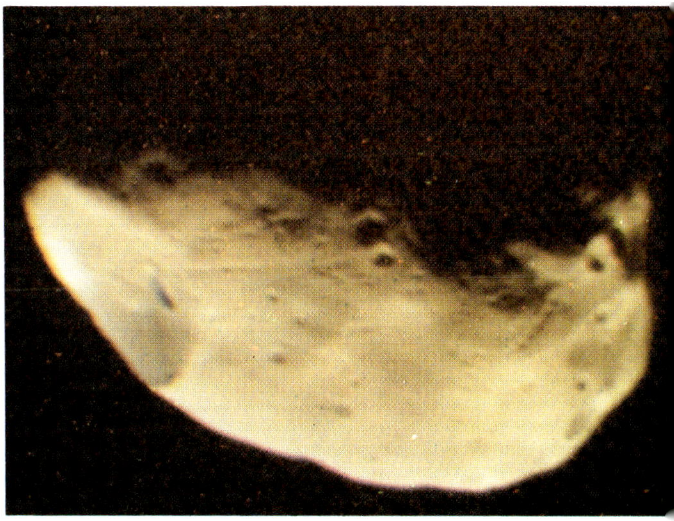

THE MINOR PLANETS

The Titius-Bode law

In 1766 the German mathematician Johann Titius brought to light an interesting numerical relationship linking the distances of the six known planets from the Sun. He took the series 0, 3, 6, 12, 24, 48 and 96, each member of which, apart from 3, has a value twice that of the previous one. Adding 4 to each he obtained 4, 7, 10, 16, 28, 52 and 100. Taking the Earth's distance as 10, it will be seen that those of the other planets fall in well with the other numbers.

One fact that stood out was that there was no planet to correspond with the value of 28. Titius suggested that there must be an undiscovered body orbiting the Sun between

Left Portrait of the Hungarian astronomer Baron Von Zach one of the chief members of the Celestial Police, the group of astronomers who organized a search for the supposed 'missing planet' orbiting the Sun between Mars and Jupiter.

Below Sizes of the four planets compared to the Moon. Ceres, the largest of the minor planets, has a diameter of only around 1,000 km (625 miles), less than a third that of our satellite. The rest of the minor planets are considerably smaller. Even if all the minor planets were collected together, their combined mass would be equivalent to only a few per cent of that of the Moon.

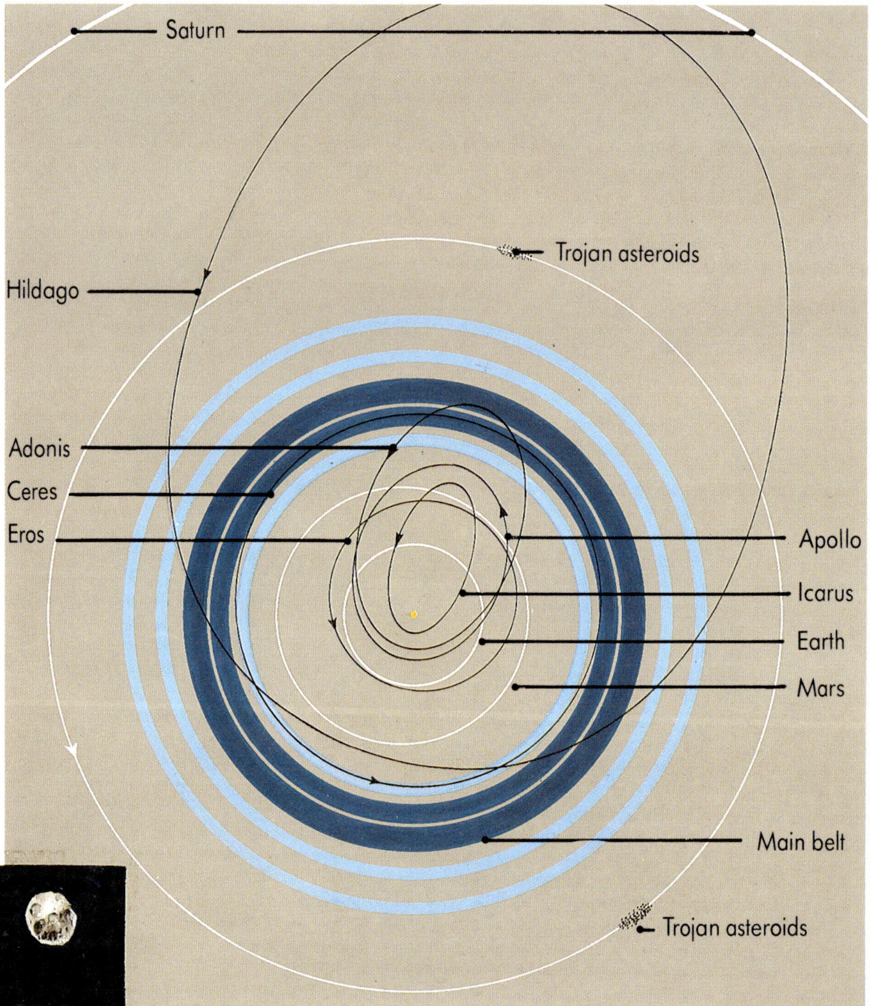

Right The German astronomer Maximilian Franz Joseph Cornelius Wolf (better known as Max Wolf) was the first to carry out a photographic search for minor planets. His efforts were almost embarrassingly successful, with over 200 discoveries being credited to his name.
Below Photographic trails of two asteroids against a background of stars.

Mars and Jupiter. He was not the first to put forward this idea. A look at any scale map of the solar system will show a marked gap between the orbits of Mars and Jupiter, and as long ago as 1596 Johann Kepler suggested that this region may play host to an extra member of the Sun's family.

At first astronomers were sceptical. However, in 1772 the German astronomer Johann Bode revived and publicized the idea. The discovery of Uranus in 1781 did much to sway opinion in its favour. Uranus was found to tie in well with the law, which gave a distance of 196 as compared with the actual value of 191.8.

The Celestial Police

In 1800 Johann Schröter called together a group of astronomers at his private observatory in Lilienthal, Germany, with the purpose of collaborating in a search for the hypothetical planet. They christened themselves the Celestial Police and decided to split the zodiacal region of the sky into a number of areas, each of which would be searched by more than one astronomer. Schröter and his team could not hope to do this alone, and many requests for help were sent out to other observers.

As luck would have it, the first minor planet came to light in January 1801, discovered quite independently of the Celestial Police by Giuseppe Piazzi, the Director of Palermo Observatory in Sicily. He came across an 8th-magnitude starlike object in Taurus that did not appear on any of the star charts of the time. Subsequent observation showed that the object was moving through the sky, and Piazzi wrote to tell a member of the Celestial Police, the Hungarian Franz Xavier von Zach. However, by the time von Zach received his letter the object had moved behind the Sun and was no longer visible. Von Zach was convinced that Piazzi had found the missing planet: the mathematician Karl Gauss calculated the orbit from the few observations available and predicted when and where it would reappear. In December von Zach spotted it almost exactly where Gauss said it would be. The orbital distance was found to be 412 million km (257 million miles), a value of 27.7 on the Titius -Bode scale.

Ceres was small by planetary standards, and subsequent searches by the Celestial Police revealed three more objects in rapid succession. Heinrich Olbers discovered Pallas in Virgo in March 1802. Karl Harding discovered Juno in Pisces in September 1804. Olbers made yet another discovery in March 1807, that of Vesta, which, like Pallas, was seen in Virgo. After the discovery of Vesta the Celestial Police made no more finds and disbanded in 1815.

Further discoveries

The next discovery was made by Karl Hencke, who had carried out a 15-year search for further minor planets. In 1845 he located 9th-magnitude Astraea in Taurus. He and others went on to discover yet more.

John Russel Hind located 10 minor planets. Hermann Goldschmidt found 14 (some from his window above the Café Procope in Paris!). Carl Luther tracked down a total of 24, and Johann Palisa, by sheer dedication, discovered 121 minor planets. All these early discoveries were made visually by astronomers who spent many hours at the telescope.

The advent of photography

In 1891 things changed remarkably when the German astronomer Max Wolf made the first photographic discovery of a minor planet, Brucia, the 323rd known. By 1900, Wolf's method had brought the total number of known minor planets to 452. By 1923 over a thousand had come to light. Their images appeared on photographic plates that were part of sometimes completely unrelated research and astronomers began to consider minor planets as a positive nuisance! However, the study of these tiny bodies may tell us much about the early history of the solar system.

JUPITER–THE GIANT PLANET

Jupiter is the king of the planets. Situated fifth in order from the Sun, it is a huge world with a mass 318 times that of the Earth and an equatorial diameter over 11 times that of our planet. Its volume is 1,430 times that of the Earth. The mass of Jupiter comprises some 70 per cent of the entire mass of the solar system excluding the Sun. Jupiter orbits the Sun at a mean distance of 778 million km (484 million miles) once every 11.86 years.

Despite its great size, Jupiter rotates faster than any other planet, the equatorial rotation period being 9h 50m 33s, as compared to 9h 55m 41s in the polar regions. The very quick rotation period has resulted in Jupiter becoming flattened, or oblate. The equatorial diameter is 143,000 km (89,000 miles) as compared to the polar diameter of 135,000 km (84,000 miles). Jupiter's pronounced equatorial bulge is visible through any telescope.

From Earth, Jupiter is one of the brightest planets, and can reach magnitude –2.6 at opposition. Telescopically it is a colourful sight, its disc being crossed by numerous 'belts' (dark bands) and 'zones' (light bands), which take on a multitude of colours including red, orange, brown and yellow. The zones are regions where gases from within the planet are

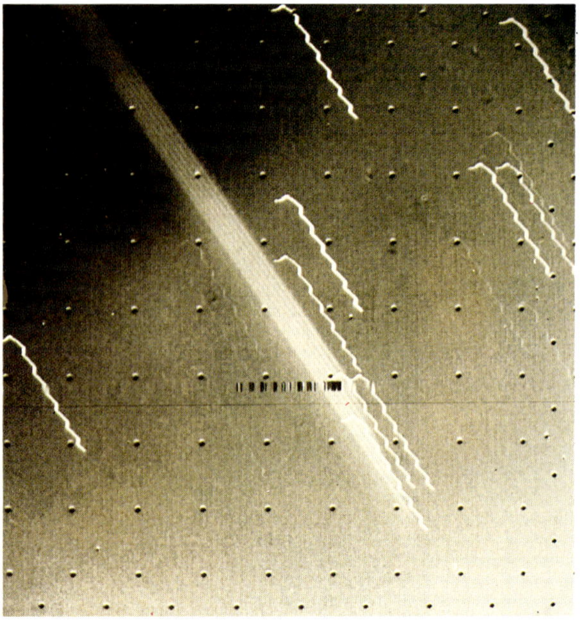

Above A Voyager 1 image, taken on 4 March 1979, revealed for the first time that Jupiter had a very thin, faint ring system. Six exposures of the ring are seen as a multiple image near the centre. The wavy star trails are the result of oscillations in the spacecraft; the dots are camera calibration points.

Right Composite picture of Jupiter together with the four Galilean satellites built up from separate Voyager images. Io can be seen at upper left, with Europa (centre), Ganymede (lower left) and Callisto (bottom right).

rising to the surface to cool; the belts are regions where cooler material is descending.

The Great Red Spot

Another feature conspicuous through earth based telescope the great Red Spot, located in the Jovian southern hemisphere and observed almost constantly since it was first seen by Cassini in 1665. This huge feature can grow to a length of 40,000 km (25,000 miles) with a width of 14,000 km (8,750 miles). Although its cause has yet to be determined, it is certainly a phenomenon of the Jovian atmosphere.

The Jovian interior

The cloudtops that we see are merely the outer layer of Jupiter's thick atmosphere. The planet comprises three main regions. On the outside is a layer comprised primarily of hydrogen 20,000 km (12,500 miles) deep. At the base of this layer, the pressures are so great that the hydrogen atoms are stripped of their electrons, which move around independently. This layer of so-called liquid metallic hydrogen is some 40,000 km (25,000 miles) deep and sits on top of a rocky core made up of iron and silicates.

Below This Voyager 2 image shows the Great Red Spot, now believed to be a huge whirling storm system. Other, smaller scale atmospheric structures can also be seen.

Below right Jupiter's swirling cloud belts and Great Red Spot can be seen in this Voyager 1 image, which also shows Io against the Jovian disc and Europa to the right.

The Galilean satellites

Jupiter has a total of 16 satellites, the four largest of which were discovered in 1610 by Galileo. (It has been suggested that an independent discovery of these four satellites may have been made by Simon Marius.) Their names are Io, Europa, Callisto and Ganymede, and they are known collectively as the Galilean satellites. Io has a diameter of 3,630 km (2,256 miles) and orbits Jupiter once every 1.77 days at a mean distance of 422,600 km (262,200 miles). It has the highest density of the Galilean satellites and is subject to frequent volcanic activity. Europa is the smallest of the Galilean satellites, with a diameter of 3,140 km (1,951 miles). It is covered by a layer of water ice thought to be around 100 km (60 miles) thick. This icy layer has many long cracks. Both Ganymede and Callisto also have crusts of water ice, but these are heavily cratered. Ganymede, the largest Jovian satellite, with a diameter of 5,276 km (3,278 miles), is also the largest satellite in the solar system. In fact, its diameter exceeds that of Mercury. Together with its craters, Ganymede has regions of grooved terrain. Callisto resembles Ganymede in many ways, with impact craters being distributed over a dark crust. The main difference in appearance between the two satellites is that there is no grooved terrain on Callisto. There is, however, the Valhalla Basin, formed by the impact of an asteroid-sized body long ago in Callisto's history.

Smaller satellites

Together with four smaller satellites (Metis, Adrastea, Amalthea and Thebe), the Galilean satellites orbit Jupiter in or very near the plane of its equator. These are the innermost of the Jovian satellites. The remaining eight satellites orbit the planet in two distinct groups. The orbital planes of Leda, Himalia, Lysithea and Elara are inclined at 24.8–29° to the Jovian equator. They all lie between 11 and 12 million km (7–7.5 million miles) from the planet. The orbits of Ananke, Carme, Pasiphae and Sinope are inclined at 147–168°, at 21–24 million km (13–15 million miles) distance.

SATURN–THE SPECTACULAR PLANET

To many observers, their first telescopic view of the planet Saturn is an event they will never forget. Even a small telescope will reveal the planet's beautiful ring system. Although many pictures of this celestial showpiece have appeared, there is nothing to compare with a first-hand sight of the planet, set against the backdrop of a velvet-black sky.

Saturn is second in size only to Jupiter: its equatorial diameter is 120,000 km (74,560 miles). A rapid axial rotation period of 10h 39m 22s (equatorial value) has resulted in a noticeably oblate appearance: the polar diameter is just 108,600 km (67,000 miles). This degree of polar flattening exceeds even that of Jupiter. Saturn has a total mass of over 95 times that of the Earth and outweighs all the other planets, with the exception of Jupiter, put together. However, one peculiarity of Saturn is its low density, amounting to around 0.7 g/cm^3, roughly half that of Jupiter. This is less than the density of water, and means that Saturn must be composed of light elements. Saturn orbits the Sun once every 29.46 years at a mean distance of 1.427 billion km (887 million miles).

Above Three of Saturn's satellites – Tethys (top), Dione and Rhea – are visible on this Voyager 2 image. The shadow of Tethys can be seen as a dark, circular patch on Saturn's southern hemisphere.

Above The complexity of Saturn's ring system can be seen in this false- colour Voyager 1 image, taken from 717,000 km (440,000 miles).

Looking inside Saturn

Like Jupiter, Saturn has an outer layer of hydrogen, although this is thought to be somewhat thicker than that of Jupiter. Beneath this is a region of liquid metallic hydrogen, which in turn envelops a rocky core, believed to be much larger than Jupiter's. Saturn's core contains around 21 per cent of the total mass of the planet: 6 per cent is the corresponding figure for Jupiter.

As with Jupiter, the outer visible layer of Saturn's atmosphere is crossed by dark and bright bands, although these are nowhere near as conspicuous or colourful as those of Jupiter. Gravity plays an important part here. The vastly greater pull of Jupiter's gravity has compressed the outer cloud layers into a total depth of around 75 km (45 miles). On Saturn the gravitational pull is much weaker, resulting in a reduced compression effect and a combined depth of the

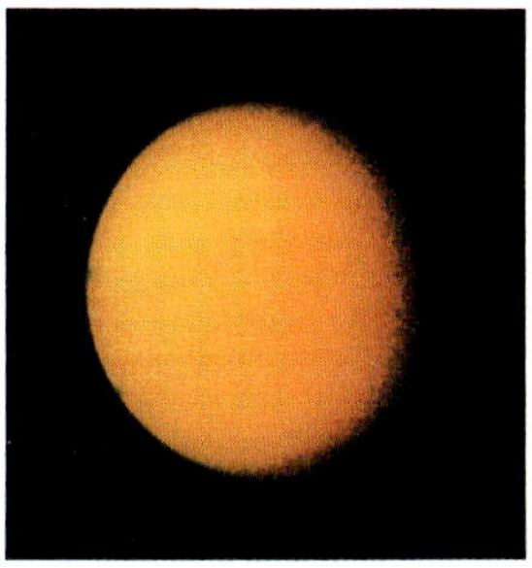

Left Titan is the only satellite in the solar system with a substantial atmosphere. Its reddish clouds completely hide the surface from view.

layers of around 300 km (190 miles). The deeper layers therefore tend to be somewhat obscured.

The atmospheric content is also different: Jupiter's atmosphere contains 82 per cent hydrogen and 17 per cent helium; Saturn's contains 88 per cent hydrogen and 11 per cent helium..

The ring system

From Earth we can see the main sections of the ring system, including the bright Ring B, the fainter Ring A and the dim Crepe Ring, otherwise known as Ring C. When the ring system is suitably presented to us, the famous Cassini Division, separating Ring A from Ring B, comes into view. Ring A also contains the Encke Division, discovered by Johann Encke in 1838.

The rings themselves are composed of countless tiny particles that range in size from several metres down to a few microns. Closer examination by space probes has revealed that each of the main sections of the ring system is composed of many hundreds of narrow, closely spaced ringlets

The probes also discovered new rings. The F Ring is only 100 km (65 miles) wide and consists of a number of intertwined strands. The D Ring is the innermost ring, extending from the C ring down to the cloudtops. The outermost G and E Rings are both extremely faint and lack the ringlet structure predominant in the brighter rings.

The satellites

Saturn has a total of 21 known satellites, the largest of which is Titan, with a diameter of 5,150 km (3,200 miles). Titan has an atmosphere, in which nitrogen is the most abundant gas (90 per cent), followed by methane and argon. The atmosphere is so thick that Voyager was unable to see down to the surface.

The surface pressure on Titan is 60 per cent greater than that of the Earth, and the surface temperature is –177 °C (–287 °F). These conditions suggest that methane ice may be found at Titan's poles, with rivers and lakes of methane at lower latitudes. There could even be falls of methane rain.

Apart from Titan, there are a further six satellites of substantial size: Phoebe, Mimas, Enceladus, Tethys, Iapetus and Rhea. Most of the 14 other satellites are irregularly shaped. As with Jupiter, the retinue of satellites around Saturn resembles a miniature solar system.

Right A cross-sectional view of Titan's atmosphere shows a surface temperature of 96K that is, 96° above absolute zero, which is –177°C (–287°F). The white line indicates temperature changes with increasing altitude. Conditions within the troposphere (below 40 km altitude) suggest that methane clouds and rain may form, leading to a weather system based on methane in much the same way that the Earth's meteorology is based on water. Methane ice may also exist in Titan's polar regions with methane rivers and lakes found at lower latitudes.

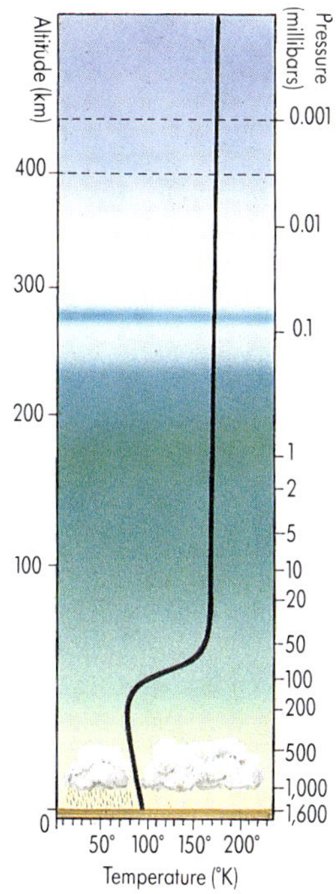

THE OUTERMOST PLANETS

Uranus

In ancient times, Saturn was the farthest known planet. When William Herschel discovered a seventh planet, Uranus, in March 1781, he effectively doubled the size of the known solar system. Herschel thought at first that he had discovered a comet.

Although Uranus can attain naked-eye visibility, its maximum magnitude is only 5.6. It is not surprising, therefore, that it was not recognized as a planet until Herschel's fortuitous discovery. When viewed telescopically, Uranus displays a greenish disc with an angular diameter of less than 4".

Composed mainly of hydrogen and helium, Uranus is a gas giant with a diameter of 50,800 km (31,572 miles). It orbits the Sun once every 84.01 years at a mean distance of 2,870 million km (1,784 million miles). Observation has shown that the planet rotates once every 17h 14m. The temperature at its surface is in the region of –210 °C (-346 °F).

Uranus possesses an unusual axial tilt, amounting to just under 98°, putting its poles very close to the plane of its orbit around the Sun. The poles point alternately towards the Sun: northern summer lasts for 42 Earth years, with the Sun above the horizon all the time. During this period the south polar region is subjected to a continuous winter night. This situation is then reversed.

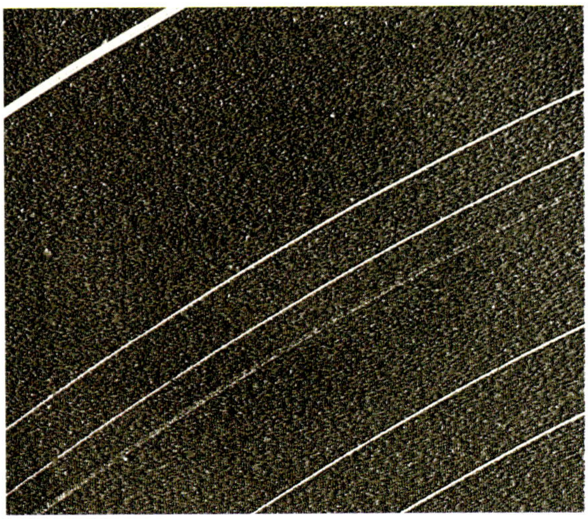

Above Voyager 2 image showing the Uranian ring system, with several of its 10 rings clearly visible. The 10th ring, discovered by Voyager, is practically invisible here, but lies between the epsilon (top) and delta rings.

Of Uranus' 15 known satellites, 10 were discovered by Voyager 2 in 1986. These are only a few tens of kilometres across. The largest of all the satellites is Titania, which has a diameter of 1,610 km (1,000 miles) which was discovered by William Herschel in 1787. He also discovered Oberon in the same year and in 1802 he discovered a third satellite, Umbriel.

Uranus also has a system of 10 rings, first observed from Earth in 1977 during the occultation of a star by the planet The light from the star was seen to blink several times both before and after going behind the disc of Uranus, indicating .the presence of rings The ring system circles Uranus between 42,000 and 52,000 km (26,100–32,300 miles) from the centre of the planet.

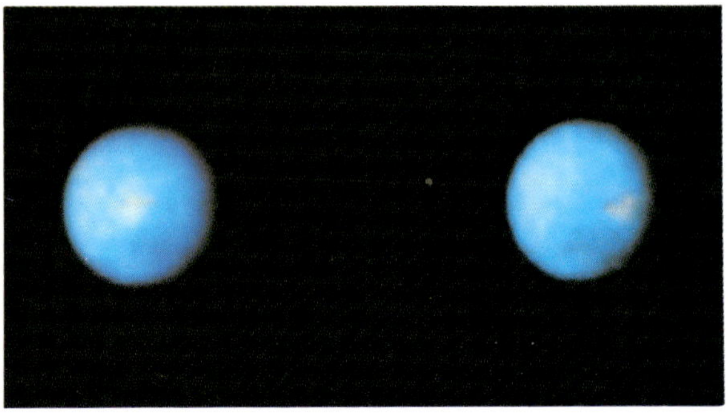

Above A bright cloud feature can be seen moving across the face of Neptune on these two images taken about two hours apart on 23 January 1989 by Voyager 2.

Neptune

Observations of Uranus made during the years following its discovery revealed that it was straying from its predicted path, compelling the conclusion that it was being perturbed by a more distant and as yet undiscovered planet. The problem of calculating the position of this other planet was taken on by the young English astronomer and mathematician John Couch Adams. After months of hard work he felt he had fixed the position accurately. He contacted the then Astronomer Royal, George Biddell Airy, who took no action. Unknown to Adams, the French mathematician Urbain Leverrier had carried out a similar series of calculations and had arrived at an almost identical position for the new planet. Leverrier's calculations were sent to the Berlin Observatory, where the planet was quickly located in almost the predicted position.

Neptune can almost be classed as a twin of Uranus. It is slightly smaller, with a diameter of just under 49,500 km (31,000 miles). Its axial rotation period is around 18h 26m . It

Above and above right This pair of photographs, taken a day apart, shows Pluto's motion against the background of stars.

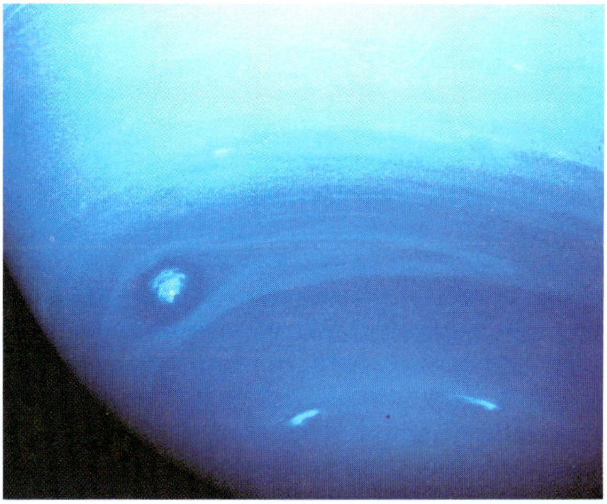

Right Neptune astounded astronomers by having a very vigourous weather system. It was discovered that the surface of Neptune was wracked with 400 mph (750kph) winds and storms that have lasted hundreds of years.

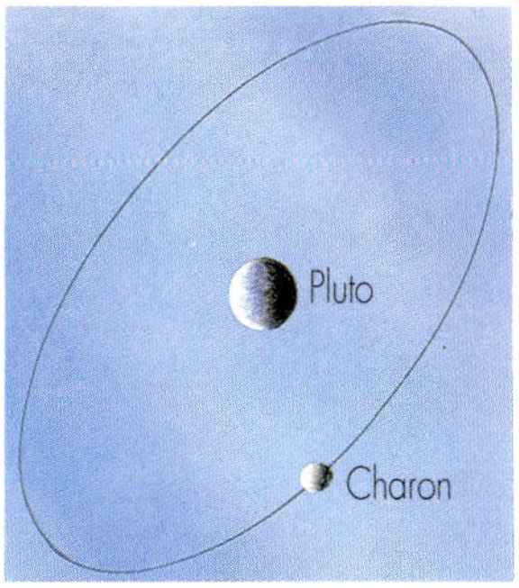

Left The comparative sizes of Pluto and Charon are shown in this diagram, which illustrates the orbital motion of Charon.

orbits the Sun every 164.79 years in an almost circular path and at a mean distance from the Sun of 4,497 million km (2,795 million miles). When seen through a telescope Neptune appears as a pale bluish disc with a maximum angular diameter of 2.3". Triton is the larger of Neptune's two known satellites, with a diameter in the region of 3,500 km (2,200 miles).

Pluto

Discrepancies in the movements of Uranus were still apparent even after the discovery of Neptune, and a systematic search for a trans-Neptunian planet was made by Percival Lowell. This proved negative, but a subsequent and extremely thorough photographic search by the young American astronomer Clyde Tombaugh eventually paid off when the new planet came to light in 1930. It was given the name Pluto, and was found to have the most eccentric orbit of any planet in the solar system. It lies at a mean distance from the Sun of 5,900 million km (3,667 million miles). But for 20 years in each revolution, Pluto comes within the orbit of Neptune. This situation has prevailed since 1979 and will continue until 1999.

Pluto is the smallest planet, with a diameter of around 2,300 km (1,400 miles), about one sixth that of the Earth. In 1978, James W Christy of the US Naval Observatory discovered a slight elongation in a photographic image of Pluto. Other astronomers had also noted this elongation and concluded that Pluto had a satellite. Named Charon, it orbits Pluto at a mean distance of 19,100 km (11,870 miles) over a period of 6d 9h 17m. This period is identical to the rotational period of Pluto. Charon is around half the size of Pluto, so the Pluto–Charon system is more realistically regarded as a double planet.

The discovery of Charon enabled astronomers to calculate Pluto's mass, which is only 0.003 of the Earth's. Pluto's density turns out to be less than twice that of water, a value consistent with a planet composed largely of frozen methane. This low mass means that Pluto could not have caused the perturbations of Uranus and Neptune on which Lowell based his calculations. Only by coincidence was Pluto near the predicted position. The planet that Lowell predicted may still await discovery. Future research may bring a trans-Plutonian planet to light. Any gravitational deviation inflicted on the Pioneer and Voyager satellites which are currently heading out of the Solar System may be the first sign of Lowell's predicted planet.

COMETS

The appearance of a great comet, with brilliant head and enormous tail stretching across the sky, can be an awe-inspiring sight. However, comets are not all that they seem: the rarefied gas and dust that make up a cometary tail are so thinly spread that conditions there are little removed from a vacuum. However, this does not detract from their visual splendour, and it is easy to understand why primitive peoples were struck with fear when a bright comet appeared. Such superstitions still exist among modern peoples.

The cometary nursery

A vast cloud of primeval material is thought to be located beyond the orbit of Pluto and to stretch to a distance of around two light years from the Sun. It was in 1950 that the Dutch astronomer Jan Oort first proposed its existence. Possibly formed from particles left over from the formation of the planets, it is thought that Oort's Cloud completely surrounds the solar system and that the clumps of icy material we see as comets originate from within it. About a dozen new comets are discovered by astronomers each year, and for this annual tally to be maintained, the reserves held in the Oort Cloud must be substantial.

Above The European Space Agency probe Giotto, one of five probes launched to intercept Halley's Comet during its last approach in 1985-6.It was launched on 2 July 1985 and achieved its 'close encounter' with the comet on 13 March 1986

Above The force of the solar wind results in comet tails always pointing away from the sun.

Below Comet Bennett photographed from Arizona on 5 April 1970.

The gravitational influence of a passing star may cause the expulsion of material from Oort's Cloud. Some of the clumps released will stray into space, but a number will fall towards the inner reaches of the solar system, slowly at first but with increasing velocity.

The structure of a comet

As it approaches the Sun, the body is warmed and its icy outer layers are vaporized. A cloud of material builds up around what will become the comet's nucleus. This cloud is known as the coma and it hides the nucleus of the comet from Earth-based observers. The coma is acted on both by the solar wind and by radiation pressure as the comet gets closer to perihelion, the point of closest approach to the Sun. Material is blown away from the head of the comet, usually to form two tails: one consisting of ionized atoms (atoms that have lost one or more electrons) and one made up of tiny dust particles. They always point away from the Sun.

A feature invisible to Earth-based observers is the hydrogen envelope, a gaseous sphere millions of kilometres in diameter that surrounds the nucleus. It is formed as the gas is generated by the decomposition of water molecules that escape as the Sun's energy vaporizes the icy material within the comet.

Once the comet begins to retreat from the Sun the tail gradually disappears. This is followed by the shrinking and disappearance of the coma, leaving the icy nucleus to journey on.

After its encounter with the Sun, a comet may make its way back to Oort's Cloud, or, if it passes close to one of the major planets, it may enter a smaller, closed orbit, periodically returning to our neighbourhood.

The orbits of comets

A comet loses mass each time it passes through the inner regions of the solar system. Comets with very short periods change rapidly, and eventually become faint telescopic objects. Many comets have met such a fate – notably Encke's Comet, which, when first spotted some 200 years or so ago, was reasonably conspicuous. However, its orbital period is so short (3.3 years) that it is subjected to an almost continuous barrage by solar energy and is losing most of its material into space.

Encke's Comet has the shortest known orbital period of all comets. Other short-period comets include comets Tempel 2 (5.3 years) and Wirtanen (5.9 years). (As a general rule, a comet is named after its discoverer, but in some cases after the astronomer or mathematician who predicted its return following previous sightings.)

Other comets take much longer to orbit the Sun and survive longer. An example is Halley's Comet (76 years). The last return to perihelion of Halley's Comet was during 1985–86, and records of it go back well before the birth of Christ.

Some comets have much longer periods, so long that we cannot measure them accurately and they are always apt to take astronomers by surprise. One such was the Daylight Comet of 1910 (not to be confused with Halley's Comet, which appeared later in the year), probably the brightest to be seen this century.

Cometary catastrophes

The material in a comet can become rapidly depleted if it passes very close to the Sun. Comets which pass very close to the sun are termed sun grazers.

A notable example of a comet disrupted by the Sun was Biela's Comet, which was seen to split in two in 1846. The 'twins' were seen again in 1852. However, this was their last appearance as comets; in 1872, when they were due to return, a bright meteor shower was seen in the region of sky from which they were to have come. Comets and meteors are intimately connected: meteors are caused by the debris of comets that have died.

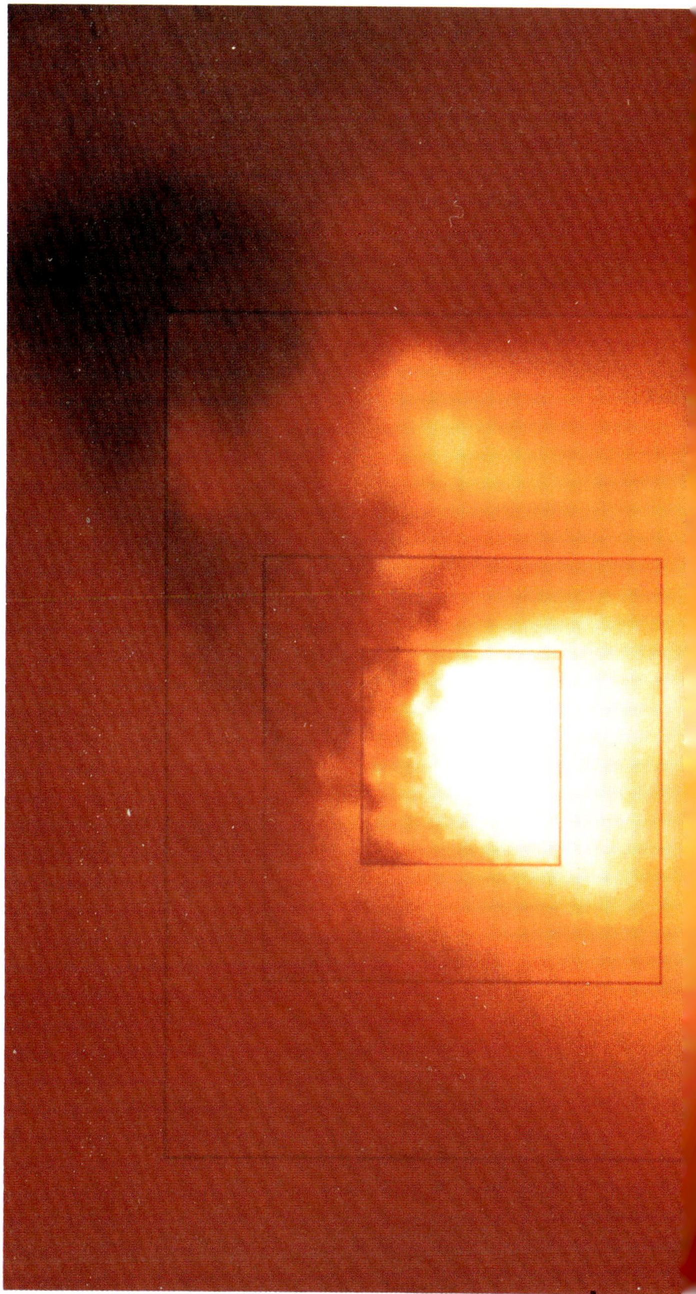

Above The dark potato-shaped nucleus of Halley's Comet is seen to the left of this Giotto image. Two bright jets of dust extend from the lower right of the nucleus toward the Sun.

METEORS AND METEORITES

On any clear night of the year a sometimes brilliant, rapidly moving streak of light may be seen against the background of stars. This is a meteor (or shooting star) and is caused by a tiny particle of dust, or meteoroid, entering the atmosphere from interplanetary space as a result of the Earth's gravitational pull. The speed of entry of the meteoroid can be anything up to 70 km (40 miles) per second. It collides with air molecules, becomes heated by friction and burns up. Countless numbers of these tiny particles are orbiting the Sun, rather like miniature planets. When in space they are much too small and faint to be seen, revealing themselves only when they enter the upper atmosphere. The frictional heat generated destroys the particle long before it reaches the ground. It was not until the beginning of the 19th century that the true nature of shooting stars became fully understood.

Below On 10 August 1972 an extremely bright fireball, roughly midway between the Sun and full Moon in brightness, was seen in full daylight from the western United States and Canada. This photograph was taken from Grand Teton National Park, Wyoming.

Meteor showers

There are two main kinds of meteor: shower and sporadic. Sporadic meteors can appear on any night of the year and from any direction. Shower meteors, on the other hand, are associated with comets. The Eta Aquarid meteor shower is linked with Halley's Comet, while the most active shower of all, the Perseids, is associated with Comet Swift–Tuttle. During its repeated passages through the inner solar system, material from a comet spreads out along its orbital path. The Earth passes through the orbital paths of certain comets at certain times of the year and larger than average amounts of particles then enter the Earth's atmosphere, resulting in a comparatively high number of meteors.

Particles travel around a comet's orbit in parallel paths. As a result, the meteors in a shower seem to emanate from the same point in the sky, known as the radiant. The Eta Aquarids radiate from a point in the constellation of Aquarius close to the star Eta Aquarii, while the Perseids radiate from a point in the constellation Perseus. The Quadrantid meteor shower, active in January, radiates from a point in the now obsolete constellation of Quadrans Muralis.

The richness of a meteor shower is measured by its so-called zenithal hourly rate (ZHR). This is a measure of the number of meteors that would be seen by an observer watching the shower under ideal seeing conditions with the shower radiant at the zenith. However, these conditions are never attained, and the actual observed hourly rate is less than the ZHR. The most reliable annual shower, the Perseids, has a ZHR of around 70. Not included are meteors below naked-eye visibility, which are extremely numerous.

Meteorites

These are larger bodies that enter the atmosphere and survive the journey to the Earth's surface without being destroyed. Meteorites can be broadly divided into three classes: stones, irons and stony-irons. The most common are stony meteorites, accounting for around 95 per cent of observed falls. Stony meteorites are again divided into chondrites and achondrites, each class having its own characteristics. Iron meteorites constitute around 5 per cent of observed falls, and are divided into over a dozen different groups. There are just two groups of the much rarer stony-irons.

Very large meteorite falls are uncommon, yet when such an event occurs havoc can be created. Probably the best example of a meteorite crater is the Barringer Crater, Arizona, over a kilometre (0.6 miles) in diameter and almost 200 metres (660 feet) deep. It was formed by a meteorite impact that took place thousands of years ago. Other large meteorite craters are found at Wolf Creek in Australia, Odessa in Texas and Campo del Cielo in Argentina.

Origins of meteorites

Meteorites are comparatively large objects that travel around the Sun in Earth-crossing orbits. There are many meteorite falls per year, and the study of meteorite paths prior to atmospheric entry has revealed that many could have originated in collisions between larger bodies within the asteroid belt. These findings are borne out through examination of meteorites themselves. Their ages are around 4,500 million years, and it is thought that they originated at the same time as the other members of the solar system.

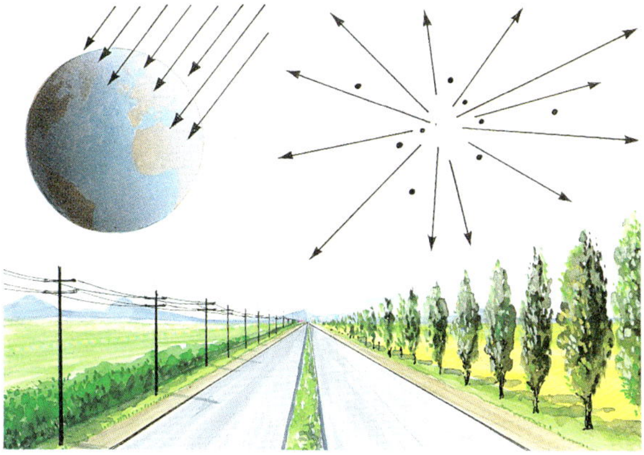

Above The radial effect of meteor showers is analogous to the parallel lanes of a straight road appearing to merge in the distance.

Below The bright almost vertical streak seen here is a Geminid meteor, photographed on 14 December 1980.

Below The three main streams, Quarantids, Geminids and Perseids, responsible for meteoric showers in relation to the orbits of Earth and Jupiter. Some of the streams are associated with certain sorts of meteors: the Geminids with short-period comets and the Perseids with long-period comets.

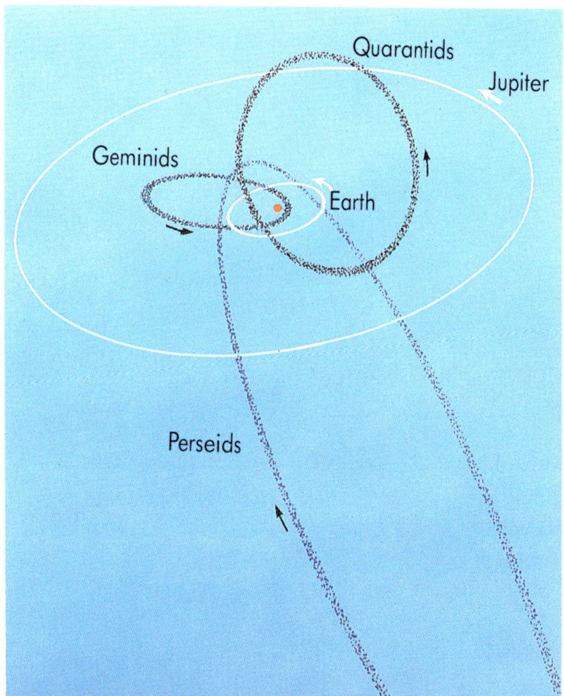

ECLIPSES AND OCCULTATIONS

Solar eclipses

Although the Moon is much smaller than the Sun, it is also a great deal closer. As a result, both the Sun and Moon have almost identical apparent diameters, and when the Moon passes between the Earth and the Sun, all or part of the Sun's light is blotted out. This event is known as a solar eclipse.

There are three different types of solar eclipse. Total eclipses occur when the lining-up of the Sun, Moon and Earth is exact and the Moon completely hides the solar disc. Partial eclipses take place when the lining-up is not exact and only part of the Sun is hidden. Annular eclipses, like total eclipses, occur during a precise lining-up of the three bodies, but when the Moon is at or near apogee, the farthest point in its orbit from the Earth. In this case not all of the solar disc is hidden, and the Sun is visible as a bright ring around the Moon. (The Latin *annulus* means ring.)

Above Two views of the total solar eclipse of 16 February 1980, showing (top) the inner solar corona and (above) solar prominences protruding over the edge of the lunar disc.

During a solar eclipse the Moon's shadow sweeps across the Earth's surface. It has a dark central region, or umbra, and a surrounding lighter region, or penumbra. An observer situated within the path of the umbra (the path of totality) will witness a total solar eclipse, while those within the penumbral regions will see only a partial eclipse.

Lunar eclipses

Lunar eclipses occur when the Moon passes into the Earth's shadow. The Moon rarely becomes completely invisible, as some sunlight is usually bent, or refracted, onto the lunar surface by the Earth's atmosphere. Generally, the Moon takes on a deep coppery-red colour during a lunar eclipse.

Above The total lunar eclipse of 6 July 1982. The photograph shows well the distinctly red colour of the Moon as sunlight is refracted onto its surface by the Earth's atmosphere.

There are three different types of lunar eclipse: a total lunar eclipse takes place when the Moon passes through the umbra of the Earth's shadow; a partial eclipse occurs when only part of the Moon passes through the umbra; a penumbral eclipse takes place if the Moon passes through the penumbra only, resulting in a darkening so slight that the eclipse can be very difficult to detect.

The maximum number of lunar eclipses that can occur during any year is three, while the maximum number of solar eclipses is five. The latter can be seen only from areas within or near the path of totality, but lunar eclipses are visible from anywhere on the hemisphere facing the Moon at the time. It follows that, from any particular location, lunar eclipses are far more common than their solar counterparts.

Solar eclipses can take place only at new Moon, and lunar eclipses only when the Moon is full. But the plane of the Moon's orbit is tilted with respect to that of the Earth around the Sun, and it is only when the Moon is near the point in its orbit at which it crosses the plane of the Earth's orbit that the three bodies become sufficiently aligned to produce some form of eclipse. The occurrence of eclipses is governed

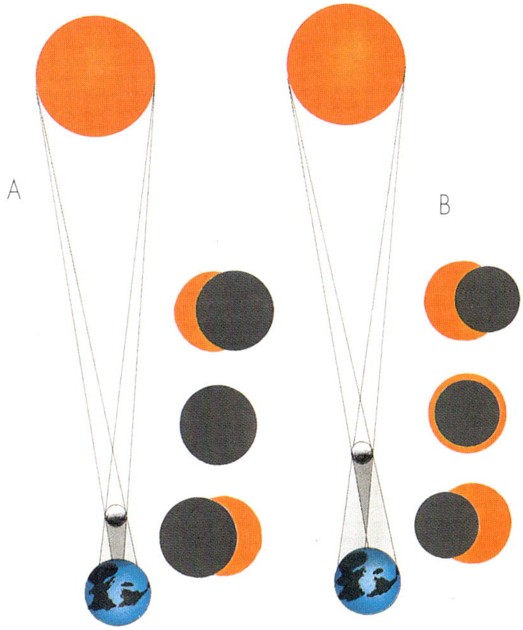

Above Unlike a total solar eclipse (A), the apparent size of the Moon during an annular eclipse (B) is insufficient to completely cover the solar disc.

Below Partial eclipse of the Sun, photographed on 21 June 1982.

Above Progress of the annular solar eclipse of 24 December 1974.

Below The tilt of the moon's orbit usually takes it above or below the earth's shadow (A), lunar eclipses (B) occuring only when it enters the shadow.

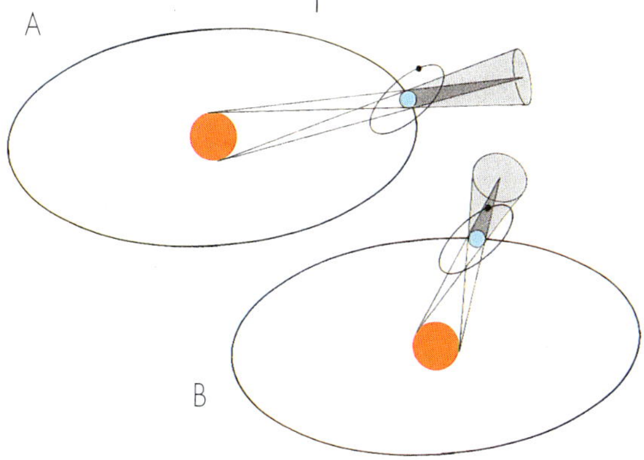

by a well defined cycle of around 18 years and 11 days duration, called the Saros period.

Occultations

An occultation occurs when a nearby body passes in front of a more distant one, temporarily hiding it from view. The most obvious example is a solar eclipse, although many other types occur. For example, because of its large apparent diameter, the Moon occults a great number of stars during its travels across the sky, although only a small number of these are visible to the naked eye. On infrequent occasions the Moon can occult a planet, while very rarely a planet can occult a star. Careful observation of occultations helps astronomers to make accurate determinations of the Moon's orbital motion.

Occultations can help astronomers in other ways. For example, the atmosphere of a planet can be studied when that planet occults a star. As the star nears the limb of the planet, it will be dimmed, by an amount depending upon the density of the planet's atmosphere. Unexpected discoveries can be made during occultations, such as that of the Uranian ring system in 1977.

PHENOMENA OF LIGHT

Aurorae

The Van Allen radiation belts are two large, doughnut-shaped regions in which protons and electrons from the solar wind are constantly travelling back and forth between the magnetic poles of the Earth. Protons are concentrated in the inner Van Allen belt, which is some 3,000 km (1,900 miles) thick and extends to a height of around 5,000 km (3,000 miles) above the Earth's surface. The outer Van Allen belt is around twice as deep and reaches out to a distance of 19,000 km (12,000 miles). It is here that electrons are concentrated.

Occasionally the solar wind can increase in intensity, as during periods of maximum sunspot activity. The result can be an overloading of the Van Allen belts and an ejection of charged particles into the Earth's upper atmosphere. Travelling at high speed, these particles collide and react with air particles. Atoms of oxygen and nitrogen are excited to fluorescence producing the aurorae we see.

Aurorae occur at heights of 100–1,000 km (60–600 miles) and can take on any of a number of different forms, including arcs, crowns, bands and rays. They can appear particularly bright when solar activity increases. Generally speaking, aurorae are seen at fairly high latitudes, although when solar activity is strong they can be seen over areas closer to the equator.

Below A solitary spruce tree is silhouetted by the beautiful blue and white bands of an auroral display photographed near Fairbanks, Alaska.Auroral displays are more common at higher latitudes.

Above Noctilucent clouds photographed over Adelaide Island, Antarctica. They consist of ice crystals that have formed around grains of dust that are probably meteoric in origin.

Vivid displays of aurorae may sometimes be seen from city areas. What at first may be no more than a glow on the horizon, visible only when the sky is dark, may extend upwards to form an arc stretching across the polar sky. Ray formations may emerge, eventually forming a gigantic rayed arc. Even more impressive are rayed bands, which form when the rays pull away from the arc and resemble a huge cosmic curtain fluttering in the sky. These ray formations follow the lines of force of the Earth's magnetic field.

A vivid auroral display is something that will stay in the memory, and a nightly glance at the poleward horizon may bring rich rewards.

Zodiacal light

Visible as a faint cone of light extending upward from the horizon, the zodiacal light is caused by sunlight reflecting from countless tiny particles scattered along or near the plane of the ecliptic. It can be seen in the west after sunset and in the east before sunrise, and is most noticeable in spring and autumn. At these times the ecliptic is nearest to being perpendicular to the horizon as seen from mid-northern or mid-southern latitudes. From the tropics the ecliptic is always steeply inclined to the horizon and the zodiacal light is visible all year around. From far northern and southern latitudes the ecliptic is always so close to the horizon that the zodiacal light's feeble glow is never seen.

The light's prominent wedge shape shows that the interplanetary dust is scattered unevenly, with a greater concentration nearer the Sun. The glow that we see comes from dust spread out to the orbit of Mars, beyond which it thins out dramatically.

The zodiacal light may be as much as 20° wide at its base

and may stretch to a height of between 40° and 60° above the horizon. From really dark observing sites, it may be seen stretching completely around the sky. This apparent extension of the light is referred to as the zodiacal band. Its width is usually between 5° and 10°.

Dust grains between the planets do not remain there indefinitely. In the case of the smallest grains, the almost imperceptible force of sunlight eventually blows them into interstellar space; the same force causes larger particles to slow down and fall into the Sun. But the dust is constantly being replenished, primarily by debris from cometary tails.

The gegenschein

The gegenschein, or counterglow, is visible as a faint patch of light directly opposite the Sun in the sky, and is even more difficult to see than the zodiacal light and zodiacal band. It has, in fact, been described as the most elusive of celestial objects. Its origin is similar to that of the zodiacal light: it is due to light backscattered from interplanetary dust particles. However, the dust that gives rise to the gegenschein lies beyond the Earth's orbit.

The gegenschein is elliptical and measures some 10° x 20°. It is at its highest and most prominent at midnight and is best seen between February and April and between September and November.

Noctilucent clouds

These are clouds that form at very high altitudes from water ice frozen onto a dust core, probably meteoric dust. In general appearance they resemble cirrus clouds. They quite often display a wave or rippled structure and can contain veils, bands, billows and whirls, structures that may be due to air flow.

Lying at heights of around 80–85 km (50–53 miles), they are seen high over the poleward horizon during the hours around midnight, between May and August, at latitudes between 45° and 70°. They are pearly white or blue and are illuminated by the Sun, which is located between 6° and 16° below the observer's horizon.

Rainbows

By far the most common and widely observed atmospheric optical phenomenon is the rainbow, formed when falling rain is illuminated by sunlight. Light enters the raindrops, is reflected internally at least once, and emerges. The light leaves the raindrops in every direction, but there are concentrations at fixed angles. The direction of such a concentration depends upon how many internal reflections have taken place. The single rainbow, or primary bow, is caused by one internal reflection. A secondary bow, produced after two internal reflections, can often be seen outside the primary bow. It has a reversed colour sequence. Both bows are seen opposite the sun in the sky.

Moonlight may also give rise to rainbows. However, because our eyes are not sensitive to colours at low light levels, these generally appear white. For the same reason all but the brightest stars in the sky appear white.

Solar and lunar coronae

A solar or lunar corona takes the form of circles of light around the Sun or Moon when it is seen through clouds containing water droplets or ice crystals of uniform size. It is made up of a series of rings ranging in colour from blue on the inside to reddish on the outside. Its diameter is generally around 2°, or four times the apparent diameter of the Sun or Moon. Outside the aureole may be seen a series of larger rings, again ranging from an inner blue one to an outer red one. Identically sized droplets would produce pure colours: a range of droplet diameters will result in the ring colours becoming less distinct.

Solar coronae are not seen as frequently as their lunar counterparts. This is because the Sun is usually too bright to permit viewing of the corona. Things are easier if the Sun is covered by cloud, or if you stand in such a position that the Sun's disc is behind an object such as a telegraph pole. Incidentally, don't confuse this kind of corona with the outer atmosphere of the Sun, which is also called the corona.

Below The zodiacal light is seen here reaching up from the horizon through Gemini, Auriga and Taurus.

THE BIRTH OF STARS

The lifetime of a typical star is measured in billions of years. It is not surprising, therefore, that the stars we see today are virtually unchanged from those listed in the early catalogues, drawn up thousands of years ago. How then can astronomers hope to learn anything of a star's birth, evolution and death?

Fortunately, stars do not go through their life cycles at the same rate, and they were not all born at the same time. It is therefore possible to find stars at many of the stages of their evolution and to try to piece together the life cycle of a star from its first appearance to its eventual demise..

The nebulae

Scattered throughout the sky are vast interstellar clouds of gas and dust. It is inside these clouds, or nebulae, that stars are born through the process of gravitational collapse. They are composed mainly of hydrogen, the most abundant element in the universe. Whether stars are formed, however, depends on the temperature within the cloud. Too high a temperature will result in the cloud's constituent atoms moving around too quickly for collapse to occur.

The first stage in the formation of a star cluster from a nebula is fragmentation, in which clumps of matter form from denser portions of the cloud. These denser regions are the result of the stability of the nebula being disrupted, perhaps through the impact of shock waves from nearby supernova explosions, or even radiation pressure from nearby young, hot stars.

The clumps continue to collapse, and their densities and internal temperatures increase. Internal pressure increases until it balances gravity and fragmentation ceases. The nebula now contains a number of hot and relatively dense stable regions, called protostars. Astronomers believe they have identified places where protostars have formed or are forming. Many bright nebulae are seen to contain small, roundish patches of dark nebulosity, starkly silhouetted against the brighter background. Around 200 of these so-called Bok globules have been catalogued. Their masses range from a few to 200 solar masses, and their diameters range from 0.1 to 2 light years. Through investigation at

Above Widely regarded as one of the most beautiful objects in the sky, the Orion Nebula is one of the most visually accessible regions of star formation. It contains many young, hot stars, including the famous multiple star Theta Orionis. The energy from this multiple provides virtually all the ultraviolet energy that causes the Orion Nebula to glow.

Right This photograph clearly shows the bright, pinkish glow of the Orion Nebula (M42), seen just to the left of centre below the three stars forming the Belt of Orion.

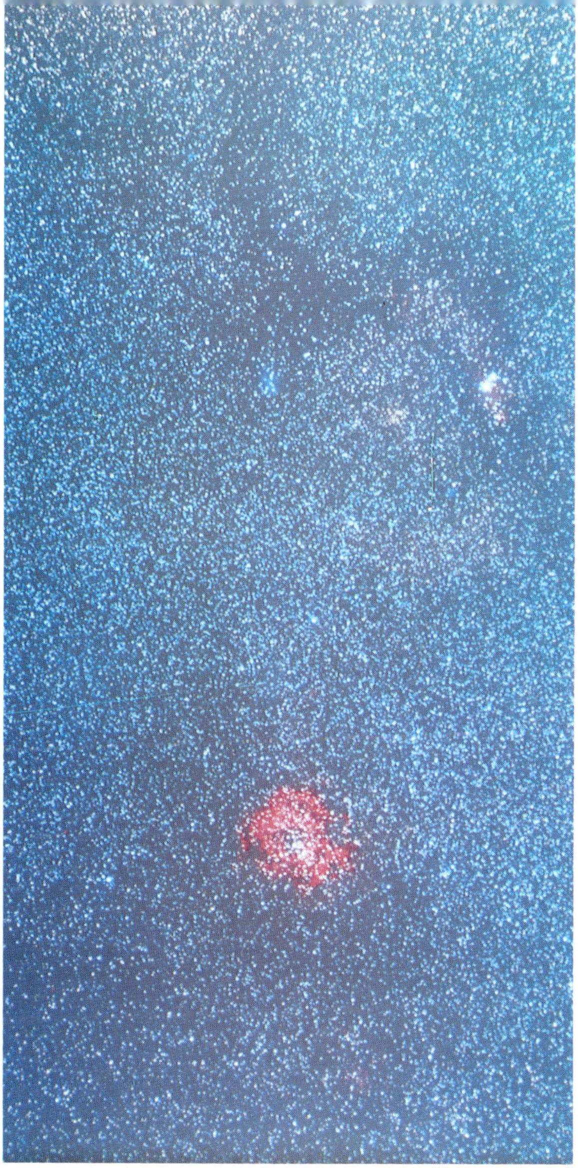

Above The Rosette Nebula in Monoceros, seen here just below centre, is a huge cloud of dust and hydrogen gas some 55 light years in diameter and shining from a distance of over 2,500 light years. The Rosette Nebula has been found to contain a number of tiny dark spots, or "globules", believed by astronomers to be new stars in the process of formation.

Above right The emission nebula NGC 6357 in Scorpius, also known as the Ghoul's Head Nebula. It is typical of nebulae surrounding young, hot stars.

infrared wavelengths, we know that their internal temperatures are sufficiently low to permit the formation of protostars.

The star begins to shine

The mass of the protostar dictates the next stage of development. In protostars with masses comparable to that of our Sun, nuclear reactions are triggered off at the core when its temperature reaches a value of 15 million °C (27 million °F). During these reactions, four hydrogen atoms are combined to form one atom of helium. However, because the resulting helium atom is lighter than the original four atoms of hydrogen, a little mass is left over from the reaction. This is converted to energy that gradually makes its way to the surface of the star and escapes as light and heat. The resulting outward-acting radiation pressure prevents any further gravitational collapse and the star becomes stable.

FROM MAIN SEQUENCE TO PLANETARY NEBULA

Solar-mass stars contain enough hydrogen fuel to ensure that they will continue to shine for around 10 billion years before further changes take place. Our Sun is roughly halfway through this stage of its evolution.

Stars of greater mass than that of the Sun consume their energy at a much quicker rate. A star of six solar masses may create energy from fusion of its hydrogen fuel for only a few tens of million of years. On the other hand, stars with less than one solar mass have much longer lifetimes.

The conversion of hydrogen to helium occupies the largest part of a star's life. As the ratio of hydrogen to helium within the star falls, there is a slight change in its outward appearance. The star becomes a little brighter and redder. Eventually, however, a star's store of hydrogen becomes depleted, and it enters the next stage of its evolution.

The fate of the Sun

Our Sun is doomed, five billion years from now, to swell into a red giant, swallowing up Mercury, Venus and even the Earth. Its surface temperature will fall from its present 6,000 °C (11,000 °F), to 3,500 °C (6,300 °F), but because of its huge size it will become a hundredfold brighter, and life will be wiped off the Earth before finally our planet is swallowed up.

The same will happen to any star of roughly the Sun's mass. The star's problems begin when its hydrogen fuel runs low and helium production decreases. The star now has difficulty in supporting its outer layers, which tend to press downwards. The core becomes slightly more compressed and so gets warmer. Hydrogen burning continues in a shell surrounding the core, and it is within this region that most of the star's energy is produced.

After a few million more years, all hydrogen fuel in the core is exhausted. Because no heat is being produced in the core, gravity once more tries to take over. The core contracts and heats up. This helps the star to counteract the inward pull and thereby maintain equilibrium.

Red giants

The core eventually becomes compressed to only a small fraction of its original size, with a corresponding increase in its internal temperature and pressure. This produces an increase in its energy output, which forces an expansion of the star's outer layers into surrounding space. As the star

Left Planetary nebulae are not all symmetrical shells of gas, as this image of the Bug Nebula (NGC 6302) in Scorpius shows.

Below The star that ejected the glowing gases forming the Helix Nebula (NGC 7293) in Aquarius can be clearly seen in this photograph.

grows to many times its original size, its outer layers cool to red-hot, around 3,500 °C (6,300°F). The star is now classed as a red giant. There are many examples of red giants in the sky, notably Aldebaran from main sequence to the brightest star in Taurus, and Arcturus, the leading star of Boötes.

The temperature in the core of the red giant rises, eventually reaching a value of 100 million °C (180 million °F). At this stage, a further round of nuclear reactions is triggered. Now the helium in the core begins to be converted into carbon. But eventually the helium fuel runs out, and the core once more contracts. In a low-mass star there will be no further nuclear reactions, and it will slowly contract and cool down, ending up as a white dwarf. More massive stars evolve differently from here on: the carbon core contracts further, initiating further nuclear fusion and enabling the star to continue shining.

Planetary nebulae

Before a star cools and contracts to become a white dwarf, radiation pressure from the core can blow away its tenuous, bloated outer layers to form an expanding shell of gas, known as a planetary nebula from its disc-like appearance in a telescope. Famous examples of planetary nebulae include the Ring Nebula in Lyra and the Owl Nebula in Ursa Major.

Above This photograph of the constellations Monoceros and Orion shows the bright red supergiant star Betelgeuse, seen near the top of the picture, a little way to the right of centre. Also seen are the Orion Nebula, visible just below the three stars forming the Belt of Orion and the Rosette Nebula, the bright red patch of light located to the upper left of centre.

The temperature of the star's newly exposed surface is high, anything up to 100,000 °C (180,000 °F) or more. The ultraviolet energy from the star ionizes the gas in the surrounding nebula, causing it to emit visible light. Nearly a thousand planetary nebulae are known.

Radiation pressure from the central star forces the material in a planetary nebula outwards, thereby enriching the interstellar medium. Planetary nebulae are relatively short-lived, with average lifespans of several tens of thousands of years. Around 10,000 planetary nebulae are thought to exist within our Galaxy alone, with several new ones forming every year.

WHITE DWARFS, NEUTRON STARS AND BLACK HOLES

White dwarfs

Beyond the red giant stage a dying star takes on even stranger forms. When nuclear reactions finally cease, gravity becomes the only source of energy left to it. A star that is not too massive (more than 1.4 times the mass of the Sun) will collapse until it becomes an incredibly dense 'white dwarf'. During this process, the star's component atoms become tightly packed together. So severe is the compression that the star is crushed to immense densities. A star similar to our Sun becomes a million times as dense as water and is packed into a sphere with a diameter of only a few thousand kilometres.

Gravitational energy released during the collapse is converted into heat and the white dwarf continues to shine. However, this energy eventually radiates into space, leaving a dead star called a black dwarf.

Stars above 1.4 solar masses cannot change to white dwarfs unless they lose some of their mass beforehand. This can happen if the star's outer layers are shed into space to form a planetary nebula.

Above Sirius, the Dog Star, lies at the centre of this photograph. Its white dwarf companion star (not shown here) is know as Sirius B or 'The Pup'. Discovered in 1862, it was the first white dwarf known.

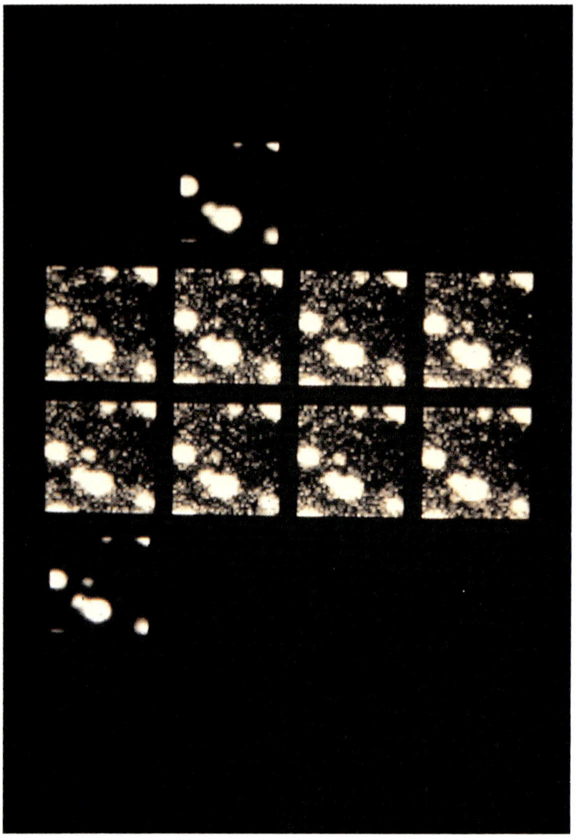

Above A series of images of the 24th - magnitude Vela pulsar, sen as a faint object just left of centre, undergoing brightness changes as it flashes every 0.089 seconds. Flash minimum (top) and maximum (bottom) are also seen.

Neutron stars and pulsars

Stars of between 1.4 and 3 solar masses collapse beyond the white dwarf stage. The pull of gravity on these stars is so great that their constituent protons and electrons are smashed together to form neutrons, giving rise to a neutron star. Neutron stars have such high densities that 15 cubic cm (1 cubic inch) of their material has a mass of around 15 million tonnes. Typically, neutron stars have diameters of only a few tens of kilometres.

Neutron stars existed in theory before any were actually identified. They represented the hypothetical end of stars with over 1.4 solar masses. Observational evidence had to wait until 1967, when astronomers detected bursts of radio emission from an area of sky that contained no visible source. These signals had an extremely regular period, measured at 1.3370109 seconds.

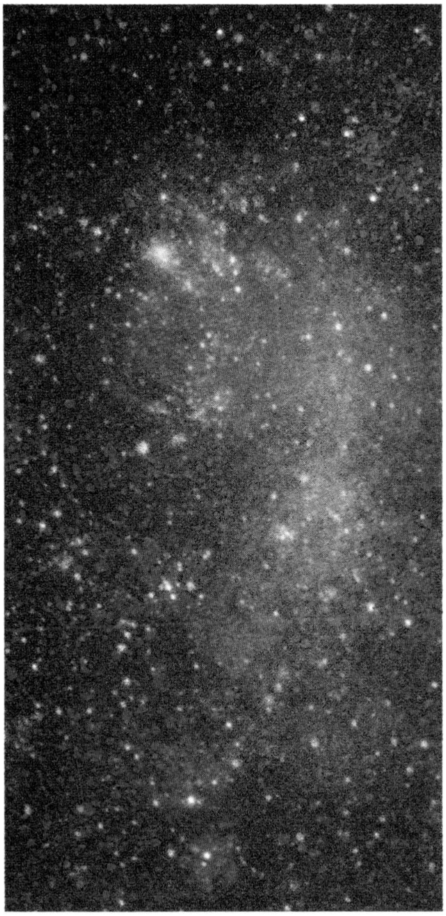

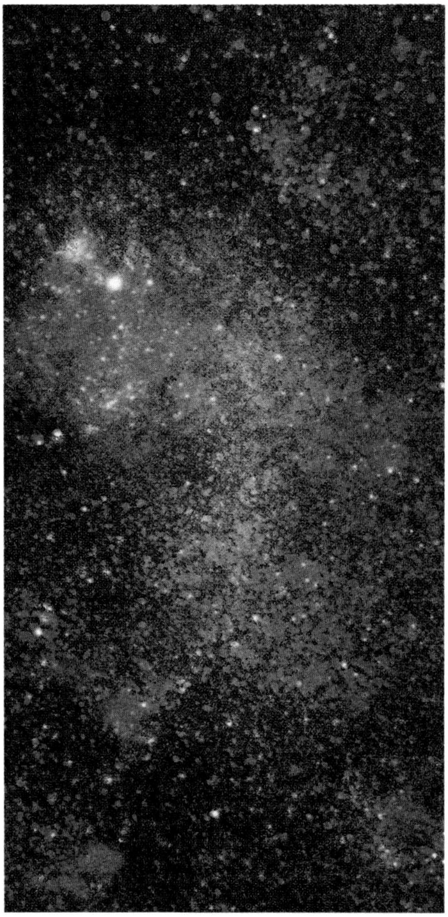

Left A pair of images showing the area around the Tarantula Nebula in the Large Magellanic Cloud. The left-hand image was taken before the appearance of supernova 1987a, which can be clearly seen on the right-hand image, just above centre and near the right edge. This photograph was taken on 27 February 1987, a few days after the discovery of supernova 1987a. Resulting from the explosion of a supergiant star, this was the first supernova to become visible to the naked eye for almost 400 years.

At first it was thought that the signals were emanating from a pulsating star. The object was given the name pulsar, and a search through previous records revealed three more. Since then, many have been found, notably one at the heart of the Crab Nebula in Taurus.

In 1054, Chinese astronomers recorded the appearance of a new and very bright star in the constellation of Taurus. The object they saw was in fact a supernova, an event that occurs as the result of the gravitational collapse of a very massive star. The collapse is so forceful that there is a rapid increase in the star's internal temperature. Violent nuclear reactions occur, which throws the outer layers of the star off into surrounding space. For a time the exploding star can outshine the rest of the galaxy of which it is a member. The core collapses to form a neutron star.

The Crab Nebula is actually the scattered remains of the 1054 supernova, and the pulsar inside it has now been identified as a rapidly spinning neutron star. It emits a beam of radio waves that sweeps over the Earth during each revolution, giving rise to a pulse of signals 30 times per second. Several hundred pulsars have now been found, although few have been identified optically.

Black holes

Stars that have masses of more than eight times that of the Sun may collapse beyond the white dwarf and neutron star stages. An irresistible gravitational contraction produces a sphere of increasing density and decreasing size. As the density grows, the escape velocity of the star also increases, until it eventually exceeds the speed of light. To an observer, the star would simply disappear, after which the collapse would continue to its limits.

Evidence for the existence of black holes may come from the study of binary stars. Binary systems containing a white dwarf, a neutron star or a black hole can emit bursts of X-rays when material is pulled from the surface of the larger star by its denser companion. This material collects in a ring, or accretion disc, surrounding the dense star and becomes very hot before it spirals down onto its surface, emitting X-rays. Bursts of radiation at these wavelengths have been detected from certain binary systems with one very massive component. Most of these systems contain neutron stars, but a number are thought to contain black holes. One binary system that may contain a black hole is the X-ray source Cygnus X-1.

WHAT STARLIGHT TELLS US

If starlight is passed through a prism it is split up into a range of constituent colours. Light consists of waves, with different colours corresponding to different wavelengths. As with sound waves, the wavelength is the distance from one wave crest to the next. The electromagnetic spectrum is made up of the complete range of electromagnetic radiation. Visible light forms only a tiny part of this, ranging from short-wavelength violet through blue, green, yellow and orange to long-wavelength red. The multicoloured band of light that is produced by passing the light through a prism is called a spectrum.

Types of spectrum

Light from incandescent high-density gases, such as those that make up a star, produces an unbroken sequence of colours, called a continuous spectrum. However, if the gas whose light is being examined is of a low density, such as that found in a nebula, the spectrum will take the form of a series of bright individual lines. A particular set of these lines will be produced by a particular element. This is called an emission spectrum.

The tenuous gas above the photosphere of a star, if it could be seen in isolation, would produce a bright-line emission spectrum. However, the gas is actually seen against the background of the star's much brighter continuous spectrum. In these circumstances the gas absorbs light at precisely the wavelengths at which it would otherwise emit light. The result is that a dark line spectrum appears

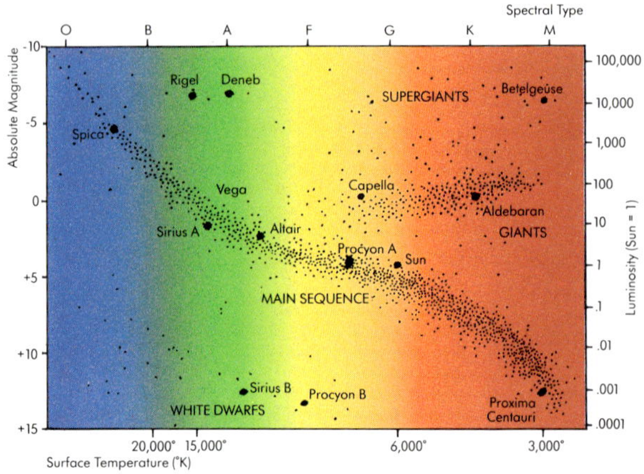

Above The Hertzsprung–Russell (H–R) diagram plots the spectral types and surface temperatures of stars (horizontal) against their absolute magnitudes and luminosities (vertical). It can be seen that stars are grouped into areas, with most stars distributed along a narrow band known as the main sequence. Stars on the main sequence (including the Sun) are classed as dwarfs.

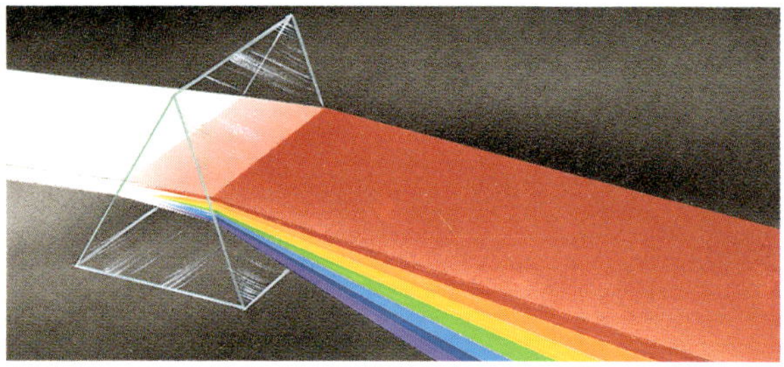

Above White light is dispersed into a spectrum when passed through a prism, with colours in the order red, orange, yellow, green, blue, indigo and violet.

Below A double rainbow seen over the dishes of the Very Large Array (VLA) radio telescope at Socorro, New Mexico. Rainbows occur when sunlight illuminates falling rain. After entering the raindrops the light is internally reflected and dispersed into its component colours before re-emerging.

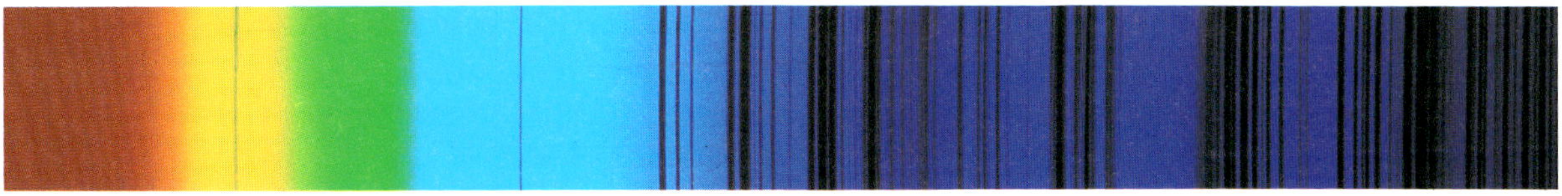

Top A spectrum of sunlight, with a number of absorption lines visible. Although around 20,000 lines have been observed, only the major ones are shown here.

superimposed on the star's continuous spectrum. Each line is indicative of the presence of a particular element within the atmosphere of the star being observed.

The examination of spectra of stars and other celestial objects is known as spectroscopy. The spectra are obtained with a spectroscope, an instrument that is attached to the telescope and splits the starlight up into its individual wavelengths. The spectroscope normally employs not a prism but a device called a diffraction grating, consisting of a flat mirror or piece of glass on which closely packed straight lines are engraved. On being either reflected or transmitted by the grating, light is broken up into a spectrum.

Spectral classes

In the early 1900s Annie Jump Cannon and her colleagues at Harvard Observatory drew up a classification of spectra. It identified stars according to their temperatures, with spectral classes being designated by letters from the sequence O, B, A, F, G, K and M (R, N and S were added later). The hottest stars, with surface temperatures exceeding 35,000 °C (63,000 °F), are classed as O, while the coolest M, R, N and S stars have surface temperatures of around 3,000 °C (5,400 °F) or less. These broad classifications have been further subdivided by the insertion of a number, ranging from 1 to 9, after the letter. For example, the Sun is classed as a G2 star.

Star colours

The hottest stars, of spectral classes O, B and A, are blue-white or white. Typical examples are Iota Orionis (O9), Spica (B1) and Delta Cygni (A0). Below these we have the yellow stars of spectral classes F and G, including Polaris (F8) and the Sun (G2), followed by the orange K-type stars, such as Dubhe in Ursa Major (K0). Finally we have the red stars of types M, R, N and S: well known examples are Antares in Scorpius (M1) and Betelgeuse in Orion (M2).

The light from stars fainter than first magnitude is not strong enough for colour to become apparent to the naked eye, but binoculars and telescopes will often reveal it. For example, binoculars will bring out the strong colour of Mu Cephei (M2), which was nicknamed the Garnet Star by William Herschel.

The Hertzsprung–Russell diagram

During the early 1900s the American Henry Norris Russell and the Dane Ejnar Hertzsprung independently realized that when the magnitudes and colours of a number of stars were plotted against each other a regular pattern emerged. In modern versions of their diagram, hot stars are usually plotted towards the left-hand side of the diagram with cool stars near the right, and bright stars are placed near the top with faint stars near the bottom.

Extending from the upper left to lower right of the Hertzsprung–Russell (HR) diagram is a band of stars called the main sequence of which our sun is a member Towards the upper right are the supergiant stars, which are so large that they have high luminosities, even though some, such as Antares and Betelgeuse, are fairly cool. Supergiants can have diameters anything up to 1,000 times that of the Sun. Some supergiants, such as Rigel in Orion (B8) and Deneb in Cygnus (A2), also have high surface temperatures, their positions near the upper left-hand corner of the diagram reflect these characteristics.

Just below the red supergiants are the red giants, which have similar surface temperatures but are smaller, and consequently less bright, than the supergiants. Their diameters are anything from 10 to 100 times that of the Sun. A typical example is Aldebaran (K5), the brightest star in Taurus. In the lower left-hand corner of the diagram we have the white dwarfs. These have high surface temperatures but are also faint, because of their small sizes.

MEASURING STELLAR DISTANCES

To assess the true brightness of a star or other celestial object and to gain a picture of the structure of our Galaxy and the universe beyond, we must have ways of measuring distance. The most straightforward method is to measure a star's parallax, its apparent shift against the background of more distant stars when viewed from two different positions in the Earth's orbit. The principle of trigonometrical parallax has been known for a long time, but several attempts by different astronomers were made before it was successfully used to determine the distance to a star.

Trigonometrical parallax can be used only for stars out to a distance of around 70 light years or so. There are somewhere in the region of 1,400 stars within 70 light years of the Earth, nearly a thousand of which have had their distances calculated with a high degree of accuracy.

The moving cluster method

The distance scale can be extended by studying the motions of open clusters. For practical purposes the members of a cluster can be regarded as travelling together along parallel paths. But because of the effects of perspective they will in general seem to be converging towards, or diverging from, some point in space. Their proper motions (angular displacements) can be found from observations over a number of years. These can be projected forwards (or backwards) to find the point in the sky towards (or from) which the stars seem to be moving. Each star's radial velocity (the component of velocity towards or away from us) can also be found by measuring the Doppler shift of its spectral lines (see page 46). By combining the stars' radial velocities with their angular velocities and true direction of motion their distances can be calculated.

To carry the cosmic distance scale beyond this, other methods must be used. Sometimes a comparison can be made between a star of unknown distance and another of the same type at a known distance. By assuming that two stars of similar type will have similar luminosities, astronomers can calculate the distance to the more distant star by comparing the two apparent brightnesses. In later sections we shall encounter still further methods of distance determination.

The brightness of the stars

As long ago as 150 BC the Greek astronomer Hipparchus devised a system in which the brightness of a star was designated by a number. He divided the stars into six classes, the first containing the brightest objects in the sky and the sixth the faintest.

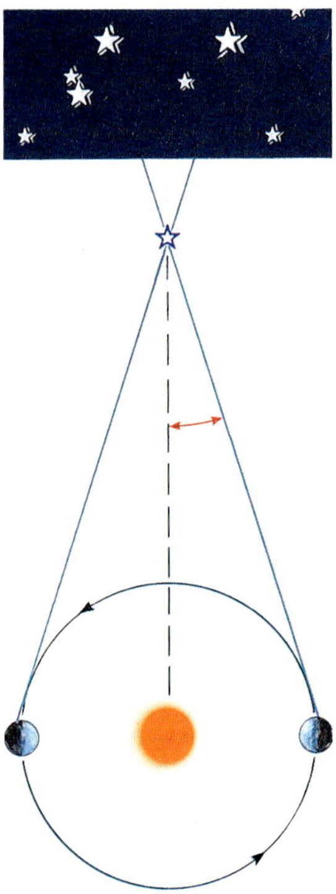

Left If a nearby star is viewed from opposite points in the Earth's orbit its distance can be calculated by trigonometry If the radius of the Earth's orbit is known and the angle of shift against the background stars is measured.

Below The stars that make up constellations are generally not close to each other, but merely lie in roughly the same line of sight as seen from Earth. An example is Crux, whose main stars lie at distances varying from 59 light years for Epsilon to 434 light years for Beta.

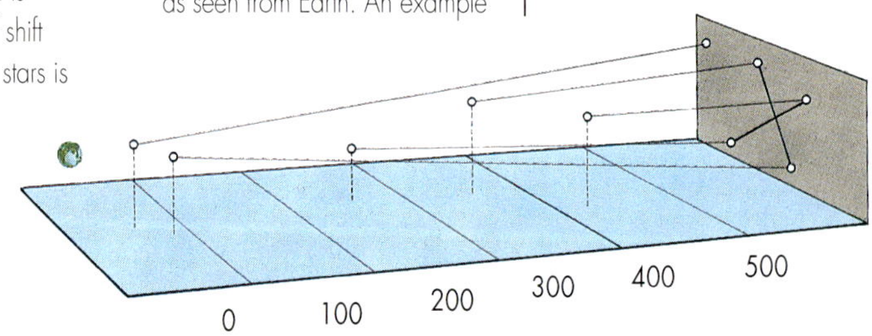

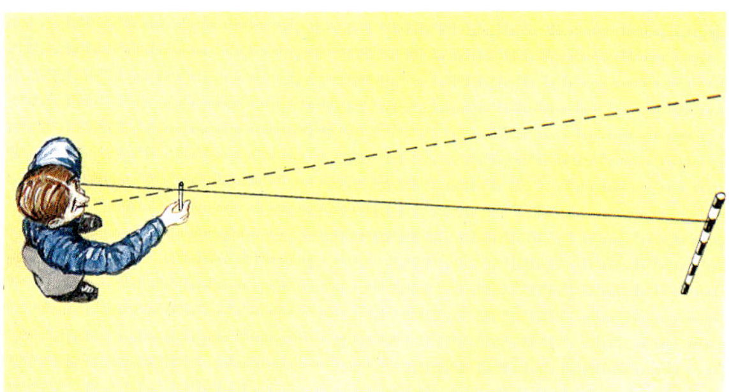

Left A pencil viewed alternately with each eye will seem to shift in relation to the background. Nearby stars also seem to move in relation to more distant ones in the course of a year because of the movement of the Earth. This is known as parallex.

Right The German astronomer Friedrich Wilhelm Bessel, who became the first astronomer to determine the distance to a star by trigonometric parallax.

Today we use the same basic system, although with modern instrumentation brightness can now be measured to within 0.01 of a magnitude. The brightest objects in the sky are given negative magnitudes to fit in with the current scale. For example, Sirius, the brightest star in the sky, has a magnitude of –1.42, closely followed by Canopus (magnitude –0.72) and Alpha Centauri (magnitude –0.27).

A star of 1st magnitude is defined as being 100 times as bright as one of 6th magnitude. It follows that the brightness ratio between successive magnitudes is 2.512: in other words, a star of magnitude 2.00 is 2.512 times as bright as one of magnitude 3.00 and so on.

The magnitudes of all celestial objects have been measured. The Sun has a magnitude of –26.8, while the full Moon has an average magnitude of –12.7. Venus, the brightest of the planets, can attain a magnitude of –4.4, while Uranus can reach naked-eye visibility at magnitude 5.6. Pluto, on the other hand, has a maximum magnitude at opposition of around 14.

The faintest objects photographed so far have magnitudes of around 26. A pair of 7x50 binoculars will show stars down to around 9th magnitude, whereas a 60-mm ($2\frac{1}{2}$-inch) telescope will reveal stars a magnitude fainter.

Absolute Magnitudes

The absolute magnitude of a star is defined as the apparent magnitude it would have if viewed from a standard distance of 10 parsecs or 32.6 light years. (A parsec is the distance at which the Earth–Sun distance of 1 astronomical unit would have an apparent angular size of 1".)

As we have seen, the star with the highest visual magnitude (apart from the Sun) is Sirius, which is 0.7 magnitudes brighter than Canopus. But Canopus lies at a distance of 1,170 light years, while Sirius is 8.7 light years away. If both stars were placed at a distance of 10 parsecs, the visual magnitude of Sirius would be +1.4 while that of Canopus would be –8.5 – over 600 times as luminous!

Bolometric magnitude

The apparent and absolute magnitude systems express a star's brightness in terms of its output of visible light. However, although certain stars or other celestial objects may appear faint at visible wavelengths, their outputs of other radiation may be much higher.

In order to allow for this, astronomers assess the bolometric magnitudes of stars and other objects. Bolometric magnitude is a measure of the total amount of radiation at all wavelengths received from a star, expressed on the stellar magnitude scale. Different types of detectors are required to receive these different forms of radiation. By definition, the bolometric magnitude of a star is its apparent magnitude determined from measurements over all wavelengths, made above the atmosphere.

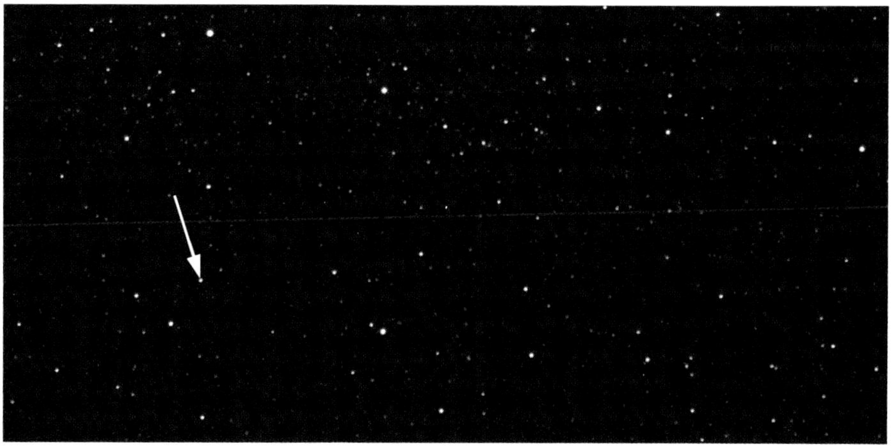

Right Photograph of the constellation Cygnus, the Swan, 61 Cygni is at the right corner of the triangle on the left of the page. Lying at a distance of just over 11 light years, 61 Cygni is a binary star. It is historically significant in that it was the first star to have its distance determined through measurement of its parallax shift, by Friedrich Bessel in 1838.

DOUBLE AND MULTIPLE STARS

The Sun is a solitary star. However, most of the stars we see are members of multiple star systems, ranging from clusters, sometimes huge, down to double (binary) stars.

Although there are a huge number of systems in which the member stars are physically associated, quite often stars that appear close together are not actually related to each other. In these so-called optical doubles the two stars lie in the same line of sight as seen from Earth, their apparent association being nothing more than a chance alignment. A good example is the wide naked-eye pair Alpha^1 and Alpha^2 Capricorni: this is a case of two stars appearing to be close together, though in reality one (Alpha^1) is many times farther away than the other.

Originally it was believed that all double stars appeared as such because of this line-of-sight effect. However, observations by Sir William Herschel led to the discovery of true, physically associated binary systems. In 1802 he made the announcement that: '. . . many of them (double stars) have actually changed their situation with regard to each other, in a progressive course, denoting a periodical revolution round each other'.

Binary stars consist of two stars in orbit around their common centre of gravity. Their periods of revolution can be anything from less than an hour to many thousands of years. The binary with the shortest known orbital period is the X-ray star X-1820-303 in the globular cluster NGC 6624, almost 30,000 light years away in Sagittarius. In this system the two stars orbit each other once every 11m 25s!

Moving towards the other extreme, the two components of Delta Serpentis are thought to orbit each other over a period in excess of 3,000 years. Periods of such duration are difficult to measure, and it is impossible to say which binary systems have the longest periods. In systems where the components are separated by large distances the periods of revolution may amount to millions of years.

Spectoscopic binaries

There are a great number of binary systems in which both components are clearly visible in telescopes. But in many cases the stars are so close to each other that even the world's largest telescopes are unable to resolve both components. In these cases it is only through the use of the spectroscope that we are able to identify them.

Stellar spectra consist of a line spectrum superimposed on a continuous spectrum (see page 42). Depending upon whether a star is moving towards or away from us, the lines

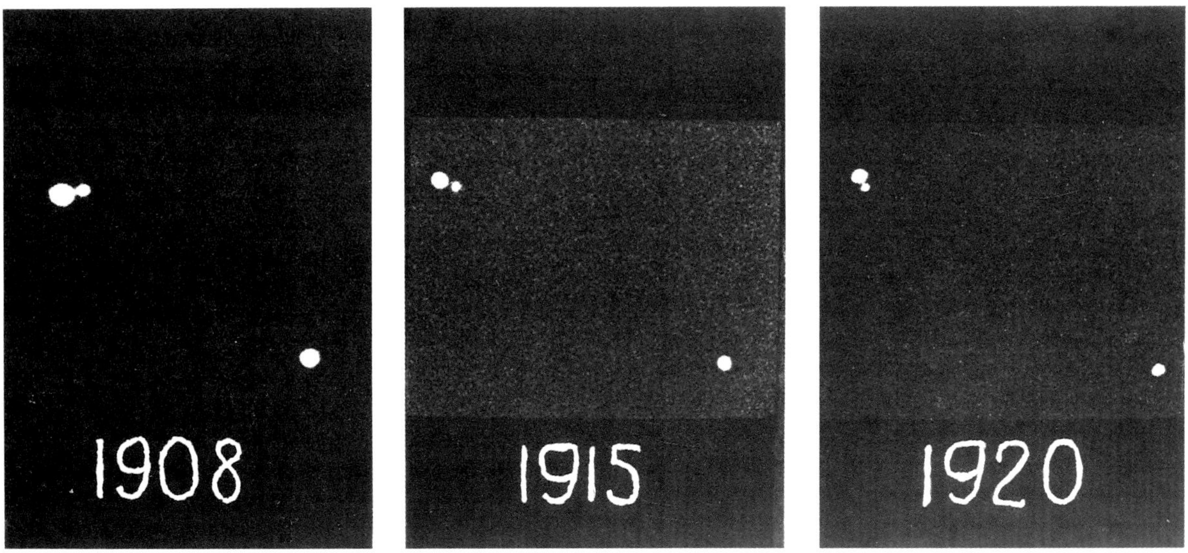

Below The changing appearance of the visual binary star Krueger 60 is seen here on photographs taken in 1908, 1915 and 1920. Krueger 60 is one of the nearest binary star systems nearest to us, lying at a distance of 13.1 light years and located roughly 1° to the south of Delta Cephei. The two red dwarf components orbit each other once every 44.46 years. The fainter component is a flare star, one of a class of variable stars that undergo sudden, rapid and unpredictable increases in luminosity, These are thought to be caused by outbursts on their sufaces similar to solar flares observed on the Sun, though vastly greater.

of the emission are shifted towards the blue or the red end of the spectrum. In the case of a receding star, the wavelengths of light are stretched a little, producing a shift of the spectral lines towards the red, or long-wavelength, end. The lines in the spectrum of an approaching star are shifted towards the blue, or short-wavelength, end. This effect is known as the red (or blue) shift, the amount of the lines' displacement being an indication of how quickly a star is travelling towards or away from us. The greater the spectral shift, the higher the velocity of the star The phenomenon is also known as the Doppler effect, after the 19th century physicist Christian Johann Doppler.

In the case of a binary system in which the orbital plane is roughly lined up with the Earth, there will be times when one component is moving towards us and the other away. When this happens, the spectral lines of the approaching star will be shifted towards the blue end of the spectrum and those of the receding star toward the red. In other words the two sets of spectral lines will become separated, creating a sort of concertina effect. When the two stars are moving across our line of sight the spectral lines will appear single.

Around 1650 the Italian astronomer Giovanni Riccioli discovered an optical companion to Mizar, thus making Mizar the first double to be discovered with a telescope. The two components, Mizar A and Mizar B, are currently separated by 14.4". There has been little change in their relative positions since discovery, just a slight increase in position angle. This indicates that the orbital period is many thousands of years. In 1889 the American astronomer Edward Charles Pickering noticed that the spectral lines of Mizar A periodically doubled. He came to the conclusion that Mizar A consisted of two components too close to be resolvable with any telescope. The orbital period of the Mizar A system is 20.5386 days, the separation of the components being of the order of 30 million km (18 million miles). Mizar A was the first binary to be detected spectroscopically.

Multiple star systems

Subsequent observation has shown that Mizar B is also a spectroscopic binary, its two components orbiting their common centre of gravity every 175.55 days. Nearby Alcor, itself a spectroscopic binary, is also associated with Mizar, since they are both members of the Ursa Major Moving Cluster, a group of stars travelling together through space. The true separation of Alcor and Mizar is in the region of a quarter of a light year.

Other examples of multiple star systems include the sextuple system Castor in Gemini and Alpha Centauri, the closest naked-eye star to Earth. Alpha Centauri is a triple system, the two main components of which orbit each other every 79.9 years. Alpha Centauri is regarded as one of the finest binary systems in the sky.

The Alpha Centauri system is accompanied by the magnitude 10.7 red dwarf Proxima Centauri, situated about a sixth of a light year from its brighter companions, and orbiting them with a period in the region of half a million years. Proxima Centauri was discovered by the Scottish astronomer Robert Thorburn Ayton Innes in 1915. It is marginally closer to us than is Alpha Centauri and is actually the closest star to the Earth.

Invisible companions

Sometimes a star's companion, though too faint to be seen, reveals its existence by the disturbance it causes in the visible star's motion. Bernard's star, for example, the third-closest star system to us, 'wobbles' in its path across the sky. Analysis indicates it has two companions, presumably planets, since they have masses similar to that of Jupiter.

Right The visual appearance of double stars is given in terms of separation in seconds of arc of the 2 components and postion angle, the angle measured from North through East.

Far right The position angle and separation of binary stars are constantly changing due to the orbital motion of the system. Retrograde motion of the fainter component produces a reduction in position, direct motion producing an increase.

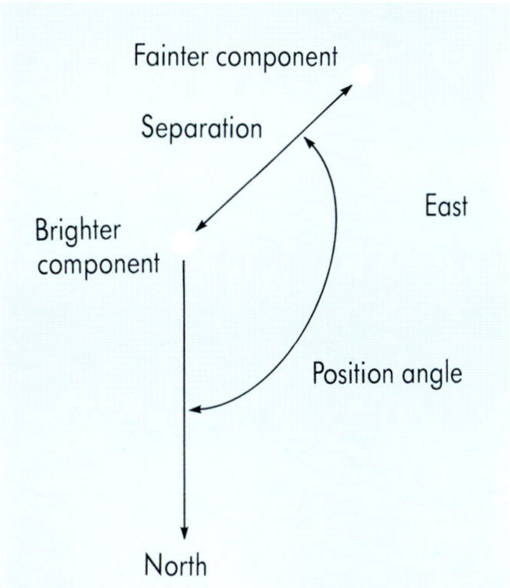

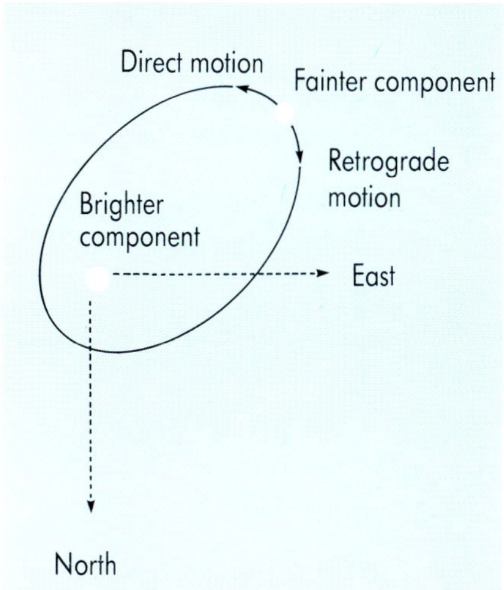

VARIABLE STARS

Although the majority of stars shine steadily, some display fluctuations in brightness over relatively short periods. These variable stars fall into two main categories: extrinsic variables undergo changes in brightness through the intervention of another object, either another star or a cloud of gas and dust; intrinsic variables change in brightness because of pulsations or eruptions taking place within the stars themselves.

A few more specialized terms are helpful in discussing variables. The light curve is a graph of changes in brightness over a period of time. The difference between minimum and maximum magnitudes is referred to as the amplitude. The time taken for a complete cycle of variations, from maximum to following maximum, is known as the period.

Bottom The light curve of the pulsating variable star Delta Cephei, characterized by a rapid rise followed by a gradual decline in brightness. The period of Delta Cephei is 5.37 days; periods of other cepheids vary from a few hours up to 50 days or more. The diameter and temperature of a cepheid changes with its brightness.

Below Diagram of the eclipsing binary Algol (Beta Persei). The orbital plane is nearly 'edge on ' to us, so the two stars are seen to eclipse each other. The light output is also reduced when the bright star eclipses the fainter companion.

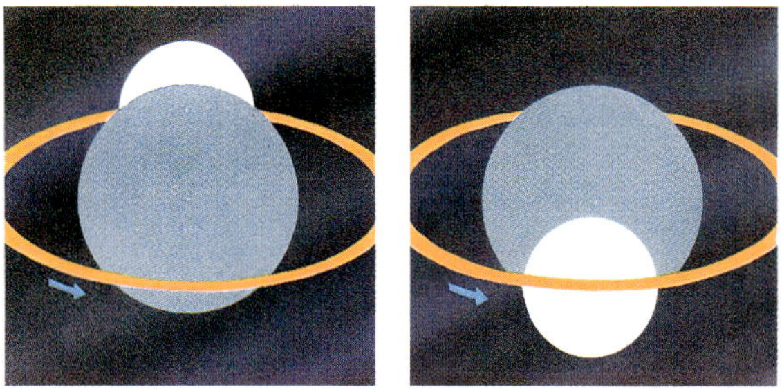

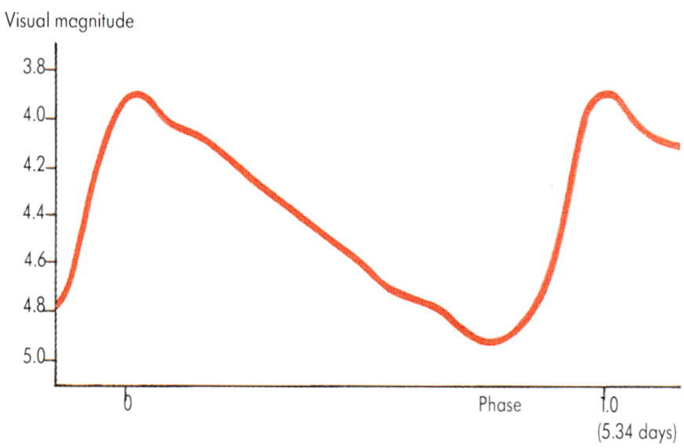

Above The eclipsing binary Algol is visible just below centre in this photograph. Algol was the first eclipsing binary to be discovered and was the prototype for the class of eclipsing binaries known as Algol variables.

Extrinsic variables

Included in this category are the eclipsing binaries and nebular variables. Eclipsing binary systems contain two components orbiting their common centre of gravity. Because the plane of their orbit is in line with Earth, each star in turn hides all or part of the other from view. These eclipses reduce the overall apparent brightness of the system.

The most famous eclipsing binary is Algol, or Beta Persei. The orbital plane of the Algol system is so inclined that the darker component passes between its bright companion and us every 2.87 days. Algol-type variables are typified by a relatively large reduction in brightness followed by a second, smaller minimum.

Beta Lyrae-type eclipsing binaries have different light curves. In these systems the two stars are so close to each other that their atmospheres mingle and the stars themselves are distorted into ellipsoids. The variations in light output are continuous, with alternate deep and shallow minima and with

Right Photograph of the area around Delta Cephei, visible near the bottom of the picture. Delta Cephei is the prototype of the class of pulsating variables known as cepheids and was the first star of its type to be discovered.

total variations of less than two magnitudes.

Similar in some respects to Beta Lyrae variables are the W Ursae Majoris systems, the components of which are also gravitationally distorted. Their periods are usually less than a day, with total amplitudes of less than a magnitude.

The T Tauri stars are typical nebular variables. They are thought to be young stars, surrounded by clouds of gas and dust thrown off as they settle down to a period of stable evolution. As you might imagine, the variations in light output caused by the interspersion of this material are unpredictable. T Tauri itself varies from around the 9th to the 13th magnitude, and can pass through the complete range in only a few weeks. The magnitude can also remain constant for prolonged periods.

By far the most famous intrinsic variables are the cepheids. These are named after Delta Cephei, the first star of this type to be recognized as a variable, by John Goodricke in 1784. Cepheids are short-period pulsating variables that are very luminous and can be seen over immense distances. Well over 500 cepheids are known to astronomers, all with periods between 1 and 55 days. The period of Delta Cephei is 5.36634 days, during which time it

Above The famous long-period variable star Mira (Omicron Ceti) is seen here in two comparison photographs. The period of the star is around 331 days. A distinct reddening is evident in the bottom picture, when Mira is fainter and cooler. The bottom one was taken on 26 November 1986 when the star was at magnitude 7 and increasing in luminosity. The top picture was taken on 29 January 1987, a few days before maximum, when the magnitude was 3.2.

varies between magnitudes 3.6 and 4.3. As its brightness varies, its spectrum alters from F5 to around G3, and its temperature may alter by around 1,500 °C (2,700 °F). Cepheid light curves are all similar, with the fall to minimum always being slower than the rise to maximum. The rise in brightness is usually smooth and steady, while the decline is usually a little irregular. The variations in brightness are usually less than 1 magnitude, although some are known to fluctuate by around $1^1/_2$ magnitudes.

The period–luminosity relationship

A vitally important link between the absolute luminosities

and periods of cepheid variables was announced by the American astronomer Henrietta Swan Leavitt in 1912. She was examining photographs of cepheids in the Small Magellanic Cloud when she noticed that those with longer periods were always brighter than those with shorter ones. Because all the cepheids under examination are at essentially the same distance from us, their apparent brightnesses reflect their true brightnesses. Leavitt concluded that those with longer periods were really more powerful.

This meant that the distance to a cepheid could be determined by measuring its period. Once the absolute brightness of the star had been determined, it was compared to its apparent brightness and the distance was calculated.

There are actually two classes of cepheid variable: Population I cepheids are located in the spiral arms of galaxies, while Population II cepheids, also known as W Virginis stars, can be found in elliptical galaxies, globular clusters and the halos of spiral galaxies. The period–luminosity relationships are different: Population I cepheids possess intrinsic luminosities $1^{1}/_{2}$ magnitudes fainter than those of Population II.

Long-period variables

The prototype long-period variable is Mira (Omicron Ceti), the brightest and most famous example. As with other long-period variables, the maxima and minima of Mira are not constant: brightness fluctuates from 3rd or 4th magnitude to 9th magnitude or less. However, on rare occasions Mira has been known to attain 2nd magnitude and once, in 1779, it almost reached 1st magnitude. The period is in the region of 331 days but, like the amplitude, is subject to variations.

Long-period variables are the most common type of variable known, with around 4,000 catalogued. They have a number of characteristics in common. They are all red giants, 90 per cent being of spectral class M. The rest are divided among spectral classes N and S, with a tiny number in class R. They undergo large changes in luminosity, with periods averaging out at between 200 and 400 days, but one cycle is often considerably different from the next.

Other types of variables

Among the many other types of variable are Beta Canis Majoris stars, which are highly luminous and vary only slightly in brightness over very short periods. The rare RV Tauri stars are also very luminous. Their light curves have alternate deep and shallow minima, although there are frequent irregularities, but successive deep minima often occur. There are two subtypes of RV Tauri stars. One, which includes RV Tauri, has short-term fluctuations superimposed upon a much longer cycle of around three years. The other type do not undergo this superimposed cycle.

Eruptive variables

This class of variable includes novae, hot stars that suffer increases in luminosity over short periods before fading back to normal. The decrease in brightness may take a number of years. There have been many spectacular novae, notably Nova Aquilae, discovered on 8 June 1918. At the time of discovery Nova Aquilae was at 1st magnitude, although within only a few hours it was close to Sirius in brightness. By examining photographs taken of the area prior to the appearance of the nova, astronomers discovered that Nova Aquilae had been an 11th-magnitude star prior to 3 June. The rise to maximum brilliance took just 6 days, the subsequent fall lasting much longer. Nova Aquilae was still at the threshold of naked-eye visibility in March 1919.

Recurrent novae are seen to brighten on more than one occasion. However, these increases are nowhere near as large as those of ordinary novae. The stars also return to former brightness at a more rapid rate. The brightest and best known example of a recurrent nova is T Coronae Borealis, otherwise known as the Blaze Star. The only other recurrent nova to reach naked-eye visibility is RS Ophiuchi.

Dwarf novae, such as SS Cygni, also undergo periodic increases in brightness, although at a much faster rate. SS Cygni itself varies between a minimum of 12th magnitude to around 8th magnitude several times a year and over a period of only a few days. The fall to minimum takes several weeks, the interval between outbursts averaging around 50 days.

The different types of nova have one thing in common: they are all members of close binary systems. The component that becomes a nova is usually a white dwarf. Material is pulled from the larger, cooler companion onto the surface of the white dwarf. This accumulates until the temperature and pressure at the base of this new layer are high enough to spark off a nuclear reaction.

Naming variable stars

The variable stars within a given constellation are assigned letters in sequence. The sequence starts at R, which is given to the first variable to be discovered within that constellation. The second to be discovered is allocated the letter S, and so on through to Z. After this a new sequence begins with RR, RS and so on to RZ. The next sequence is SS to SZ, and so on until ZZ is reached. Then the variables are named AA, AB ... AZ; BB, BC ... BZ; and so on to QZ. A variable designated QZ would be the 334th variable in a constellation (note that the letter J is never used). The next variables are then allocated numbers from 335 on, preceded by V (indicating a variable star): V335, V336, V337 and so on. Each numerical denomination is followed by the genitive form of the constellation name.

NEBULAE

Faint misty patches of light can be seen at various points in the sky. These are nebulae, a name derived from the Latin word *nebula*, meaning mist or cloud. Although some are visible to the naked eye, the vast majority lie only within the light grasp of binoculars or telescopes. Closer inspection reveals them to be huge clouds of gas and dust, concentrations of the vast amounts of interstellar material scattered throughout the spiral arms of the Galaxy. The appearance of a nebula depends upon its type. They can show up either as a dark patch superimposed on a brighter background or as a bright, luminous patch. There are three main types of nebula: emission, reflection and dark.

Emission nebulae

This type contains young, hot stars, the ultraviolet energy from which ionizes the gas within the cloud. As a result, the nebula gives off visible light. Regions within which gas is brought to fluorescence in this way are known as HII regions, and perhaps the most famous example is the Orion Nebula (M42). Visible to the naked eye as a shimmering patch of light, M42 shines because ultraviolet radiation from the group of stars known as the Trapezium ionizes the surrounding gas. The Eagle Nebula (M16) in Serpens is another example. The nebula is a scene of star formation, observation having revealed the presence of numerous small, dark 'globules', regions which are believed to be newly forming protostars. There are also many T Tauri type variables, objects thought to be undergoing gravitational contraction.

Reflection nebulae

These nebulae are usually less visually impressive than emission nebulae, their luminosity coming about through the reflection of the light from nearby stars. The light from these stars is reflected from dust particles contained within the cloud. Perhaps the most famous example of reflection nebulosity is that which surrounds the stars in the Pleiades star cluster in Taurus. The nebulosity seen here is all that remains of the original cloud from which the stars in the Pleiades formed.

Dark nebulae

These nebulae reveal themselves as dark patches silhouetted against a brighter stellar or nebulous background. These huge clouds contain no stars and blot out the light from objects beyond. The classic example is the Horsehead Nebula, situated a little to the south of Alnitak, the easternmost star in the Belt of Orion..

Above The complex nebulae NGC 6589 and 6590 in Sagittarius. The reddish regions of ionised gas contrast with the two large blue reflection nebulae at lower left.

Another equally impressive dark nebula can be found in Monoceros. Lying just to the south of the large, scattered star cluster NGC 2264 is the famous Cone Nebula, a huge pinnacle of dark material reaching up into the nebulosity surrounding the stars in NGC 2264. The Cone Nebula is beautifully silhouetted against the brighter background, its appearance in telescopes rivalling that of the Horsehead.

Many other dark nebulae are known, including the famous Coal Sack in Crux and the winding Snake Nebula in Ophiuchus. The American astronomer E E Barnard specialized in the study of dark nebulae, establishing their true nature and publishing a catalogue of these objects. As a result, many are now known by their Barnard numbers, including the Horsehead Nebula, or B33.

Stellar remnants

There are two other classes of nebulosity, both of which are formed late on in a star's life. Planetary nebulae are visible as

Right The gas in emission nebulae (A) is excited to luminosity by the energy from nearby hot stars, whereas dark nebulae (B) cut out the light from stars that lie beyond. Reflection nebulae (C) simply reflect the light from nearby stars.

shells of gas surrounding hot central stars, and are formed from the outer layers of the star, which are thrown off into space as the star itself begins the collapse into a white dwarf. Among the hundreds of planetary nebulae known are many famous examples, including the Dumbbell Nebula in Vulpecula and the Saturn Nebula in Aquarius.

Another type of stellar remnant is that created in the death throes of very massive stars. Supernova explosions have been widely observed in other galaxies, but only a few have been witnessed within the Milky Way. The most famous of these was the supernova of 1054. This huge explosion resulted in the dying star throwing off most of its material into space, the remnant visible today being known as the Crab Nebula. The most recent supernova was 1987a, which first appeared in February 1987 in the Large Magellanic Cloud.

Unlike low-mass stars, which end their careers in a much less awe-inspiring way, the amount of material in high-mass stars ensures that a prolonged series of nuclear reactions takes place. Each round of nuclear reactions involves the fusion of the remnants of the previous reaction into a heavier element. The chain of events will cease when silicon-burning forms an iron core, the iron being unable to fuel further reactions. At this stage, the core is surrounded by shells in which different elements are burning, a cross-section of the star at this stage resembling an onion.

Star death

Fresh iron is continually being deposited in the core as a result of the silicon burning just above it. Eventually, the mass of the core becomes so great that it begins to collapse. The core temperature climbs very rapidly and within less than a second, the pressure becomes so great that the collapse halts. Meanwhile, the outer layers of the star, no longer supported by nuclear reactions, fall onto the core at colossal speeds. They hit the core, producing enormous temperatures and pressures. These cause the material to bounce back, creating a wave of material that travels out towards the surface of the star. Because of the decreasing resistance experienced by the wave, its speed increases. It eventually reaches the surface, and the outer layers of the star are thrown out into space, producing the brilliant event we know as a supernova.

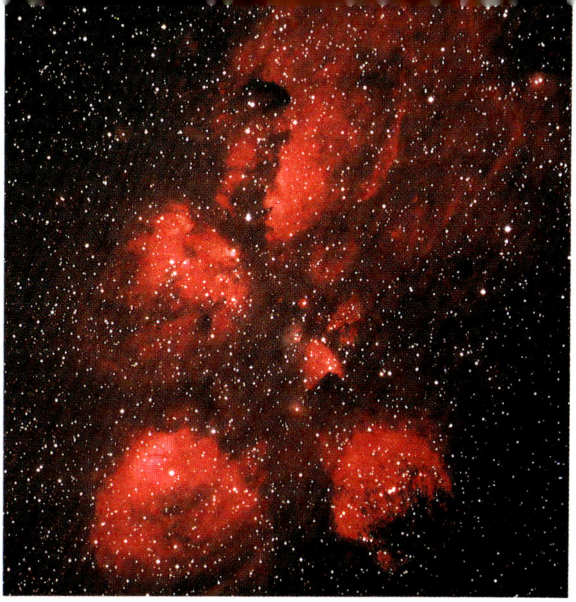

Above Lying at a distance of 5,700 light years, the emission nebula NGC 6334 in Scorpius also contains a number of dark clouds, some of which are visible in this photograph.

There are two types of supernova, which originate in different ways. Type II supernovae arise from the collapse of very massive stars and are described above. Type I supernovae result from binary systems comprising a red giant and a carbon-rich white dwarf. The dwarf 'steals' material from the tenuous outer reaches of the giant, resulting in a gaseous layer being built up on the dwarfs surface. This build-up of material eventually takes the mass of the white dwarf above 1.4 solar masses. The carbon ignites and the star is destroyed in a very short time.

Depending upon its mass, a supernova remnant may collapse into either a neutron star or a black hole. The heavy elements ejected into space mingle with the interstellar medium and find their way into nebulae that will eventually collapse into stars. Elements produced in massive stars and released into space through supernova explosions may thus contribute to the building of planetary systems.

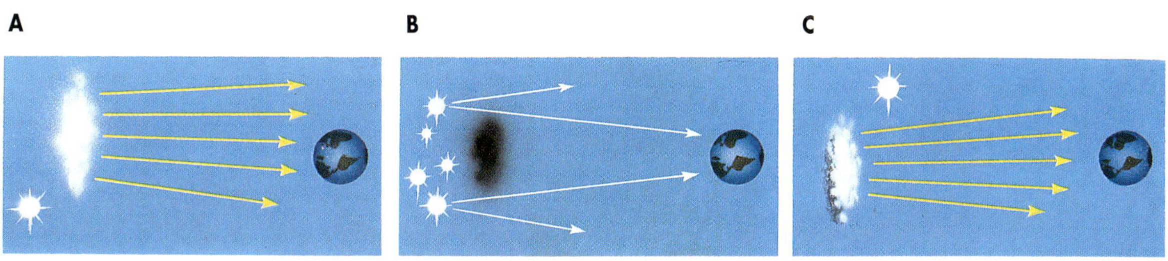

STAR CLUSTERS

Although most of the stars are scattered randomly throughout space, many are seen to be members of relatively small, compact groups. A number of these star clusters are visible to the naked eye, including the Hyades and Pleiades in Taurus, the Sword Handle Double Cluster in Perseus and the Jewel Box in Crux. Binoculars reveal many more, while the number visible through telescopes is very high.

Open clusters

There are two main types of star cluster; open and globular. Each type has its own distinctive composition, shape and general location. Open clusters are found within the spiral arms of our Galaxy and as such are often referred to as galactic clusters. They are irregular in shape with diameters of no more than a few tens of light years. They can contain anything from around a dozen to many hundreds of stars. Open clusters are generally made up of young, hot stars of Population 1, typical of those found throughout the spiral arms of the Galaxy, and they often contain traces of the original nebulosity from which the stars are formed.

Over a thousand open clusters have been catalogued, the two best known examples being the Hyades and Pleiades, mentioned above. Located at a distance of around 400 light years, the Pleiades cluster is fairly young, with an estimated age of around 20 million years. All the stars in this group were formed from the same interstellar cloud, remnants of which can be seen surrounding many of the stars in the cluster. A popular name for this group is the Seven Sisters: However, a person with excellent eyesight observing under ideal conditions can see many more, and the record stands at almost 20.

The best views of the Pleiades are to be had with binoculars or a rich-field telescope, a wide field of view being essential in order to bring out the cluster to best effect. The total number of stars in the Pleiades is not known with certainty, but the total is probably 250–500.

The Hyades cluster, located around 12° or so to the SE of the Pleiades, is notable in that it is one of the closest objects of its kind. Recent measurements put the Hyades at a distance of about 145 light years. The group contains around 400 stars, a number of which are very faint, 16th-magnitude objects, with true luminosities of less than a two-thousandth of the Sun. Normally, stars this faint cannot be seen in open clusters because of their large distances; the comparative closeness of the Hyades makes it possible to examine a larger range of typical cluster members.

Unlike the Pleiades, the Hyades are old stars, the estimated age of the group being around 400 million years. However, the oldest known open clusters are the rich and compact M67 in Cancer and the more sparsely populated NGC 188 in Cepheus. Containing some 500 stars, M67 is located at a distance of 2,500 light years and is thought to be around 10 billion years old. Located at roughly twice the

Above Globular clusters have been observed around many other galaxies, including the giant elliptical galaxy M87 in Virgo M87 plays host to a large number of globular clusters: over 500 have been detected of a total that may be as high as 4,000. This photograph shows some of these, appearing as fuzzy spots around the edge of the galaxy.

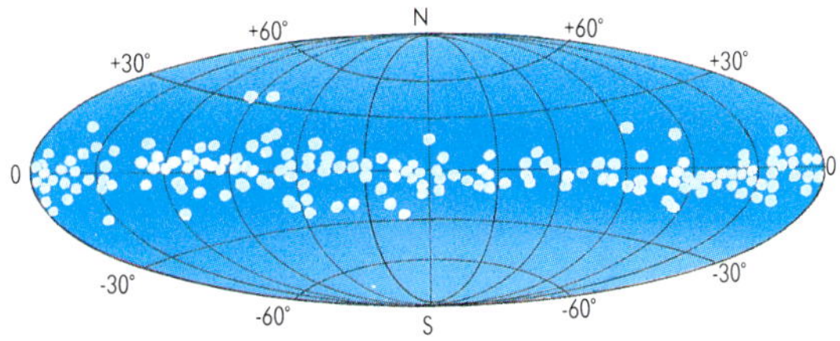

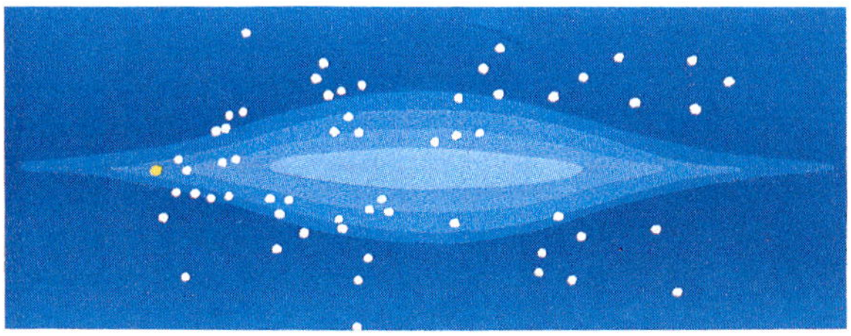

Top Open or galactic star clusters are comprised of comparatively young stars and are distributed primarily along the main plane of the Galaxy.

Above The older stars forming globular clusters lie within the galactic halo and these objects are seen outside the main galaxy.

Left The globular cluster NGC 104 in Tucana is one of the finest objects of its kind in the sky. This is thanks to the fact that it is one of the nearest globular clusters, laying at a distance of some 16,000 light years. Its diameter is around 210 light years.

distance of M67 is NGC 188, the age of which is estimated at between 12 and 14 billion years. These two objects are the two main examples of open clusters with stellar populations more typical of those found in globular clusters, globulars being generally much older than their galactic counterparts. Another thing that these two clusters have in common is a high displacement above the main plane of the Galaxy, amounting to 1,500 light years for M67 and 1,800 light years in the case of NGC 188.

Above The Jewel Box (NGC 4755) in Crux is one of the youngest open clusters known. Lying in a rich area of the Milky Way, this superb collection of stars is one of the showpieces of the southern sky. It lies about 3,500 light years from us.

Globular clusters

Globular clusters differ greatly from open clusters not only in shape and size but in distribution. As their name suggests, globular clusters are spherical collections of stars and can contain anything up to a hundred thousand or more individual members. The stars in globulars are relatively tightly packed leading to a gravitational attraction strong enough to allow the cluster to retain its shape. Globular clusters are amongst the oldest known class of object.

Whereas open clusters are found within the spiral arms of the Galaxy, and orbit the galactic centre in paths that are almost circular, globular clusters are located in the galactic halo, a spherical volume of space surrounding the Galaxy. They travel around the galactic centre in eccentric orbits that are highly inclined. Around 200 globulars are known to exist around our Galaxy, many of which are concentrated close to the galactic centre. Their diameters range from a few tens to several hundred light years. They are made up of old Population II stars of the type found in galactice nuclei.

As with their galactic counterparts, a number of globulars are visible to the unaided eye. The two brightest, Omega Centauri and NGC 104, are situated in the southern sky. Omega Centauri is considered by many to be the best example of a globular cluster. Situated at a distance of around 17,000 light years, it was first noted by the Greek astronomer Ptolemy around 2,000 years ago. NGC 104, otherwise known as 47 Tucanae, can be seen just to the west of the Small Magellanic Cloud, and is second only in magnificence to Omega Centauri.

The best example of globular cluster in the northern hemisphere is undoubtedly the Great Globular Cluster (M13) in Hercules. Just visible to the naked eye as a small, spherical patch of light, M13 is comparable in diameter to 47 Tucanae and is situated a little over 20,000 light years away.

THE MILKY WAY GALAXY

Our Sun is just one of around 100 billion stars that make up the huge spiral system of stars we call the Galaxy. Together with this colossal number of stars, the Galaxy contains vast amounts of interstellar gas and dust, concentrations of which are seen to be scattered throughout its spiral arms. New stars are continually forming from this material.

The Galaxy has three main regions: the central bulge, the disc and the halo. The spiral arms that radiate from the central bulge are, from the centre, the Norma Arm, the Sagittarius Arm, the Orion Arm and the Perseus Arm. The solar system is located in the disc between the Orion and Perseus Arms, roughly 30,000 light years from the galactic centre, or two-thirds of the way out.

Although the outer boundaries of the galactic disc are not exactly defined, its overall diameter is believed to be around 100,000 light years, with a thickness of some 3,000 light years, though this thickness varies across its width. The stars within the disc orbit the galactic centre in roughly circular paths, the stars nearer the centre completing their orbits in shorter times than those farther out. The Sun takes roughly 225 million years (a cosmic year) to complete one orbit.

Although the Galaxy is large, there are many other galaxies that are much bigger – notably the Andromeda Spiral, another member of the Local Group. There are billions of other galaxies throughout the universe. (The term Galaxy, with a capital "G", is applied only to our own system.)

The Milky Way

As we look out along the main plane of the Galaxy, we see the combined light from countless thousands of stars spread out in a band of light around the sky. This band of light is called the Milky Way. Legends relating to it have come down to us from numerous peoples, including the Chinese, American Indians, Greeks and Arabs. It has been referred to as, among other things, a Heavenly River, the Way of Heaven and the Path to the Land of the Hereafter. It was only with the advent of the telescope that Galileo was able to confirm that the light we see is that from many stars, although it appears that the idea was suggested by Pythagoras and Democritus over 2,000 years ago.

The irregular form of the Milky Way can be easily observed. The Milky Way is brightest in the regions of Cygnus and Aquila, in the northern hemisphere, and Scorpius and Sagittarius, in the southern hemisphere. The faintest regions are found in Monoceros, contrasting with the dense star fields in Sagittarius. The width of the Milky Way is quite variable: it averages about 15°, but reaches 30° in places. The plane of the Milky Way is inclined at just over 60° to the ecliptic, and passes through Cassiopeia and near Alpha Crucis, at which points it approaches to within 27° of the north and south celestial poles.

Above Cross-sectional view of our Galaxy, showing the location of the Sun, roughly 30,000 light years out from the centre.

Divisions in the Milky Way's structure can be seen in Vela, near the bright star Canopus, where it appears completely divided for a short distance, and from Cygnus to Aquila, where it is split into two lanes for a distance. This Cygnus-Aquila division is often referred to as the Great Rift. Another spectacular gap can be found in Crux in the form of the Coal Sack, a dark cloud of obscuring matter that blots out the light from the stars beyond and gives the appearance of a hole in the sky. All these divisions in the Milky Way are due to the presence of dark nebulosity located between us and the starfields beyond.

The Galactic Centre

Unlike the Galactic disc, within the spiral arms of which are found young ('Population I') stars, the central bulge is home to much older ('Population II') stars. Also, the central regions of the Galaxy contain little interstellar gas and dust. The central bulge is around 20,000 light years in diameter and some 10,000 light years thick.

The centre of the Galaxy is located in the direction of the constellation Sagittarius, although we are unable to see it at optical wavelengths, owing to the intervention of gas and dust along the Galactic plane. However, radio and infrared observations can be carried out successfully and have allowed astronomers to plot the general structure of these regions. The centre of the Galaxy has been identified with the strong radio source Sagittarius A. In fact, the Galactic centre was the source of the first-ever radio waves received from the sky, by Karl Jansky in the early 1930s.

Finally, the halo is a huge, spherical cloud of stars that completely surrounds the Galaxy. Like the central bulge, the halo contains old Population II stars, most of which are concentrated into globular clusters that orbit the galactic centre in elliptical paths.

Left The Milky Way in Scorpius with the two open clusters M6 (NGC 6405) and (below) M7 (NGC 6475) prominent to the left of centre. The two bright emission nebulae at centre of picture are NGC 6357 (left) and NGC 6334 whilst the emission nebula IC 4628 can be seen near right of picture. The bright open cluster NGC 6231 can be seen just to the right (south) of IC 4628 whilst just to the south of NGC 6231 is the naked eye double Zeta Scorpii. The brighter (lower) star is magnitude 3.6 orange subgiant Zeta 2, offering a colour contrast with the magnitude 4.8 blue-white supergiant Zeta 1, situated nearly 7 minutes of arc of the west.

Left This photograph , with north at the top, shows the Milky Way running through Crux, the constellation visible just to the left of centre. Prominent here are the Coal Sack Nebula, just to the lower left of Crux, and Beta Centauri, the bright star to the lower left. The Eta Carina Nebula (NGC 3372), the most luminous emission nebula known in the Milky Way, is seen at right of picture. Roughly mid-way between the southern end of Crux and NGC 3372 are the regions of nebulosity surrounding the open star cluster IC 2948.

GALAXIES BEYOND OUR OWN

Above The large spiral galaxy M83 (NGC 5236) in Hydra is one of the brightest galaxies in the sky. Lying at a distance of almost 10 million light years, M83 has a small but bright nucleus from which radiate well defined spiral arms containing many giant stars, star clouds, bright nebulosity and prominent dark dust lanes.

Wherever we look into the void beyond our own galactic system, the glowing shapes of other galaxies can be seen in colossal numbers The diameters of these galaxies range from several thousand to 100,000 light years or more. Each one of the galaxies revealed as luminescent blurs on long-exposure images comprises billions of stars.

Types of galaxies

Galaxies take many different forms, of which spirals like our own are just one example. The Milky Way has spiral arms radiating from a central bulge, whereas the barred spirals have arms that emanate from the ends of a bar that extends through the centre of the system. Elliptical galaxies, as their name suggests, have no spiral pattern and are uniform in appearance. Ellipticals are the most numerous galaxies, generally made up of old, cool and massive stars with little or no interstellar material. Indeed they are similar in many ways to huge globular clusters. These three classes of galaxy are further subdivided: spirals and barred spirals can have either tightly wound spiral arms, together with small or large central bulges, or more loosely wound arms with smaller central bulges. The ellipticals vary from highly elongated to almost spherical systems.

A further two classes of galaxy are recognized: irregular galaxies are loose collections of stars with no well defined shape, while lenticular galaxies resemble the flattened centre of a spiral galaxy without its spiral arms.

Evolution of galaxies

The stars in a spiral galaxy revolve around the centre in orbits that are more or less circular, the rotation being such that the arms appear to trail behind. The evolution of spirals and ellipticals is thought to have taken different tracks. Galaxies condensed from relatively dense and localized regions of material shortly after the Big Bang. Those objects that were to become elliptical galaxies formed fairly quickly, using up all of the material present to form stars.

Spiral galaxies evolved differently. Their central bulges seem to have formed in a similar way to the ellipticals, with all the interstellar material being transformed into stars. Excess material surrounding the newly formed bulge of stars then went to form a disc-shaped structure around it. Although it is not known with certainty how the spiral arms formed, one thing that is certain is that they should not be regarded as objects existing in their own right. If they were, they would have fragmented long ago as they rotated about the centre of their parent galaxy. They appear to be waves of density produced through the gravitational interaction of the stars within the galactic disc. These waves produce contractions in the gas and dust in the disc, and these regions of increased density then collapse to form new stars. These stars illuminate the surrounding clouds of dust and gas, which show up as spiral arms in the areas recently visited by the density waves. However, it should be borne in mind that huge numbers of stars together with gas and dust also populate the regions between the arms.

Galaxies emit continuous radio noise, arising primarily from their interstellar gas. Different types of atom emit different radio wavelengths. For example, hydrogen sends out radio emission at a wavelength of 21 cm. By listening in at this frequency astronomers are able to chart the positions of

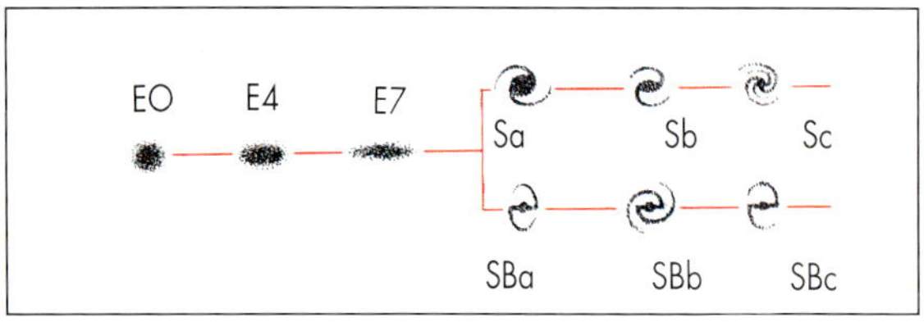

Above Galaxies are divided into types according to the system devised by Edwin Hubble. This includes elliptical galaxies (EO to E7), spirals (Sa, Sb or Sc) and barred spirals (SBa, SBb or SBc).

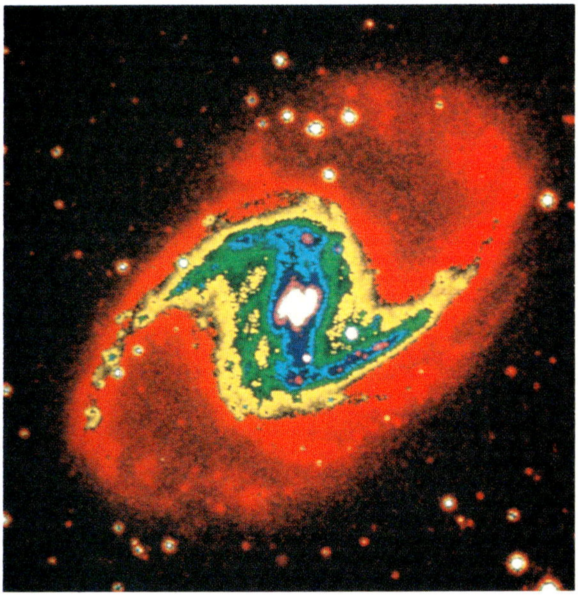

Above This image-processed optical photograph shows NGC 1365, a magnificent example of a barred spiral galaxy. The bar, running across the central region of the galaxy from top to bottom, is very well defined.

the interstellar hydrogen clouds in our own and other galaxies. The radio emission from normal galaxies comes from their optically visible regions.

Radio galaxies

A quite different type of emission is received from objects called radio galaxies. Virtually all radio galaxies are seen to be elliptical. Their radio output amounts to many times the

Above A bright jet can be seen extending from the giant elliptical galaxy M87 (NGC 4486). The material in this jet is believed to emanate from the highly active nucleus which is thought to contain a supermassive black hole.

energy output of a normal galaxy. This radio emission comes from electrons that are accelerated to colossal speeds and emanates from huge lobes situated symmetrically outside the galaxy itself. The lobes appear to have been violently ejected from the main galaxy. One of the best examples is the huge Centaurus A (NGC 5128) elliptical galaxy. Situated at a distance of around 15 million light years, Centaurus A is the nearest, and most extensively observed, radio galaxy. A series of lobes extends to 1.5 million light years from its centre.

Seyfert galaxies

Seyfert galaxies are characterized by weak spiral arms surrounding a small nucleus, which is bright and almost stellar in appearance. Seyfert galaxies are moderate emitters of radio waves. They also give out a great deal of infrared and ultraviolet energy and in some cases are strong X-ray sources.

A good example of a Seyfert galaxy is the bright and compact spiral M77 (NGC 1068) in Cetus. Here, as in other Seyfert galaxies, observation has revealed the presence of gas clouds moving at several hundred kilometres per second in the central regions of the system. The masses of these clouds are thought to equal several million solar masses and they are thought to have been ejected from the nuclear region. The enormous speeds of these gas clouds may be due to the gravitational influence of a massive object at the centre of the galaxy, such as a black hole, which may be the power source for the whole galaxy's core.

CLUSTERS OF GALAXIES

The vast majority of galaxies are grouped together in clusters, swarms of island universes bound by the gravitational influence of one or more dominant members. Our own Local Group is a good example. This is a collection of around two dozen galaxies a few million light years across. The three largest members of the Local Group are the Milky Way, the Andromeda Spiral (M31) and the Triangulum Spiral (M33). Apart from these three, most of the other Local Group members are dwarf elliptical systems. The Milky Way Galaxy and the Andromeda Spiral are seen to be central members of subgroups of galaxies. The Large and Small Magellanic Clouds are satellites of the Milky Way, while the Andromeda Spiral has many small satellite galaxies in orbit around it.

It cannot be taken for granted that galaxies lying in approximately the same direction are actually associated with each other. In order to ascertain whether galaxies occupy common regions of space, their distances must first be determined.

A group of galaxies that lie in roughly the same direction in Pegasus is Stephan's Quintet, comprising NGC 7317, NGC 7318a and 7318b, NGC 7319 and NGC 7320. The last-named possesses a much smaller red shift than its neighbours, indicating that it lies much closer to us (see page 62) and is therefore not a member of the group. Yet photographic evidence seems to show that NGC 7320 is actually connected to its neighbours by streams of gas. Evidently red-shift evidence must be used with care.

The group of galaxies closest to our own is the Sculptor Group, situated at a distance of just under 8 million light years. The dominant member is the large spiral NGC 253, discovered by Caroline Herschel in 1783. Many of the other members of the Sculptor Group are large, faint spirals.

Located just a little farther away from us is the Ursa Major -Camelopardalis Group, the dozen or so members of which are concentrated around the magnificent spiral galaxy M81 and the unusually shaped M82, both of which were discovered by Johann Bode in 1774.

A group of galaxies is dominated by the gravitational influences of its major members. It seems that the dwarf members of these systems have little or no influence on their overall structure and evolution.

Galaxy clusters

Even larger than the groups of galaxies discussed above are the clusters, which can play host to hundreds or even thousands of individual members. A fine example is the Virgo Cluster, the nearest rich cluster of galaxies, which is located at a distance of 40–70 million light years. The total membership of the Virgo Cluster is unknown, although around 2,000 individual galaxies have been recorded on photographic plates. Assuming that dwarf galaxies too dim to be detectable are predominant within the Virgo Cluster, as they are in the Local Group, then the total membership may be considerably higher.

Above Our Local Group has around two dozen member galaxies, of which shown here. The Large Magellanic Cloud (upper left) and the Small Magellanic Cloud (right) are irregular dwarf systems which are orbiting companions of our own galaxy, the Milky Way. They are named after the Portugese navigator Ferdinand Magellan who first described

The Virgo Cluster, often referred to as the Virgo–Coma Cluster, is centred on a point near the border between the constellations Coma Berenices and Virgo, and member galaxies can be seen within each constellation. Among the member galaxies of the Virgo–Coma cluster is the giant elliptical galaxy M87 (NGC 4486). M87 is one of the most massive galaxies known, with a luminosity greater than that of the Andromeda Spiral.

Even larger than the Virgo Cluster is the Coma Cluster, 350 million light years away. The cluster has thousands of members, dominated by the two giant galaxies NGC 4874 and NGC 4889. Each of these galaxies has a diameter of the order of 2 million light years and is surrounded by large numbers of smaller, more normal-sized galaxies.

Superclusters

The Virgo Cluster lies at the centre of a huge collection of galaxies known as the Local Supercluster, the diameter of which is in the region of 100 million light years. Member systems include many individual groups of galaxies, our own Local Group being situated near its periphery. The Local Supercluster also includes some solitary galaxies situated between the main groups.

Dozens of other superclusters have been found, each of which contains many smaller clusters scattered across regions of space tens of millions of light years across. Included here are the large examples in Hercules and Perseus. The Virgo Supercluster consists of just one rich cluster, the Virgo Cluster. Generally speaking, other superclusters have a higher number of rich individual clusters within their boundaries.

Just as stars are the building blocks of galaxies, the galaxies themselves, or even clusters and superclusters of galaxies, form the fabric of the universe as a whole.

Left Image-processed optical pciture of the Pavo 5 cluster of galaxies. This picture has been colour coded according to the intensity of the light from the cluster. The most intense sources show up predominantly pink, the centres of the galaxies. The least intense are blue, the faint and tenuous halos of gas that surround and link the galaxies.

Below The Local Group consists of twenty or so galaxies of which our galaxy is one of the larger members. The closest galaxies to our own are the Large and Small Magellanic Clouds. The Local Group has no apparent centre but has two major clusters of galaxies, both centred on large spiral galaxies, one our own and the other the Andromeda galaxy. However, it is still unclear whether such clusters are random associations or whether they are bound together by gravitational force.

Below X-ray clusters of galaxies Abell 1060 in Libra. This moderately-rich cluster of galaxies, 200 million light-years away, is dominated by the two elliptical galaxies in the middle of this photograph of its central portion. Satellite telescopes have detected x-rays coming from this cluster, which are believed to come from thin, exceedingly hot gas filling the space between the galaxies. The large, slightly wedge-shaped spiral galaxy, NGC 3312, is believed to be having some of its material stripped away as it moves through the background gas.

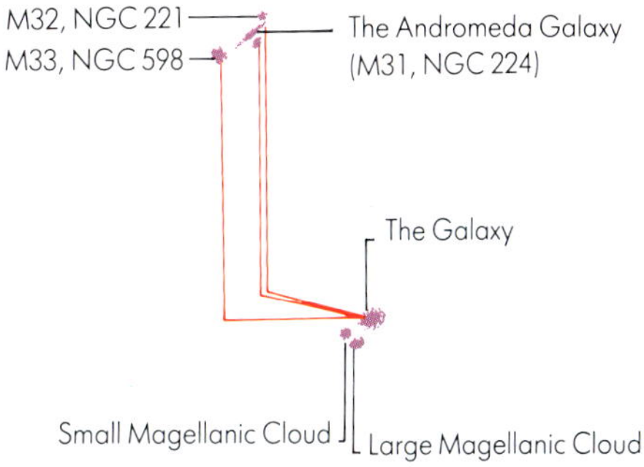

THE EXPANDING UNIVERSE

The universe was born in a colossal primeval explosion. The galaxies are the debis of that explosion, still hurtling outwards through space – perhaps for ever. Such is the story told by present-day cosmology.

When the spectrum of a galaxy is examined, we see the combined spectra of all the member stars of that galaxy. However, the main spectral lines are identifiable, and with each galaxy examined, apart from nearby galaxies within the Local Group, a red shift has been found. This implies that all the galaxies we see are actually moving away from us and that the universe is in a state of expansion.

In addition it has been found that the red shifts of galaxies farther away from us are greater than those of closer systems, meaning that their recessional velocities are higher. This relationship between distance and velocity of recession of galaxies was first pointed out by the American astronomer Edwin Hubble.

The Big Bang theory

Many ideas have been proposed to explain how the universe came into being. The idea of a primeval explosion was put forward in 1927 by the Belgian mathematician Abbé Georges Lemaître. Lemaître's idea was elaborated by later astronomers and eventually became known as the Big Bang theory. One of these theorists was George Gamow who, in 1946, suggested that the common elements were formed from the hydrogen present shortly after the initial explosion.

Further evidence for an initial high-temperature, high-density phase of the universe was discovered in 1965 by Arno Penzias and Robert Wilson at the Bell Telephone Laboratories, New Jersey. While they were mapping radio emissions from the sky away from the main plane of our Galaxy they detected radio noise that appeared to be coming from everywhere in the sky and was distributed uniformly. No matter where in the sky they pointed their antenna, they detected faint background radiation. This is now thought to be the cooled-down cosmic radiation left over from the Big Bang.

Quasars

During the early 1960's astronomers were carrying out a search for distant objects. Among the objects studied were radio sources that, from their radio properties, were believed to lie at immense distances. They were identified optically by comparison with photographs taken by the Palomar 508-cm (200-inch) reflector. They were found to be blue, starlike objects that had been thought to be lying in the Milky Way. However, when the spectrum of 3C 273 (the 273rd object in

Above The 15-metre (50-foot) long horn-shaped antenna at the Bell Telephone Laboratories station at Holmdel, New Jersey, with which Arno Penzias and Robert Wilson first detected the cosmic background radiation.

the third Cambridge catalogue of radio sources) was examined, it was found to have an extremely large red shift. Examination of spectra of further examples showed that astronomers had stumbled upon a totally new and different class of object, many of which were found to be receding at speeds of up to half the speed of light!

These objects were christened quasars (short for quasi-stellar radio sources). Almost all theorists interpret their high red shifts as meaning that the quasars are very remote, in accordance with the relationship between distance and velocity that galaxies obey. Quasars are the most luminous objects in the universe. In spite of their immense distances, they have relatively high apparent magnitudes, indicating that some powerful quasars emit more light than a galaxy like our own! Yet observation has also shown that their diameters are small – much less than a light year. Figuring out just how such objects are throwing out these copious amounts of energy is a problem for astronomers. There is mounting evidence that quasars are actually nuclei of very active galaxies, and it may well be that they are powered by massive black holes, sucking in matter and releasing energy.

The farthest known quasar at the time of writing is Q0000-26. Situated near the border between Sculptor and Cetus, the light from this magnitude 17.5 object set off towards us when the universe was only around 10 per cent of its present age. In studying this and other quasars at similar distances, astronomers are effectively looking back in time to a point only a couple of billion years or so after the Big Bang.

However, there is a limit to how far we can see. Q0000-26 is travelling away from us at something like 93 per cent of the speed of light. Eventually there will be a point at which objects are receding at the speed of light. This is the

Right Radio picture of the quasar 3c273 with regions of greatest radio intensity shown as red and decreasing through yellow, green and blue. The extended appearance of 3c273 comes from energy emitted by radio lobes located on either side of the quasar.

Below The spectra and recessional velocities of five galaxies, each photographed to the same scale and arranged (from top to bottom) in order of increasing distance. Their spectra (the elongated bands) contain prominent calcium lines which are redshifted by a greater amount the further away the galaxy is. The recessional velocity, in km/sec, is calculated from the amount of shift.

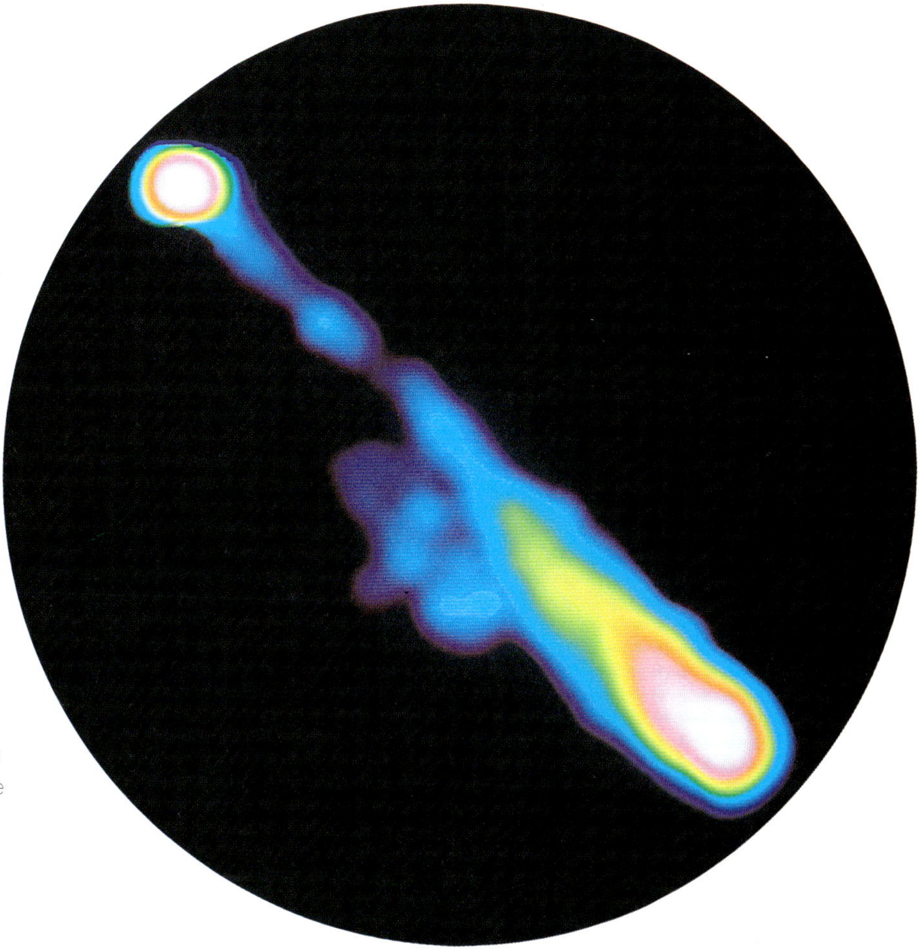

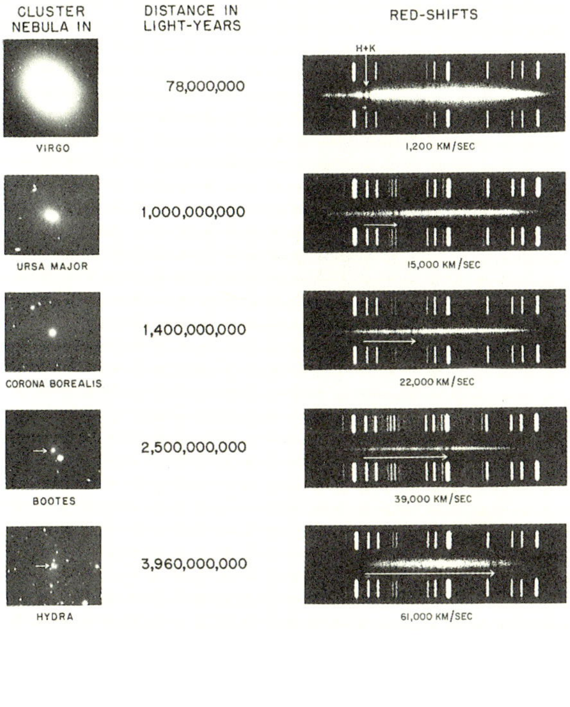

boundary of the observable universe, the region beyond which is forever hidden from view.

The Fate of the Universe

It has been suggested that the universe is actually oscillating. The expansion we see today will eventually stop and the universe will collapse upon itself. The contraction will end in another Big Bang and subsequent expansion. According to the theory, a new explosion takes place roughly every 80 billion years.

A major drawback with the idea of an oscillating universe is that, in order for the expansion to stop, gravity must overcome the outward momentum of the galaxies. However, the average density of matter in the universe does not seem to be great enough to produce a gravitational contraction. Nevertheless, many astronomers believe that there are huge amounts of as yet undiscovered invisible matter lurking throughout space. If this so-called missing mass is eventually detected, and there is enough of it, then gravity may indeed gain the upper hand and halt the expansion of the universe.

THE MOVING EARTH

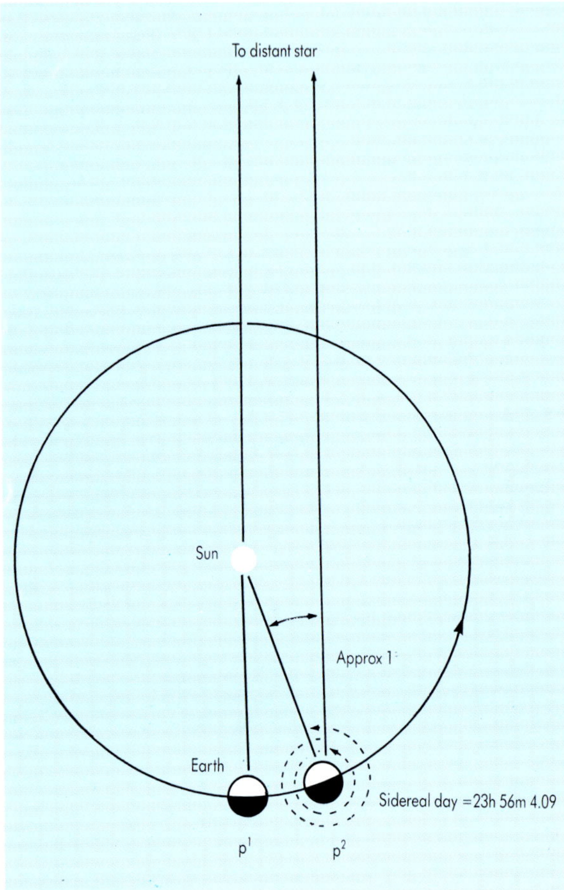

Left Astronomers use two definitions of the word 'day'. A *sidereal* day is the interval between successive passages across the meridian of a star. This is equal to the true rotation period of the earth (23h 56m 4.09s). A *solar* day is the interval between successive meridian passages of the sun (or the interval between successive noons). However, during the year the Sun appears to travel around the sky in relation to the background of fixed stars. Its rate of travel is about 1° per day in an easterly direction. As a result the solar day is slightly longer than the sidereal day. However the motion of the Sun through the sky is not uniform. This is due to two facts: the orbit of the Earth around the Sun is elliptical, and therefore its orbital velocity is not uniform;and the Sun moves along the ecliptic rather than the celestial equator, producing variations in its angular motion parallel to the celestial equator.

Below The seasons arise not as a result of the small variation in the distance of the Earth from the Sun but the tilt of the Earth's axis in relation to the plane of its orbit around our star. In June the northern hemisphere is tilted towards the Sun: as seen by anyone in this hemisphere the Sun will reach a higher position in the sky at noon than it will in December when the northern hemisphere is tilted away from the Sun. The overall effect of this is to make the days longer in June (southern winter) than in December (southern summer) because the Sun is in the sky for a longer time. The warming effect of the Sun is greater is summer because it is higher in the sky. In March and September, during spring and autumn, day and night are of more equal lengths.

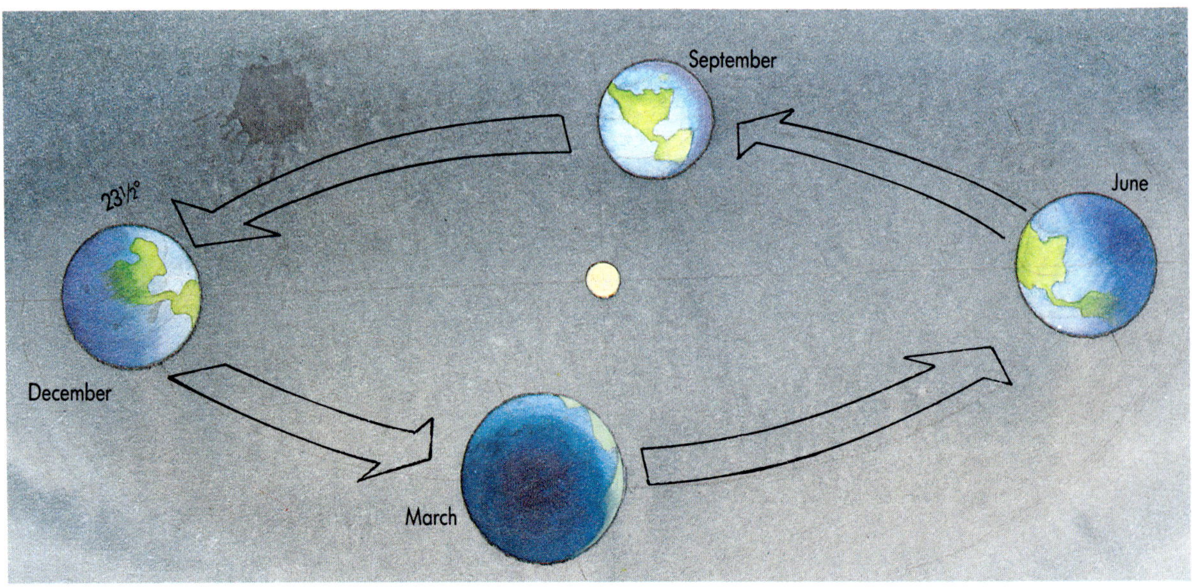

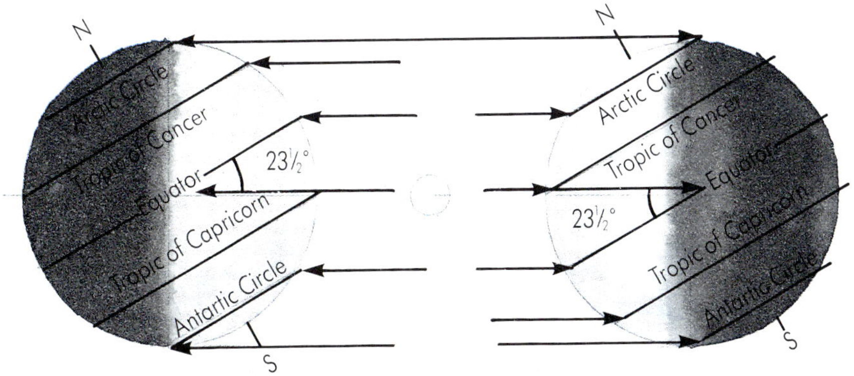

Left The maximum angular tilt of the Earth towards or away from the Sun is 23.5° and the highest and lowest latitudes from which the Sun can ever be seen directly overhead are 23.5°N (the tropic of Cancer) or 23.5°S (the tropic of Capricorn). The polar circles lie 23.5° from the poles: areas within them experience a 24 hour day or night at the solstices.

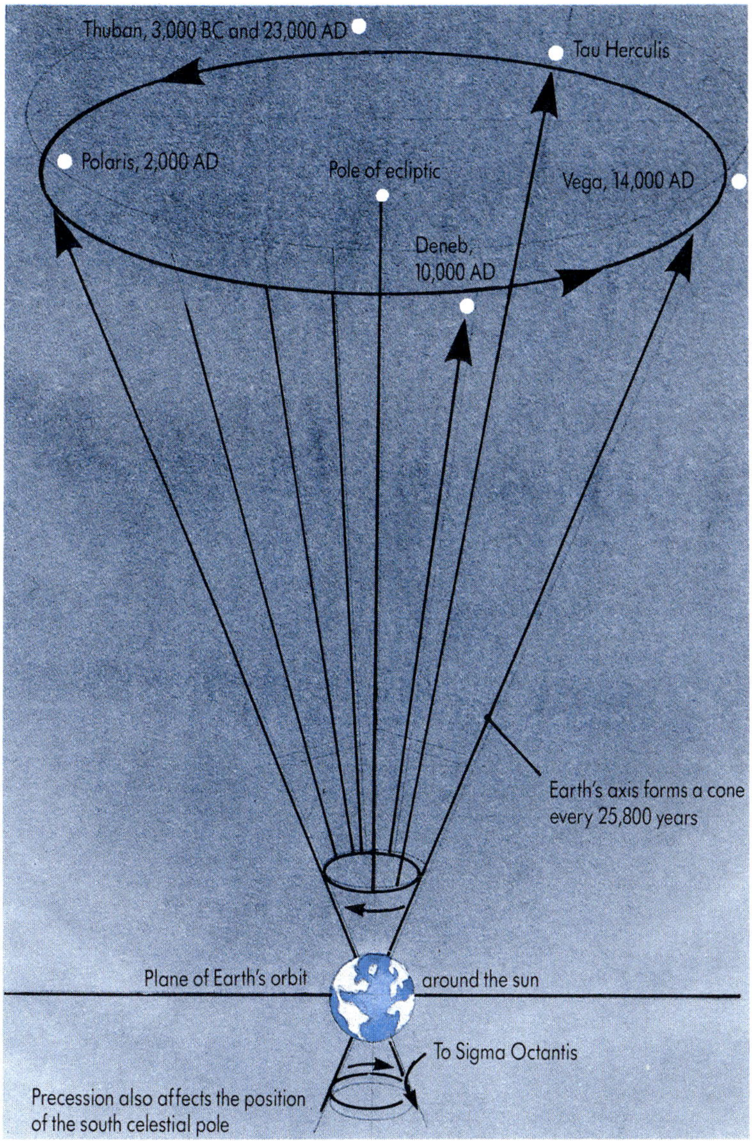

Left If the Earth's axis is projected into the sky it intersects the celestial sphere at two points. These points are situated directly above the celestial poles. At present, the position of the NCP is marked by the bright star Polaris, which lies within a degree of the true pole's position. The nearest star to the SCP is Sigma Octantis being about one degree away. Because of the gravitational influence of the Sun and Moon on the Earth's equatorial bulge, the Earth's axis wobbles.This effect is known as precession, and the result is that the positions of the celestial poles change continously. Each wobble of the Earth's axis takes 25,800 years, during which time the celestial poles trace out complete circles centred on the points on the celestial sphere vertically above (or below) the central point of the plane of the Earth's orbit around the Sun.Around 2,500BC the NCP lay close to Thuban in Draco. It will progress around the circle of precession until it returns to Thuban in AD23,000.

THE CELESTIAL SPHERE

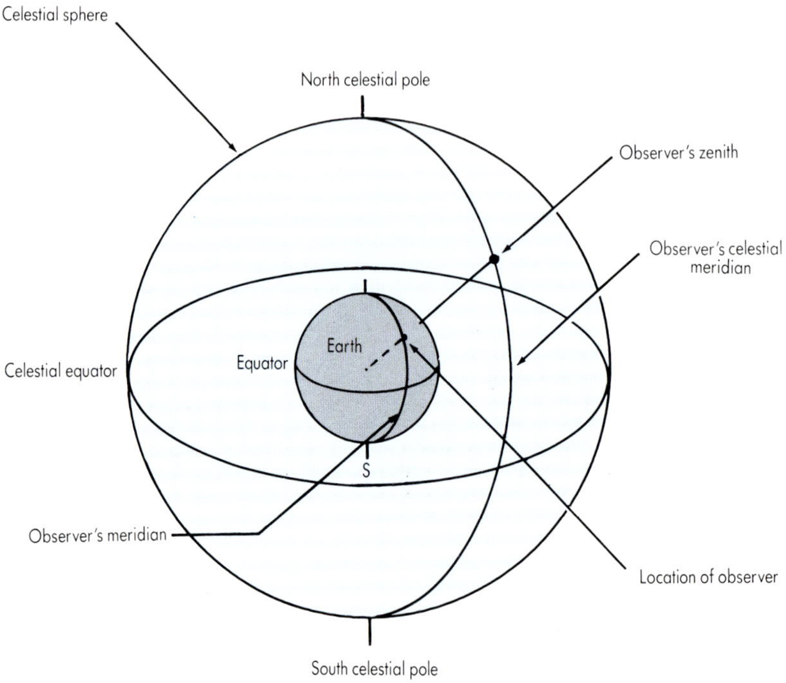

Left The celestial sphere is an imaginary sphere surrounding the Earth. Certain reference points on the sphere are defined in relation to reference points on the Earth. The celestial poles lie directly over the Earth's poles. The celestial equator lies midway beween the celestial poles and over the terrestrial equator. Other points are defined in relation to the observer. The zenith is the point directly above the observer. The celestial meridian is the circle that runs through the celestial poles and the zenith.

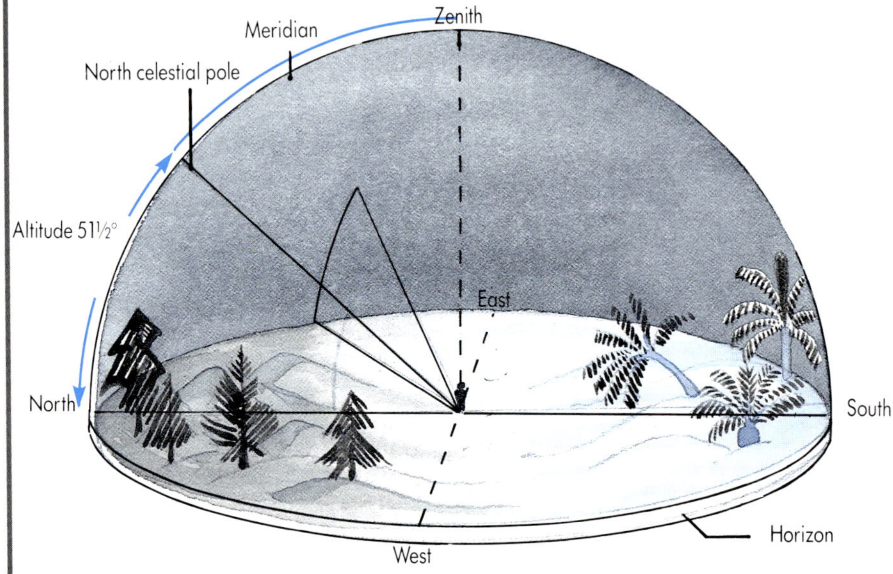

Left To an observer on the Earth, the visible sky is an inverted dome. From a point in the middle northern latitudes, as shown here, the northern celestial pole (NCP) lies at an unchanging height over the northern horizon. As the Earth rotates from west to east, all objects in the sky seem to move from east to west, revolving around the NCP. The angle between a star or other object and horizon is its "altitude" at that moment.

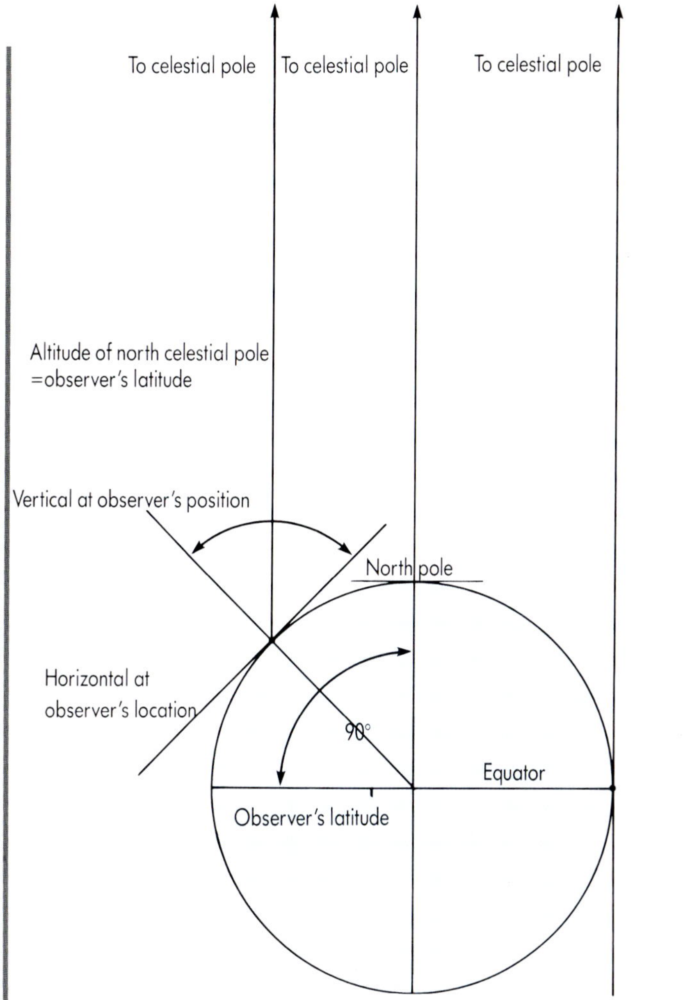

Left The altitude above the northern horizon of the NCP (marked by Polaris) is equal to the latitude of the observer. For example, at the north pole (latitude 90°N) the NCP's altitude is 90° (at the Zenith). Seen from Philadelphia (latitude 40°N) it has a altitude of 40°, and from the equator (latitude0°), it has an altitude of 0° (skimming the horizon). From below the equator Polaris will not be seen. Corresponding statements will be true for Sigma Octantis, the star closest to SCP. At the south pole it is overhead while at the equator it skims the southern horizon. From Durban, South Africa (latitude 30°S) it is 30° above a southern horizon. Furthermore, the altitude of the celestial equator as seen from New Orleans (latitude 30°N) is 90° - 30°=60°.

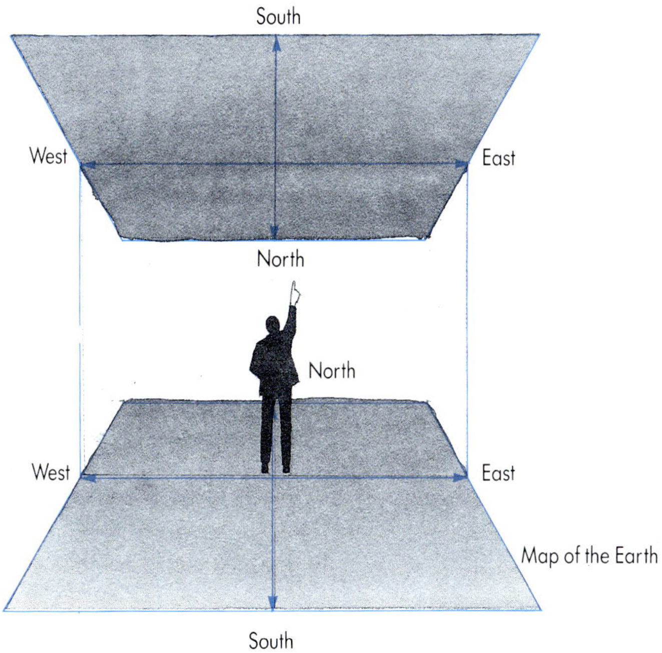

Left The points east and west appear to be reversed in relation to terrestial maps which have east on the right. The reason for this is that terrestial maps chart the planet on which you are standing whilst star charts show the sky overhead. If the star chart is held above the observer's head with the north end of the chart nearest the north horizon east and west will fall into place as, of course, will south.

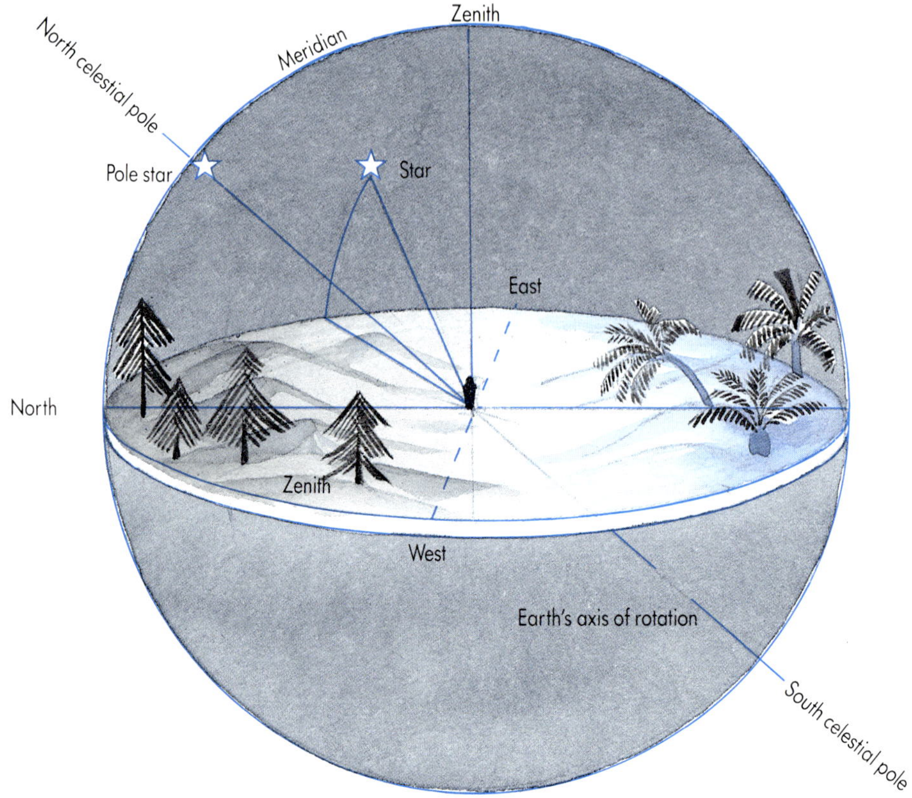

Left The celestial meridian has been extended to run through both celestial poles. The meridian is a great circle, that is, a circle on the celestial sphere that is centred on the sphere's centre. A great circle is a circle of maximum size.

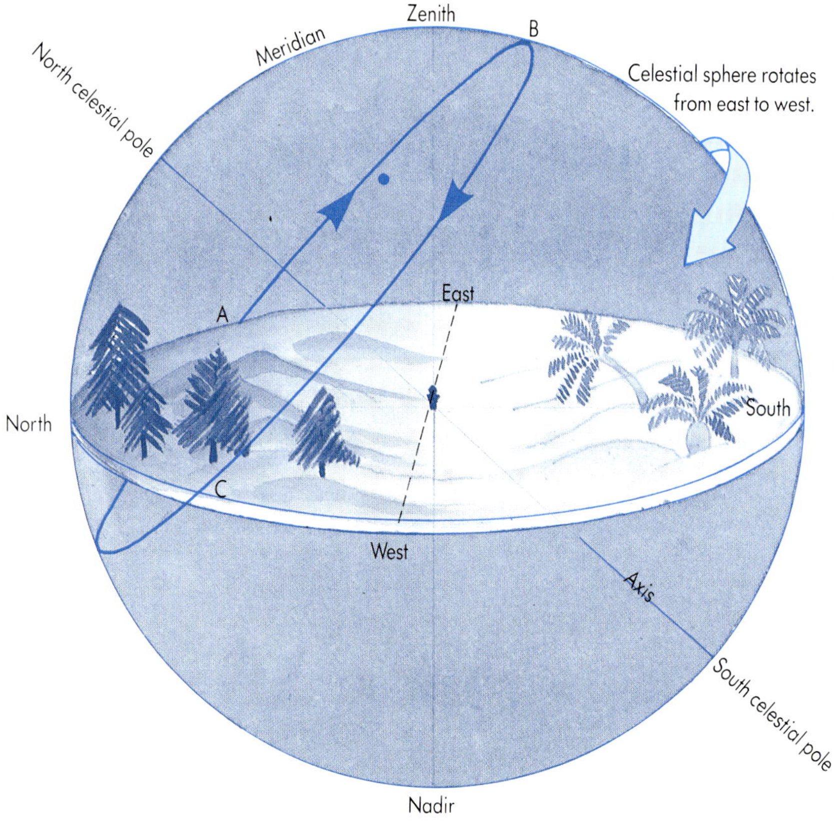

Left As the celestial sphere rotates a star rises (A), crosses the meridian (B) and sets(C). From the time it sets until it rises again, the star is hidden below the horizon. The star is said to culminate when it crosses the meridian reaching its greatest altitude. Notice also the nadir in this diagram. This is the point in the sky directly opposite the zenith, lying below the observer's feet.

Right Star A can never go below this observer's horizon. This is because any star with an angular distance from the NCP of less than the altitude of the NCP above the horizon will never set. Such stars are described as circumpolar for that observer. Star B will be above the horizon for longer than it is below. Stars on the celestial equator (C), on the other hand, spend equal periods above and below the horizon. This is the case as seen from anywhere on the Earth's surface. Stars that lie between the celestial equator and the southern horizon (D) will be below the horizon for longer than they are above it. The farther south they are the less time they are visible. Finally, stars that lie near the SCP (E) will never rise for an observer in the northern hemisphere.

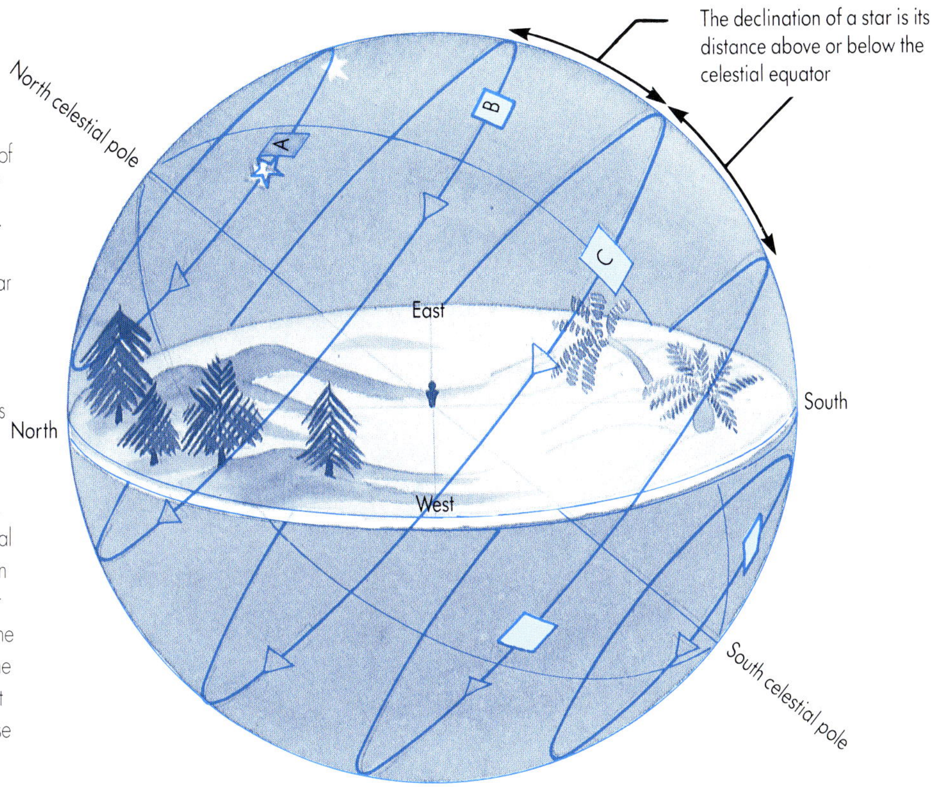

Right Locations on the Earth are expressed in terms of latitude and longitude, and a similar system exists for expressing stellar positions on the celestial sphere. One of the coordinates used is declination, which is the angular distance of an object above or below the celestial equator. This is the celestial equivalent of latitude on the earth, and is expressed in degrees (°) minutes (') and seconds (") of arc. As the celestial sphere rotates, a star traces out an imaginary circle around the sky. The other coordinate is Right Ascension, measured in hours, minutes and seconds, which is the angular distance, measured eastwards, of an object from the vernal equinox.

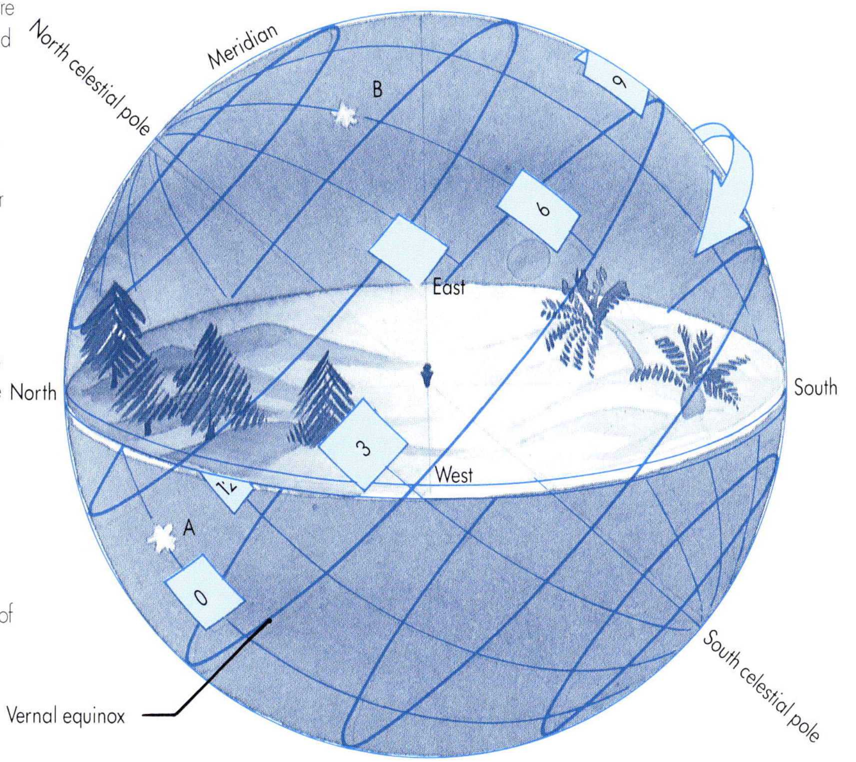

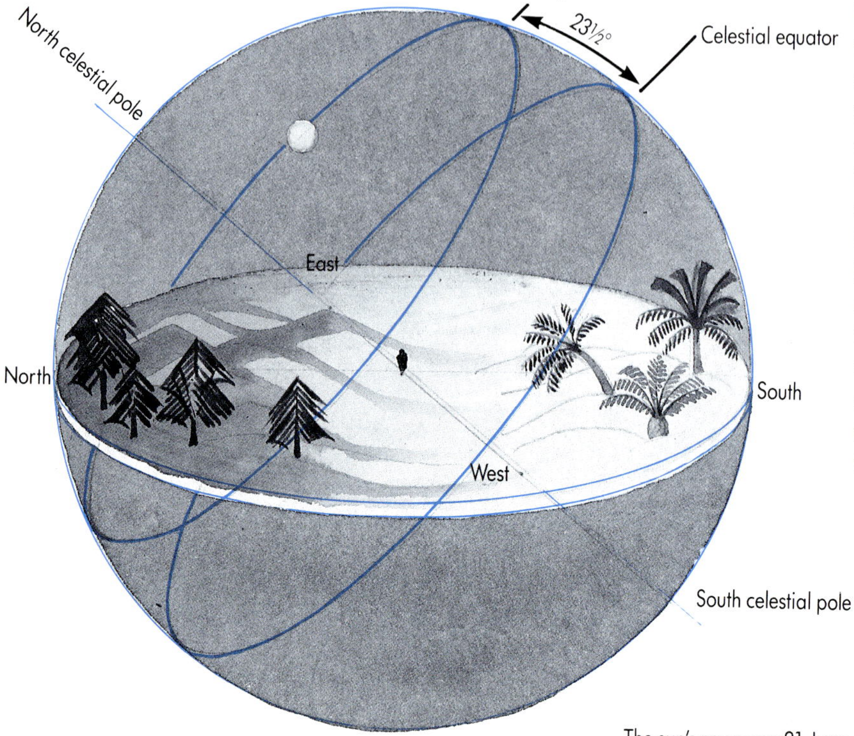

Left The path of the Sun through the sky in relation to the celestial equator at the time of the northern solstice. The Sun is now 23.5°N above the celestial equator and this marks the longest day and shortest night for the northern hemisphere. From London (51.5°N), the Sun's altitude at noon on 21 June is the altitude of the celestial equator above the southern horizon (38.5°) plus the angular distance of the Sun above the celestial equator (23.5°) totalling 62°.

The sun's course on 21 June, summer solstice, as seen from the northern hemisphere. It is at its maximum angular distance, 23½°, above the celestial equator.

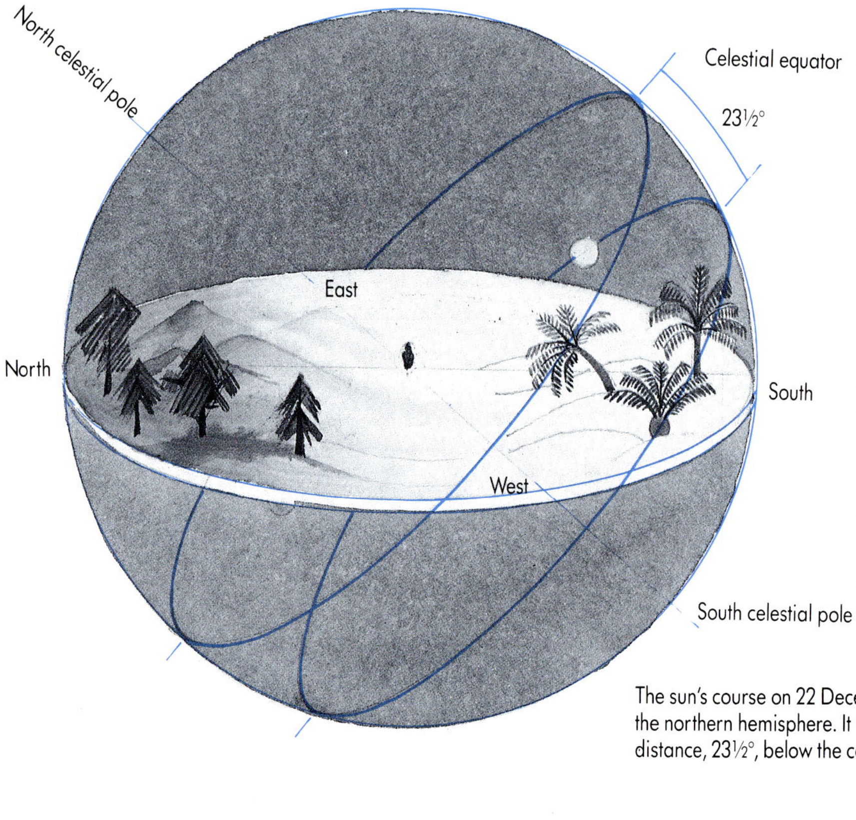

Left The course of the Sun through the sky in relation to the celestial equator at the southern solstice. Now it achieves its lowest noon altitude for northern hemisphere observers, who experience their shortest day and longest night. The lowest northern hemisphere noon position marks the highest for the southern hemisphere. For example, the altitude of the Sun at noon on 22 December as seen from Wellington, New Zealand (41°) is the altitude of the celestial equator above the northern horizon (49°) plus the angular distance of the Sun from the celestial equator (23.5° = 72.5°).

The sun's course on 22 December, winter solstice, as seen from the northern hemisphere. It is at its maximum angular distance, 23½°, below the celestial equator.

Right The course of the Sun at the vernal and autumnal equinoxes, the two points where the path of the Sun crosses the celestial equator. On these dates the Sun rises in the east and sets in the west and day and night are of the same duration. The durations of the year's longest and shortest days (and nights) depend upon latitude, greater distances from the equator producing greater differences. In the equatorial regions, day and night are of similar lengths. At the latitude of London the longest day is around 16 hours in length and the shortest around eight hours. Within 23.5° of the pole, there is at least one midnight Sun in midsummer. Conversely in winter there is one day when the sun never rises. At the poles day and night are each of six months' duration.

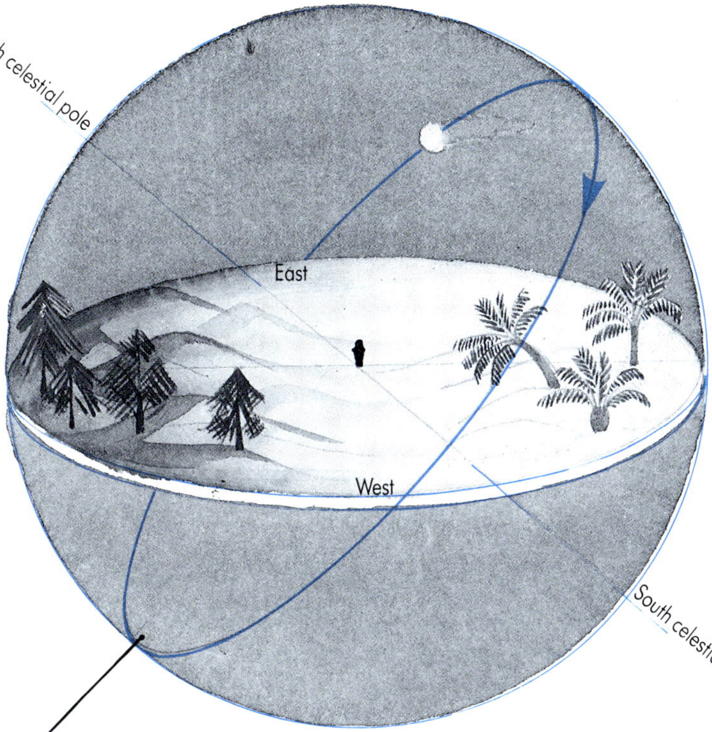

Right During the Earth's annual journey around the Sun we view our star from a slightly different position from day to day. Thus the Sun appears to travel across the sky, passing right around the celestial sphere during the course of a year. The apparent path of the Sun is called the ecliptic and the band of sky through which it passes is known as the Zodiac. As a result of the tilt of the axis the Earth in relation to the Sun it crosses the celestial equator at two points during the year. These points are known as the vernal (or spring) and autumnal equinoxes.

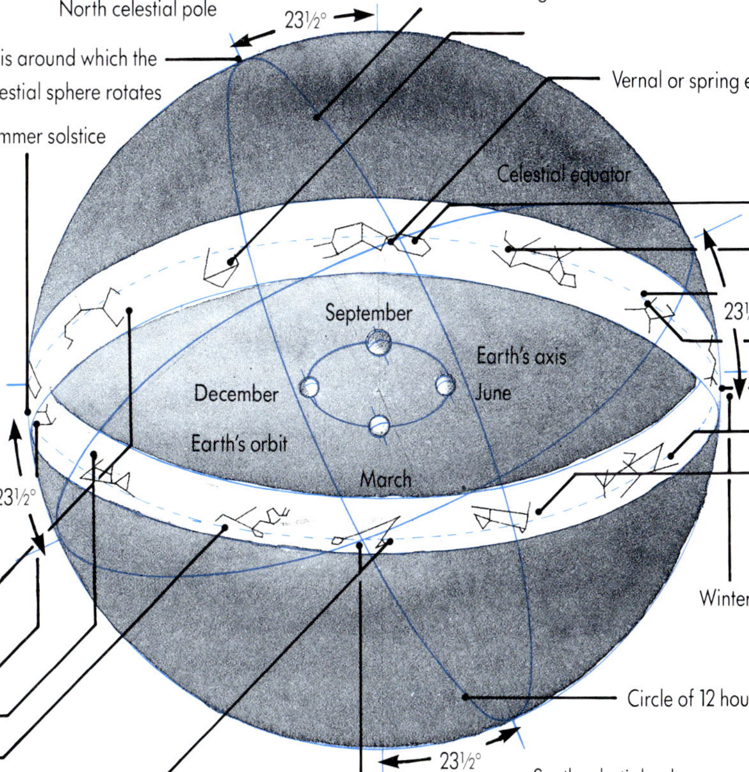

CHOOSING BINOCULARS

By far the best type of optical aid for the first-time stargazer is a pair of binoculars. They are less expensive than a telescope, have a wider field of view, are easier to use, are portable and have uses other than those relating to astronomy.

Even for the more accomplished observer, there is a great deal to be said for binoculars. Many features on the Moon can be picked out, as can a large number of deep-sky objects, and this type of instrument has been fundamental in discovering comets and novae.

Essentially, a pair of binoculars consists of two small refracting telescopes. This eliminates the sometimes tiring need to close one eye. The key to their compactness is that the light paths are folded inside the binocular barrels by a series of prisms.

The most important consideration when buying binoculars (or telescopes) is aperture (the diameter of the objective, or main, lens). This should be as large as possible, permitting more light to be gathered and fainter objects to be observed. Bear in mind, however, that binoculars with very large lenses will be heavy and difficult to hold steady. Binoculars are graded as, for example,8 x 40, which denotes a magnification of 8x and an aperture of 40 mm.

Again, the greater the magnification, the more difficult it will be to hold the binoculars steady. As a general rule, the highest magnification for hand-held binoculars should be 7x, although some observers are comfortable with 10x or even 12x. Probably the best size of binocular for general use is 7 x 50.

Another advantage of 7x50 binoculars is that their "exit pupil" matches the diameter of the pupil of the dark-adapted eye. The exit pupil of any optical system is the breadth of the beam of light leaving that system. It is calculated by dividing the magnification into the aperture: in the case of a 7x50 this is 50 mm ÷ 7 = 7 mm approximately. The aperture of the fully dark-adapted eye pupil is about 7 mm. Therefore the full diameter of the light beam leaving the binoculars can be used.

Holding the binoculars in the viewing position, but away from your eyes, will allow you to see the exit pupils as discs of light in the eyepieces. Ideally, these discs should be complete: if they appear squared off, the prisms are not allowing all the light through to the eyepieces.

Binoculars with high magnifications can be held steady with a camera tripod. A special clamp, known as a binocular adaptor, locates around the central pivot of the binocular and is fixed to the tripod by a screw on the tripod head.

Right All prismatic binoculars have folded light paths, resulting in light and compact instruments. Standard prismatic binoculars have the characteristic binocular shape and are bulkier than the roof prism binoculars pictured below.

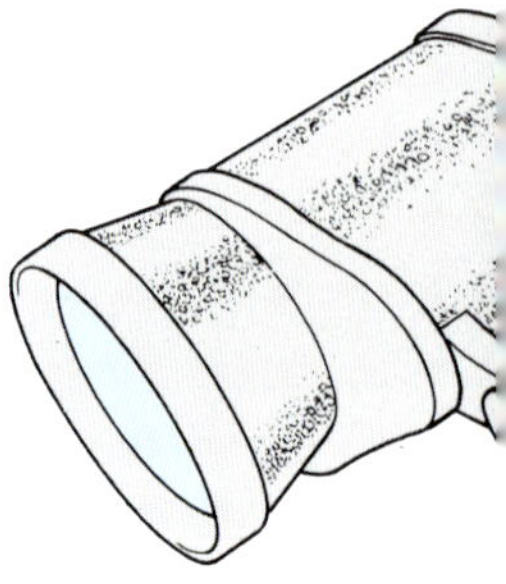

Right Binocular/tripod adaptors enable binoculars to be mounted on standard camera tripods. The adaptor clamps to the central pivot of the binoculars and locates on the camera screw on the tripod head.

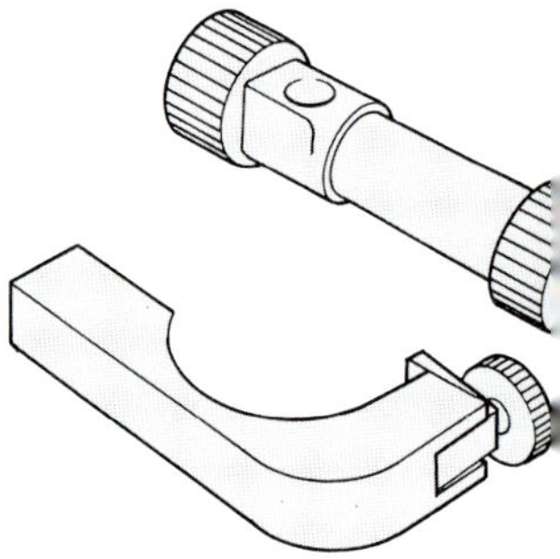

Right Roof prism binoculars have a more direct light path, which produces an instrument that is lighter and narrower than the standard prismatics..

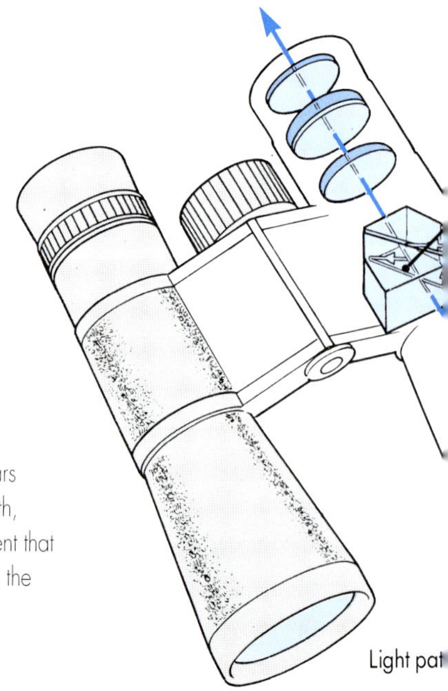

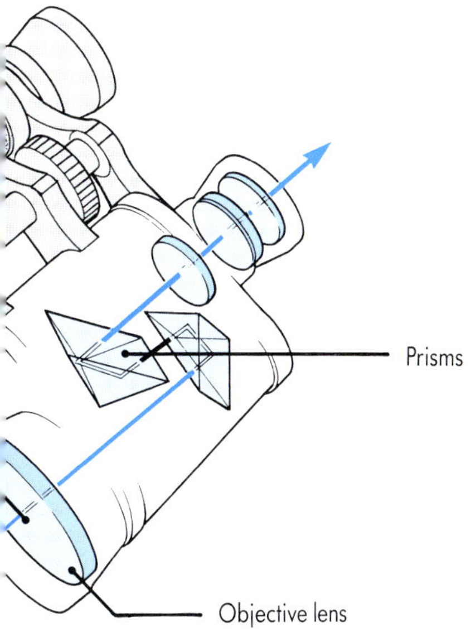

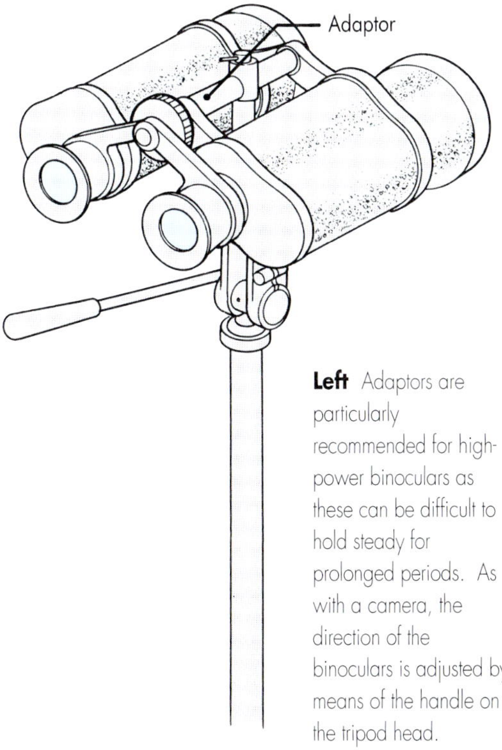

Left Adaptors are particularly recommended for high-power binoculars as these can be difficult to hold steady for prolonged periods. As with a camera, the direction of the binoculars is adjusted by means of the handle on the tripod head.

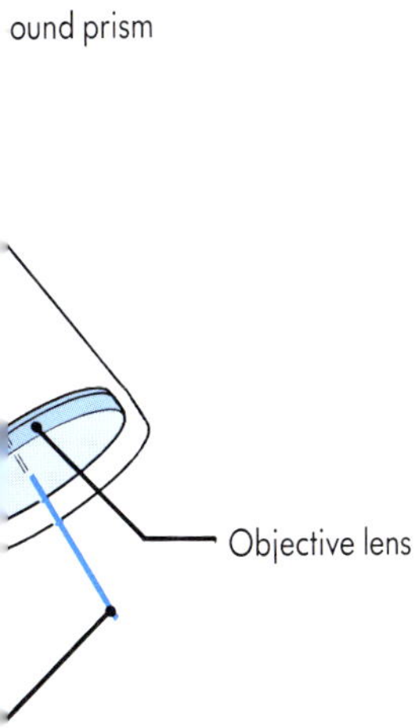

Getting value for money

You should test binoculars before you part with your money, so dismiss the idea of getting them by mail order. There is no reason why you shouldn't buy secondhand binoculars, but you must take care to ensure that they are in good working order. There are several tests that can be carried out that will help you choose a good pair.

The general standard of workmanship should be good. If you notice any dents or other damage on the lenses or barrels, discard them. Now extend the eyepieces to their full extent. Ensure that the eyepiece barrels are firm and rigid and do not tilt in any way. Try out the focusing mechanism, which should run smoothly and with steady resistance. The same applies to the central pivot, which alters the spacing of the eyepieces. This should stay firmly in place once set.

Most binoculars have anti-reflection coatings on their object glasses. These increase contrast and improve light transmission. Ideally all the other optical surfaces should also be coated. Look at the reflection of a light in the objective lens. There will be two reflections, one from the outer surface of the objective and one from the inner surface. If both surfaces are coated, then both reflections should be coloured. If you carefully adjust the position of the binoculars you will also get reflections from the prisms inside the barrels, which will indicate whether or not they are coated. Apply the same tests at the eyepiece end. If the binoculars are found to have no coatings, they should be rejected.

Focus the binoculars on a point source of light and then move it towards the edge of the field of view. The point should remain in sharp focus until somewhere around two-thirds of the way out towards the edge. Binoculars with a so-called flat field should give sharp focus regardless of the position of the point within the field. Now focus the binoculars while centred on a straight line, such as the edge of a building .Inevitably, the line will appear to be bent at the edge of the field of view. Reject the binoculars if the line becomes bent more than a third of the way in from the edge.

If the barrels are not set parallel to each other, the binoculars will produce a double image. Look through the binoculars while opening and closing your eyes. Look carefully for a momentary double image – it will become single as your eyes adjust to compensate – and reject binoculars that display this fault.

Some other hints

- Insist that you obtain a full set of lens caps and a sturdy carrying case.
- Get a carrying strap and wear it whenever you are using the binoculars.
- Be patient when buying binoculars and don't get the first pair you see.

TELESCOPES AND MOUNTINGS

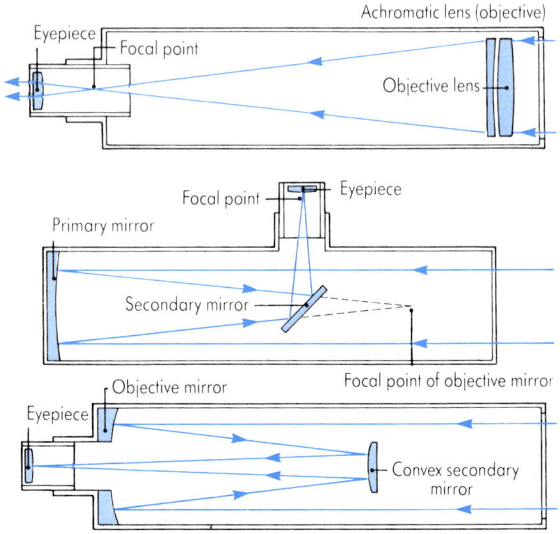

Above Light entering a refracting telescope (top) is bent by a lens to a focal point. Reflectors (centre) use a specially curved mirror to bring the light to a focus. The light is reflected back up the tube and out to the side via a secondary mirror. Cassegrain telescopes (bottom) use a special convex secondary mirror to reflect the light back through a hole in the centre of the primary. In each case the image of the object being viewed is magnified by an eyepiece.

Important though telescopes are to astronomy, the beginner must not rush into buying one. It is far better to acquaint yourself with the night sky and gain experience of naked-eye and binocular observation before committing yourself to purchasing a telescope. Too often, telescopes that are bought in haste are left to gather dust in the attic.

Once the time has come to buy a telescope, the question arises of which type to get. Many first-time enthusiasts will need a general, all-purpose instrument. Others may wish to observe double stars especially, or perhaps star clusters. Some telescopes are better suited to particular jobs than others.

Ignore claims made by manufacturers regarding the supposedly high magnifications offered by their telescopes. Aperture is of far more importance. The larger the aperture (the diameter of the object glass or mirror) the more light is gathered and, consequently, the fainter the objects that can be seen.

Refracting telescopes

There are two main types of telescope: refractors and reflectors. In a refractor the light from the object is collected by a specially shaped "objective" lens. This brings the rays of light to a focus and the resulting image is magnified by the eyepiece, which contains one or more lenses. Light-gathering power is proportional to the square of the aperture of the observing instrument: a lens twice the diameter has four (=2 x 2) times the light-gathering capability; a lens three times the diameter gathers nine (=3 x 3) times as much light. The same principle applies to all types of telescopes and binoculars.

Astronomical telescopes are usually equipped with several eyepieces. To determine what magnification any particular eyepiece will give, its focal length is divided into the focal length of the telescope objective. (The focal length is the distance from the lens to the point at which the light from a distant object is brought to focus.) For example, an eyepiece of 25 mm focal length would give a magnification of 900/25, or 36x, when used with a telescope of focal length 900 mm.

The limit of useful magnification depends upon the amount of light available: the higher the magnification, the fainter the image. A magnification of 500x would be useless with a telescope with only a 7.6-cm (3-inch) aperture.

A defect common to all refractors is that of false colour, which arises when different wavelengths are brought to focus at different points. This is known as chromatic aberration, and it can be partly remedied by using "achromatic" lenses, which have two components of different types of glass. The errors arising from each tend to cancel each other out, thereby reducing the amount of false colour.

Reflecting telescopes

Reflectors work on an entirely different principle: the light from the object being observed is collected and brought to focus by a curved mirror. The light is diverted to the eyepiece, usually mounted on the side of the telescope tube, by a small secondary mirror, or flat. Because a mirror reflects all colours in the same way, there is no chromatic aberration. However, a certain amount of false colour may be produced in the eyepiece. Because reflectors are not as robust as refractors, they will need occasional maintenance and realignment of the optical components.

The Newtonian reflector is by far the most popular type. Although Newtonian reflectors can be readily purchased, their basic design is fairly straightforward and keen enthusiasts can make their own.

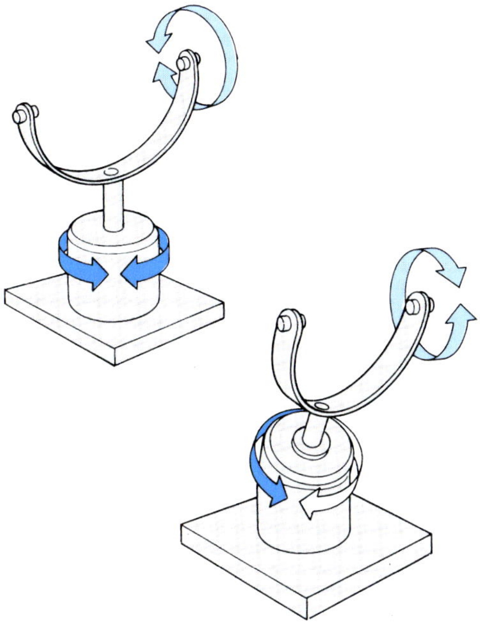

Left Altazimuth mountings (top) alllow the telescope to be moved both up and down (*altitude*) and horizontally (*alzimuth*). The main problem with this type of mounting is that the telescope has to be moved on both axes at once in order to keep the object being studied in the field of view. This problem does not arise with the equatorial mounting (bottom). Equatorial mountings have polar and declination axes. The polar axis is set up so that it lies parallel to the Earth's axis and points towards any star by turning it around both axes. The declination axis is then clamped in position and the star kept in view by moving the telescope around the polar axis only. Prolonged tracking can be carried out by use of automatic drives that compensate for the Earth's axial rotation.

Catadioptric telescopes

These telescopes make use of both lenses and mirrors, the incoming light passing through a corrector lens before being brought to a focus by primary and secondary mirrors. Because the light path is folded inside the tube, catadioptric telescopes are very compact and highly portable up to quite large apertures.

Advantages and disadvantages

Advantages of refractors include their good resolution of fine detail, making them particularly suitable for planetary work or study of double stars. They are generally robust and will stay aligned through reasonably careful handling, transportation and so on. Aperture for aperture, a refractor is more effective than a reflector, but also more expensive. This is because each component of an achromatic lens has two surfaces to figure, while mirrors have only one. This is one reason why all the world's largest professional telescopes are reflectors. The largest refractor in the world is the 102-cm (40-inch) instrument at Yerkes Observatory in the United States. It is unlikely that a larger refractor will be built. A lens has to be supported around its edge and above the size of the Yerkes instrument the lens starts to distort under its own weight. The mirrors in reflectors can be supported over their entire underside, eliminating the problems of distortion.

For the amateur astronomer the minimum really useful aperture is around 7.5 cm (3 inches) for a refractor and 15 cm (6 inches) for a reflector.

Telescope mountings

Any observing equipment with a magnification of more than 7x should have a mounting to hold it steady during use. For binoculars and small telescopes the type most commonly used is the altitude-azimuth (altazimuth) mount, which allows the instrument to be moved both vertically (in altitude) and horizontally (in azimuth).

The Dobsonian telescope is a standard Newtonian reflector on an altazimuth mounting, usually made of wood. The bearings are Teflon pads running on a Formica base. (Instructions for constructing a Dobsonian telescope appear on page 80-1.) Because the mounting is constructed from cheap materials, Dobsonian telescopes of large aperture are available at very competitive prices. For wide-field work a Dobsonian telescope may well be the best bet.

The altazimuth mounting is unsuitable for serious work. It has to be constantly adjusted in both directions in order to keep the star or other object in the field of view. Equatorial mountings are aligned with the Earth's axis and enable an object to be kept in the field of view by adjustment of one axis only. To make the job even easier, equatorial mounts can be driven automatically by a simple clockwork or electrical system or through more sophisticated computer drives. A driven equatorial mount is essential for long-exposure astrophotography.

The mounting should be as sturdy and robust as possible. Even the best telescope will perform badly if used with an insubstantial mounting. The result will be unsteady images brought about by telescope shake.

TELESCOPE ACCESSORIES

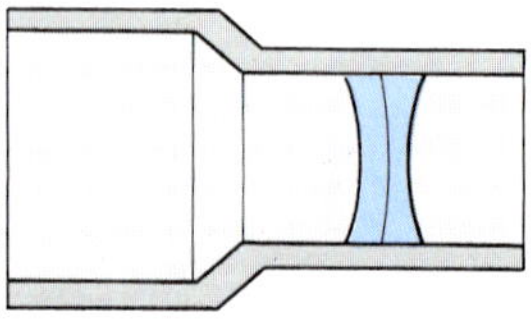

Left The Barlow eyepiece is a special lens designed for use in conjunction with normal eyepieces to increase the magnification of the eyepiece.

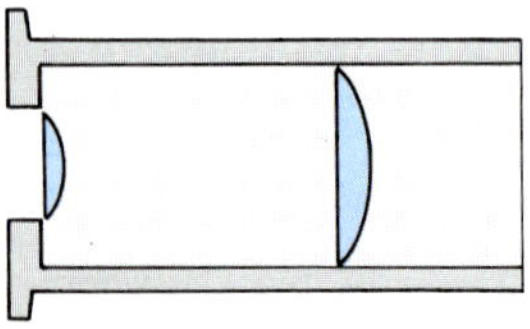

Left The Huygens eyepiece is. inexpensive and simple in construction. This type of eyepiece does not use cemented lenses and is therefore recommended for solar projection.

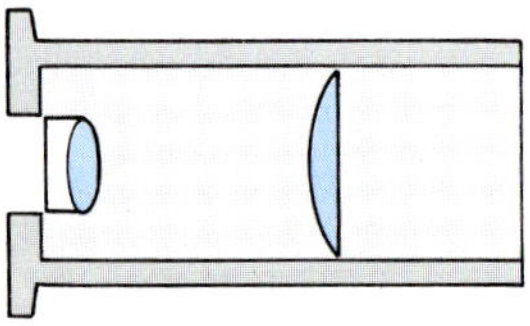

Left The Kellner eyepiece gives a wider field than the Huygens although it suffers from edge-of-field image distortion with short focal length telescopes.

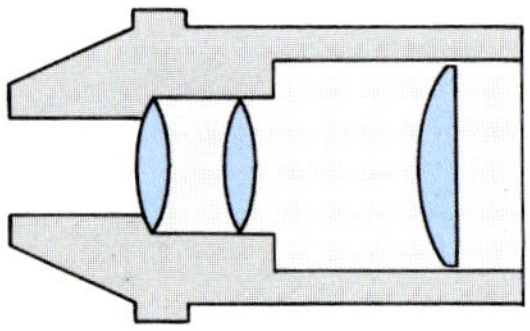

Left The Orthoscopic eyepiece is well suited for short focal length telescopes, giving a wide field of view and a fine image with good correction.

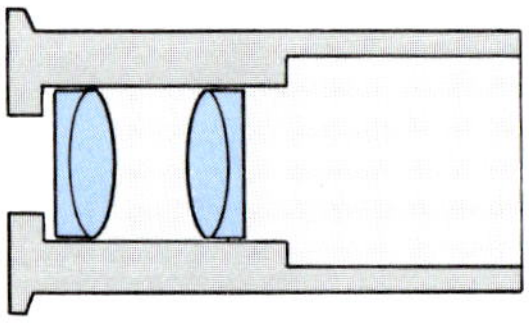

Left The Plossl eyepiece is superb for short focal length Newtonian telescopes. Good eye relief.

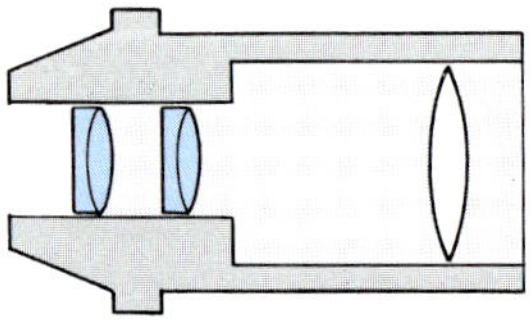

Left The Erfle eyepiece has a very wide field although suffering from severe edge-of-field image distortion.

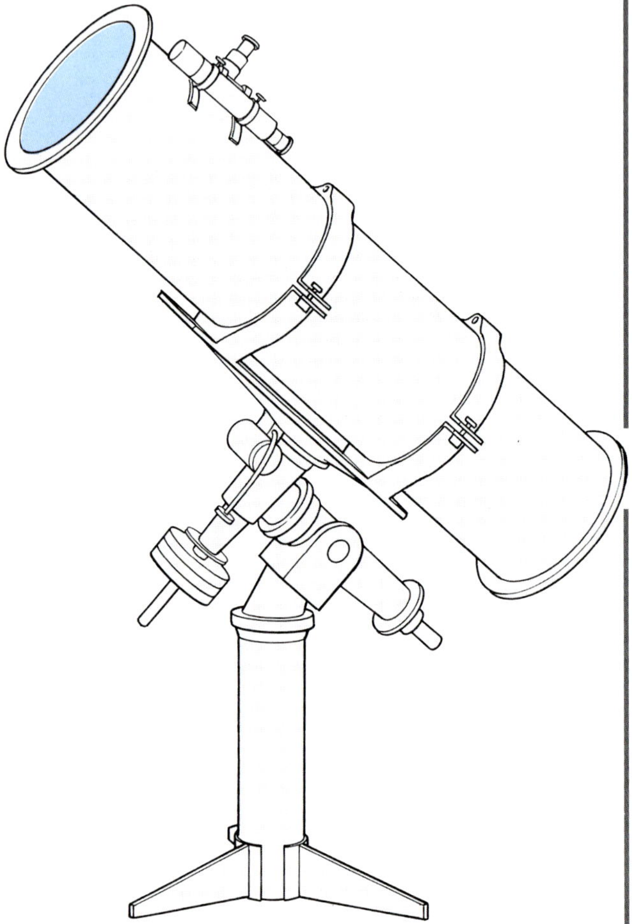

Above Equatorially mounted Newtonian reflector.

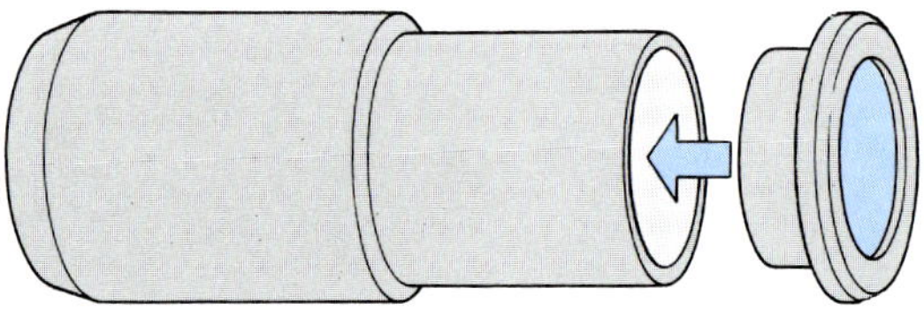

Left Special filters are now available which, when fitted to the eyepiece barrel, transmit certain wavelengths of light into the eyepiece but help to mask out artificial light pollution.

Right and below right The field of view in many amateur telescopes is so narrow that locating objects can be a problem. To make things easier view finders are available. These are attached to the telescope and work on the same principle as the sighting scope on a rifle. finders with right angle prisms make viewing at awkward angles easier.

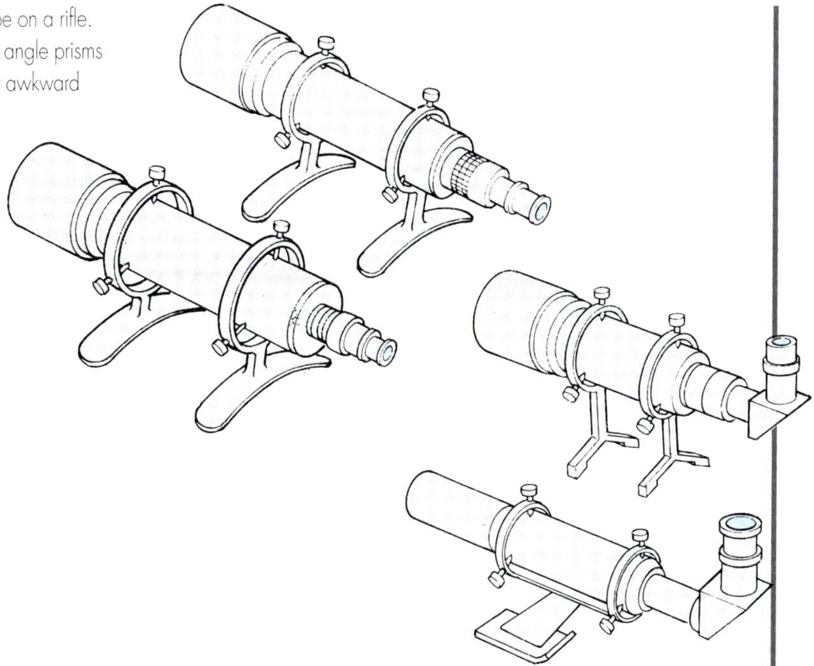

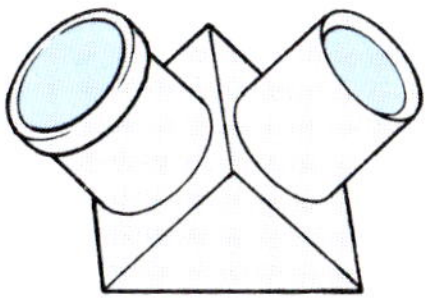

Above Right angle prisms can also be used with the main telescope for viewing at otherwise awkward angles.

Below Erecting prisms can also be used with the main telescope for viewing at otherwise awkward angles.

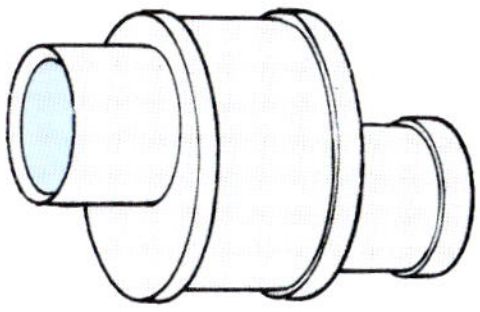

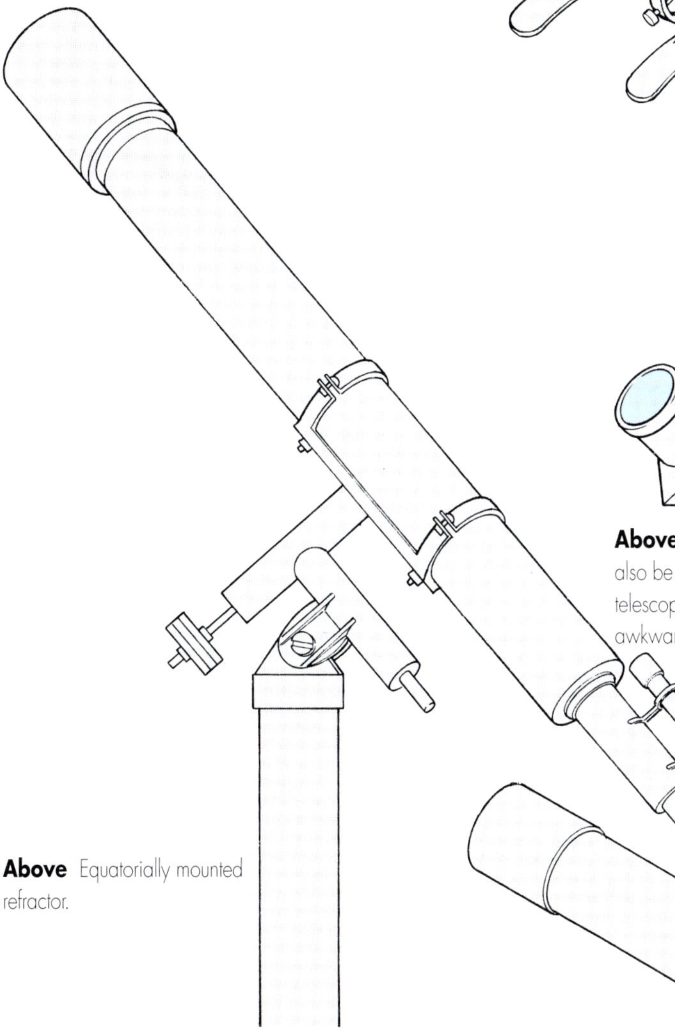

Above Equatorially mounted refractor.

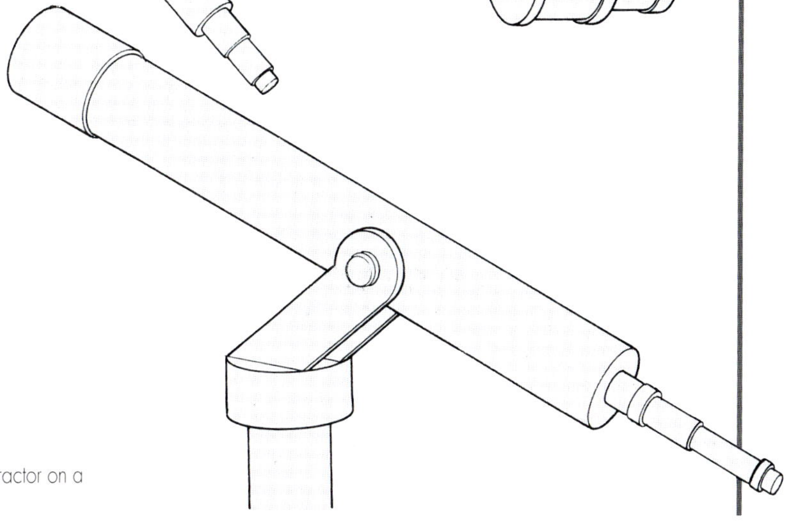

Right A simple refractor on a altazimuth mounting.

MAKING A CAMERA MOUNT

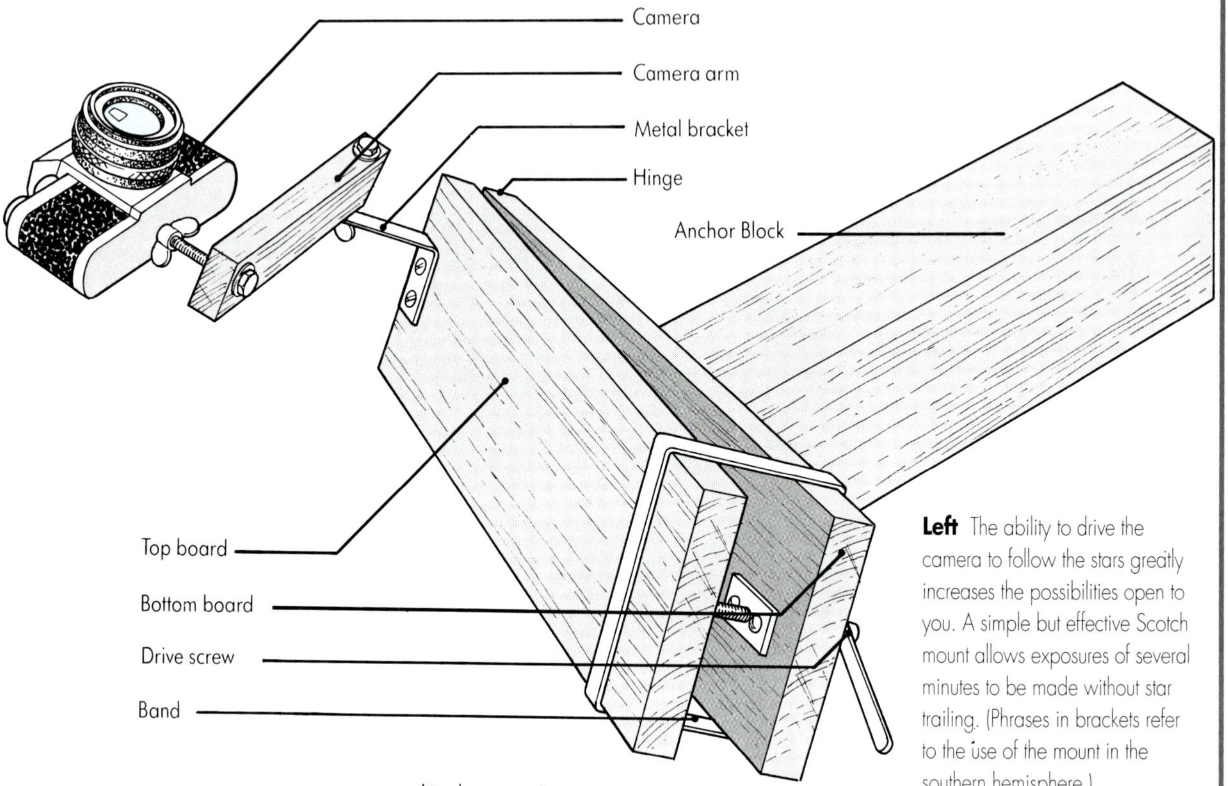

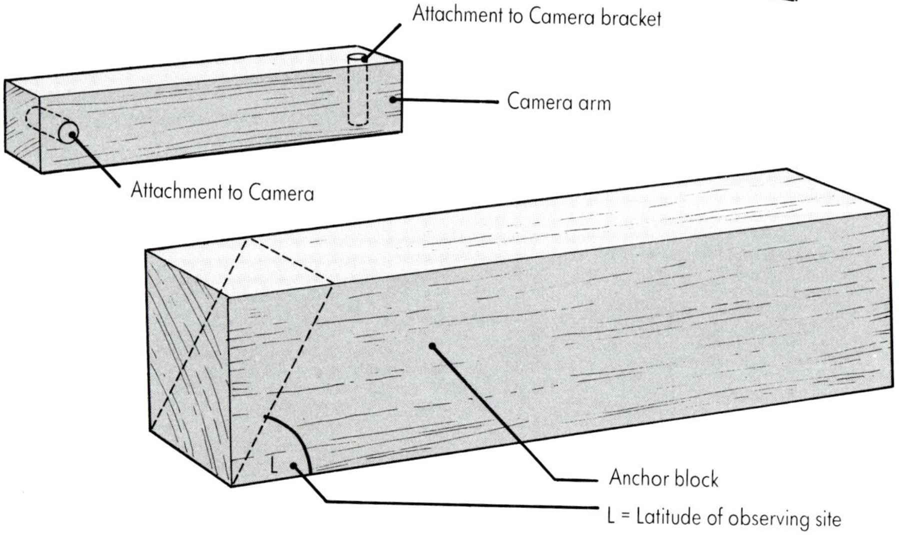

Left The ability to drive the camera to follow the stars greatly increases the possibilities open to you. A simple but effective Scotch mount allows exposures of several minutes to be made without star trailing. (Phrases in brackets refer to the use of the mount in the southern hemisphere.)
In order to use the Scotch mount set it up on a north-south line with the hinge at the south (north) end. Bolt the anchor block in place. The central axis of the hinge should point towards the north (south) celestial pole. Adjust the camera arm and lock it in position with the wing nuts. By turning the drive screw clockwise (counterclockwise) at the rate of one revolution per minute the camera tracks the stars across the sky.

Below Left Cut the anchor block at an angle equal to the latitude of the observing site, which ensures that the camera is aligned with the celestial pole.

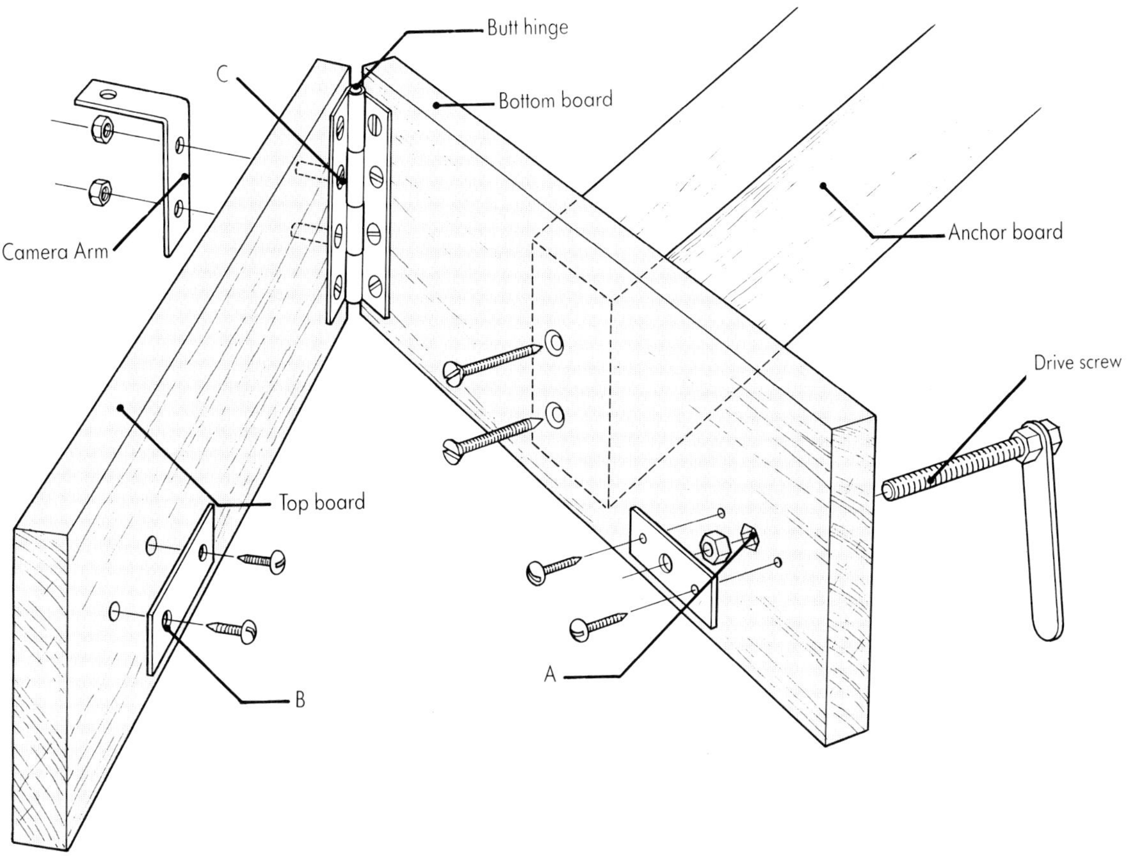

Above Attach the anchor board to the bottom board ensuring that the lower edge of the bottom board lies flush with the base of the anchor block. Then lay hinge along the end of the bottom board so that the centre of the hinge barrel runs flush with the end of the board. Drill a 6mm diameter hole in the bottom board (A). The centre of this hole should be exactly 229mm from the central axis of the hinge. An M6 nut should be wedged into this hole. The 50mm x 20mm metal plate should now be fixed over this nut. The top board metal plate (B) should be attached in a similar way. Form the camera arm bracket from steel strip and drill two holes of 5mm diameter in the 100mm long arm to match up with two of the holes the holes in the hinge. Drill a hole for the M6 bolt in the 50mm arm to attach the camera arm. The top board should be fastened to the bottom board assembly, taking care to align the edge of the board with the centre of the hinge barrel, Use two no. 6 countersunk screws together with two countersunk M5 bolts (C). The latter should be pushed through the hinge, top board and camera arm bracket attached with two M5 plain nuts.

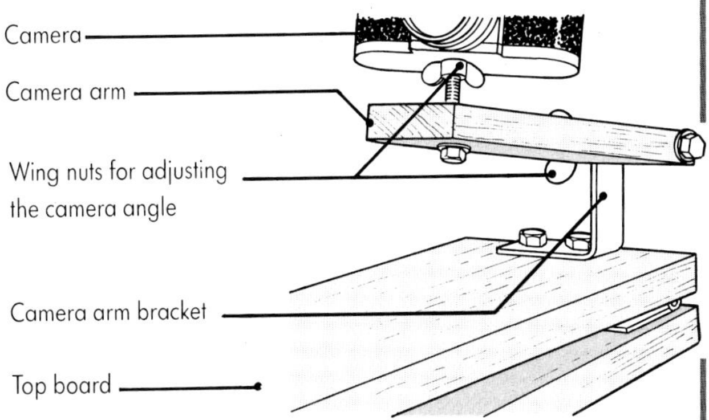

Above To attach the camera arm and camera to the top board take an M6 x 50mm bolt, fit a brass washer and pass through the hole in the 75mm side of the camera arm bracket and then through the camera arm. Secure with another washer and wing nut. Place another brass washer over the 1/4-inch BSWbolt and pass this through the other camera hole. Secure with a plain nut. Screw a wing nut onto the protruding 1/4-inch BSW bolt as shown. The camera body can now be attached to the bolt and locked into place by tightening the wing nut at the camera base. Adjusting wing nuts at both ends of the camera arm repositions the camera to any desired angle. Finally, fold the top and bottom boards together and loop a strong elastic band around them.

MAKING A TELESCOPE

In order to obtain detailed views of the night sky a good telescope is needed., The viewing of faint objects requires light gathering power. Many amateur astronomers have turned their hands to making their own telescopes and they have made some extremely fine instruments. However, not everyone has the engineering skills (or time) required to produce the huge equatorially mounted telescopes turned out by more gifted individuals. Yet there is a telescope that can be put together by virtually any keen amateur, one that makes use of some ready made parts and which requires only basic woodworking skills to assemb le. The telescope itself is of the Newtonian system, the alt-azimuth mounting a Dobsonian which is straightforward to make and sturdy in operation. It was designed by John Dobson of the San Francisco Sidewalk Astronomers.

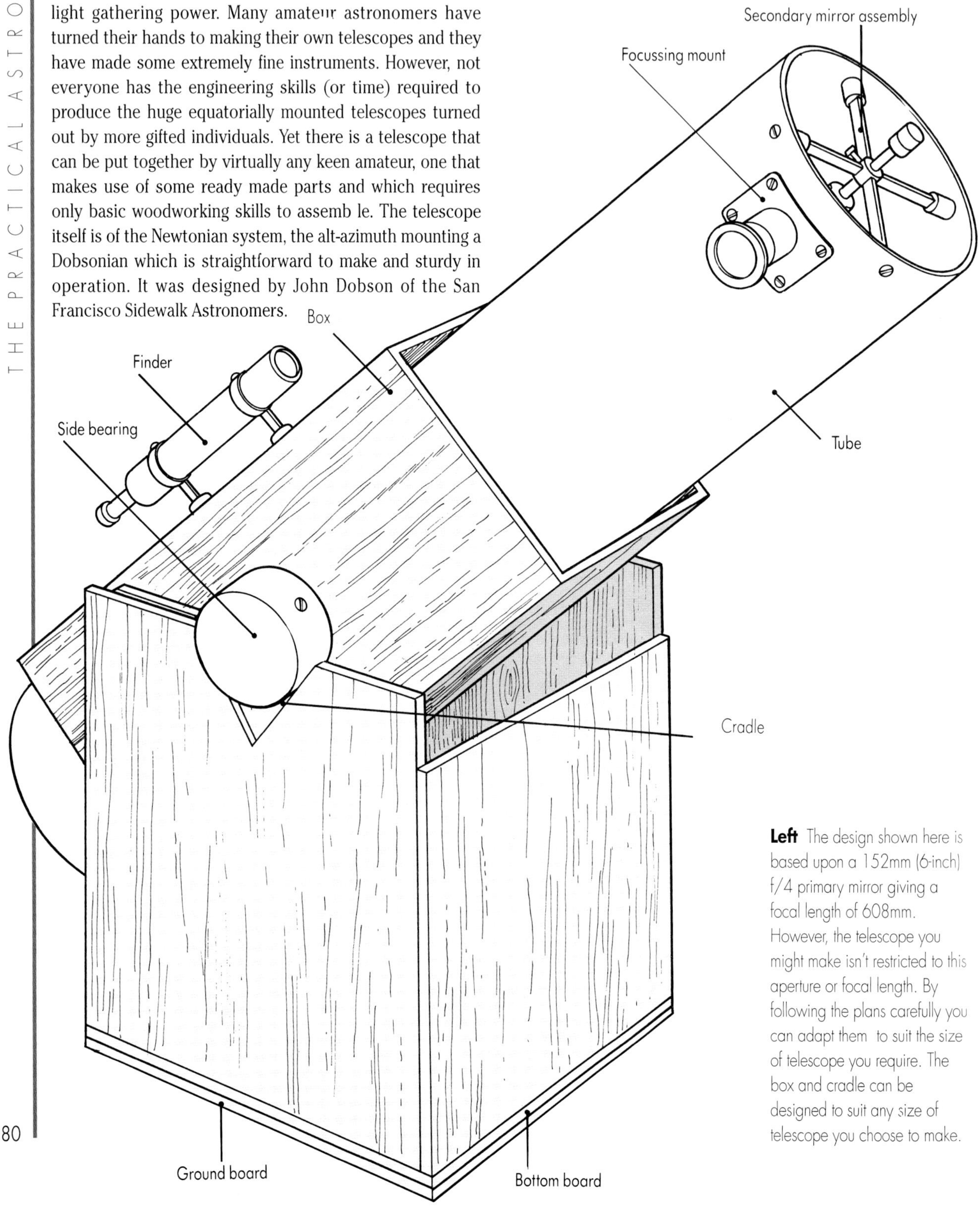

Left The design shown here is based upon a 152mm (6-inch) f/4 primary mirror giving a focal length of 608mm. However, the telescope you might make isn't restricted to this aperture or focal length. By following the plans carefully you can adapt them to suit the size of telescope you require. The box and cradle can be designed to suit any size of telescope you choose to make.

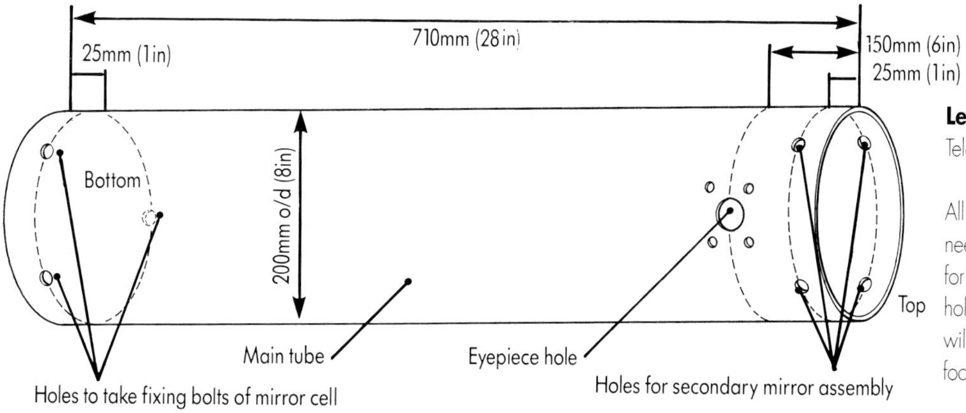

Left Assembly of Main Telescope

All holes shown in tube will need to be of diameters suitable for the items purchased. The holes around the eyepiece hole will need to be drilled to suit the focussing mount used.

Right After fixing the spider into position at top of tube, place the secondary mirror in to the holder (following the suppliers instructions) and locate shaft into hole in centre of spider.
Put a stop at the top end of the shaft as shown to prevent the secondary mirror holder from falling down the tube and possibly damaging the primary mirror. This can be made by wrapping tape around the

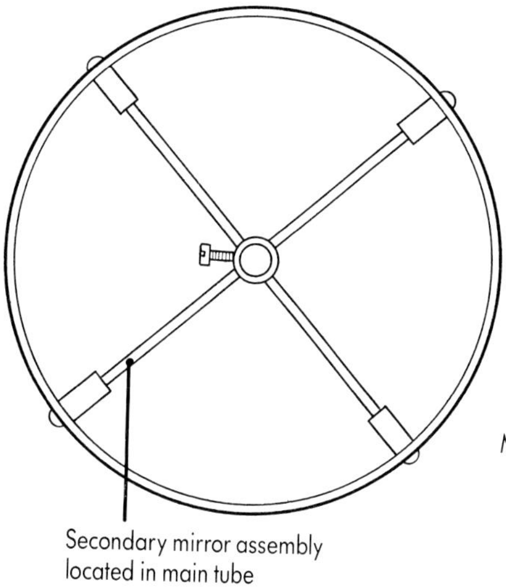

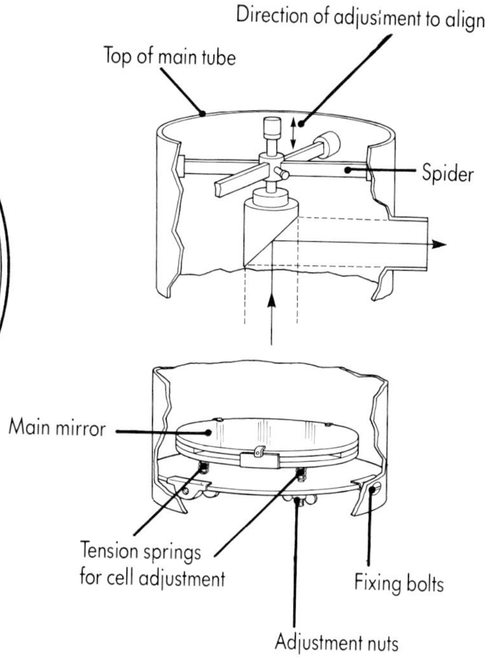

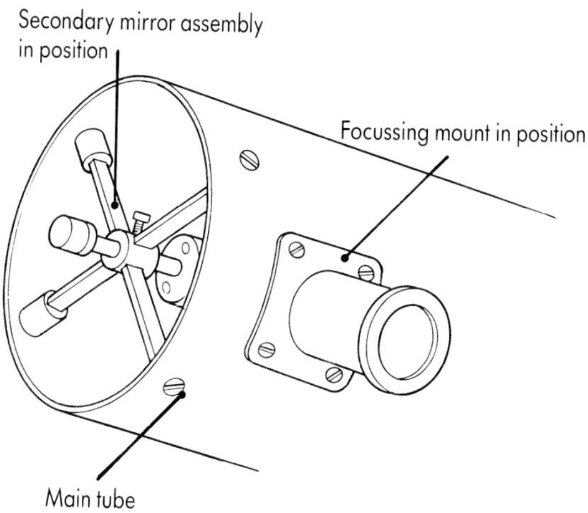

Left Bolt the focussing mount onto side of tube over eyepiece hole and adjust the height of secondary mirror until it is in the centre of the field of view when looking into the focussing mount (without eyepiece inserted).

Above Now rotate the secondary mirror shaft until the whole surface of the secondary mirror is visible through focussing mount. Using the adjusting screws, adjust secondary until the bottom end of main telescope tube is in centre of field of view. Fix primary mirror into cell and screw cell into position at bottom of tube. Using cell adjusting screws adjust position of primary mirror until the upper end of the tube is in the centre of the field of view.

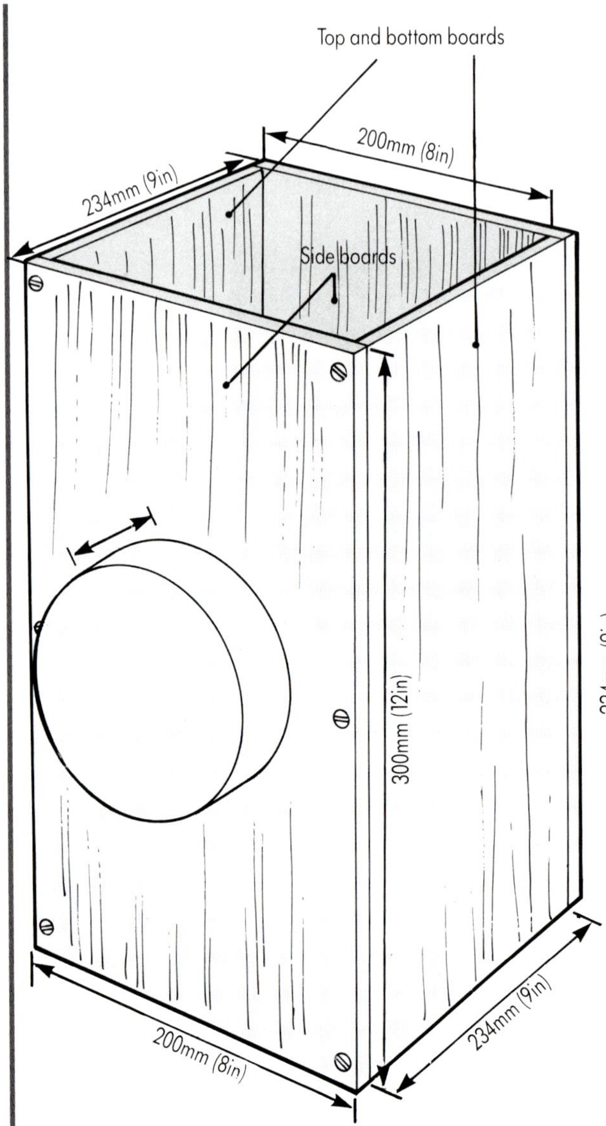

Below and left Find centres of side boards by drawing diagonal lines and draw a circle 152mm diameter aound this centre point. Cut out four plywood discs 152mm diameter to form the bearings (two discs per bearing). Form bearings by gluing two discs together, drill three holes through each bearing at 120 degrees on 45mm radius and fasten onto side boards using No 10 x 2" (50mm) screws inside circles previously drawn. Now slip the side bearing covers over the discs, drill three holes in covers, countersink and screw onto discs using No 6 x 1" (25mm) screws. Drill boards and fasten box together. Drill 1.5mm pilot holes 15mm deep in top and bottom boards in line with holes in side boards to take No 6 x 1½" (38mm) screws. This reduces risk of top and bottom boards splitting when screws are inserted.

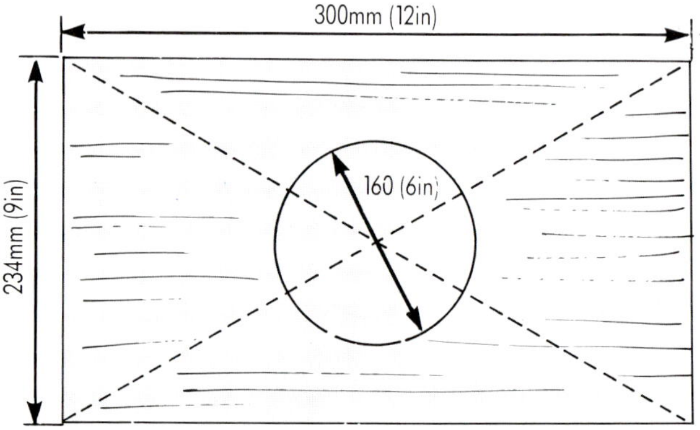

Right Cut a V into the top of each side board (top). Form centering boards by gluing two 60mm x 325mm pieces together, drill three holes and fasten to side boards using No 10 x 2" (50mm) screws leaving 17mm gap at bottom. Drill side boards , countersink, drill 1.5mm pilot holes in bottom board using No 6 x 1½" (38mm) screws. Glue Formica sheet to bottom of cradle and drill a hole ½" (12.5mm) diameter in centre of bottom board and through Formica sheet. Fasten two Teflon strips onto sides of Vs on each side board with hardboard nails.

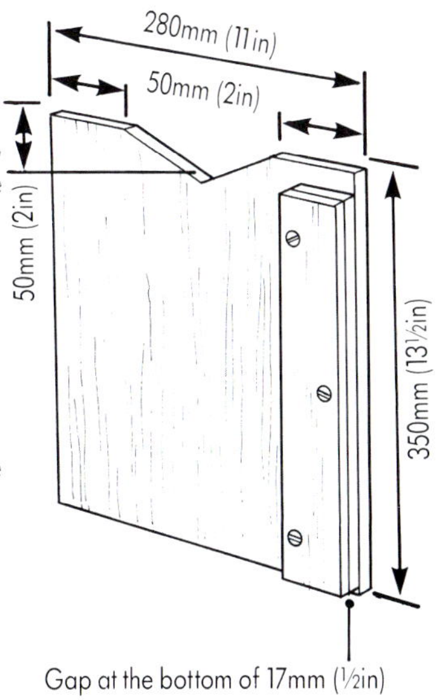

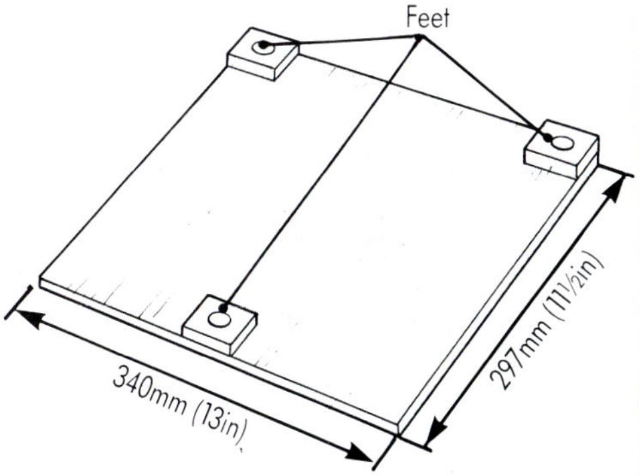

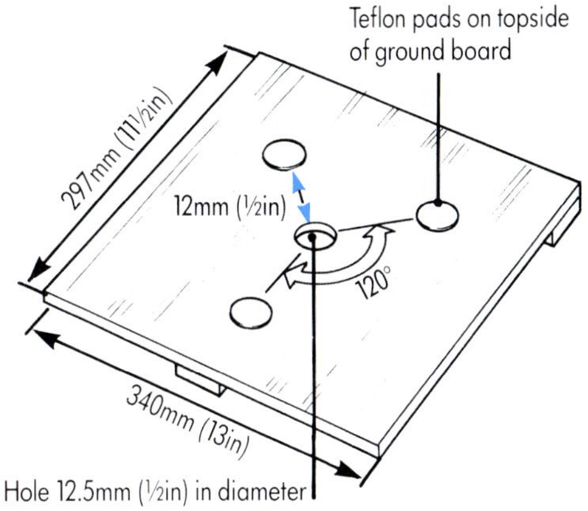

Above Drill and countersink feet and screw onto base of gound board using No 10 x 1¼" (32mm) screws. Turn ground board in line with hole in bottom board of cradle. Fasten cradle to ground board using M12 x 50mm bolt, washers and nut. The cradle will now swivel around the ground board, the formica running on the Teflon pads. This forms a very smooth, lubrication free bearing. Tighten the M12 nut until there is no wobble between the cradle bottom board and ground board.

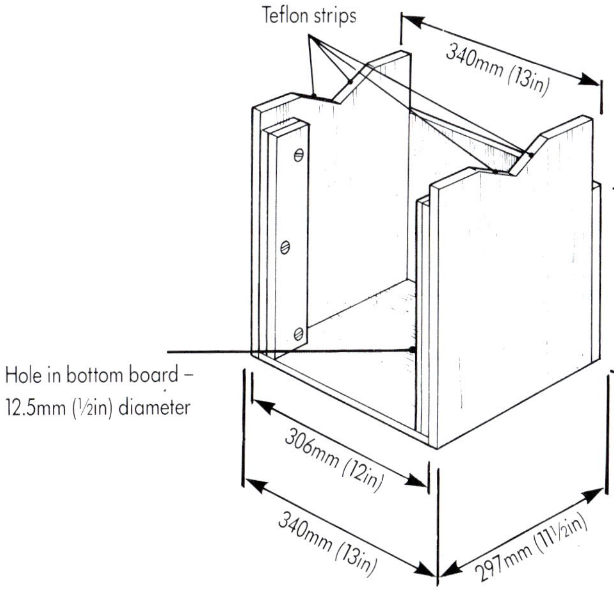

Left Locate main telescope into box. The internal dimensions of the box match the o/d of the tube, so the screws holding the box together will need slackening. Place the box into cradle, placing bearings into V's as shown. Position box on tube so that telescope balances regardless of angle to which it is set in the cradle. Tighten box screws to clamp box onto tube.

ASTROPHOTOGRAPHY

Astrophotography is the recording of astronomical images on film. Before the invention of photography and its subsequent application to astronomy in the 19th century, all observations of celestial objects were made by observers who manually recorded what they saw. Making astronomical drawings still has an important role to play and for many aspects of astronomy has advantages over photography (see page 88-91). However, the benefits of being able to record observations photographically are enormous. For example, data may be obtained for examination at a later date and over a prolonged period.

Early attempts at astrophotography were hampered by the absence of sufficiently accurate telescope drives. The early films were also 'slow' – insensitive – and were not able to record light equally well from the whole visible spectrum. Modern technology has improved this situation dramatically, and today's amateur astrophotographer can obtain images of the sky of an extremely high standard.

Getting started

In spite of the vast array of specialized equipment and advanced techniques available to the amateur astrophotographer, a great deal of useful work can be carried out with only basic equipment. The only items needed in the initial stages are a camera, tripod, cable release and suitable film.

Ideally the camera should be of the single-lens reflex (SLR) type. Usually a special B setting is provided, which allows exposures of indefinite duration to be made. Cameras with interchangeable lenses are useful, since more areas of astrophotography may be explored at a later date.

The camera is mounted on a tripod that holds it steady during long exposures. The camera is attached to this by a screw on the tripod that locates the base of the camera body. When you select a tripod, make sure that the section to which you bolt the camera can be directed towards any part of the sky, particularly overhead. The tripod should be as heavy and sturdy as possible. Although this may reduce portability, the inconvenience is worth it for the stability it provides. A cable release is used to avoid camera shake when opening and closing the shutter.

The choice of film depends upon the work being carried out. A range of different film speeds is available to cater for different observing conditions and projects. Film speeds are indicated by an ISO number (the same as the formerly used ASA number) or by a DIN number, the size of the number increasing with film sensitivity. Slow films, up to ISO 100, produce high-quality images with little graininess and good colour reproduction. However, these films have the least sensitivity to light and can only be used when recording fairly bright objects, such as the full Moon. Medium-speed films range from ISO 100 to ISO 400. They have greater sensitivity but suffer from a slight increase in graininess and lower standard of contrast. This type of film should be used when conditions are dimmer and for such projects as obtaining images of bright stars or wide-field twilight views of the Moon and planets. Finally we come to the fast films, with ratings of ISO 1000 or more. Their vastly increased sensitivity is offset by a high degree of graininess, relatively poor image quality and poor contrast.

Above An SLR camera with cable release, mounted on a sturdy tripod ready for use. This arrangement is the ideal starting point for those wishing to take photographs of the night sky. Although the camera cannot be guided to follow the motion of celestial objects, the basic setup shown here offers a great deal of scope to the astrophotographer. The wide range of possible projects includes star trails, constellation shots, satellite trails meteor photography and aurorae.

The choice of colour or black-and-white image, in either print or slide format, is really up to the individual, and is based on how final presentation of the results will be made. As a general rule, black-and-white films offer a better image contrast. In the case of black-and-white print film, the negatives make ideal slides for viewing with a projector and screen. With slides made from black and white negatives a great deal of detail can be obtained, although once the strip of negatives has been cut up it may be difficult to obtain further prints.

When taking print film for developing, remember to point out that it contains views of the night sky. Without careful scrutiny the negatives may appear to be blank and prints may not be made from them! When a slide film is being developed, it should be returned to you in an uncut form. A continuous sequence of images of the night sky makes it difficult to see the picture margins. Far better to cut the film and mount the images yourself than to run the risk of having the pictures inadvertently cut in half! Mounting slides yourself is not difficult and is safer in the long run.

First exposures

After attaching the loaded camera to the tripod and fitting the cable release, set the camera focus to infinity and ensure that the aperture is at its widest setting. There are several different settings denoted by a sequence such as 16, 11, 8, 5.6, 4, 2.8, and 2. The smaller the number, the wider the camera aperture, and the more light reaches the film. The aperture should be as wide as possible. Of course, this may not always apply – for example, when recording really bright objects such as the Sun or full Moon.

Probably the most popular subjects for first-time astrophotographers are star trails. Stars appear to rise in the east, travel across the sky and set in the west. "Circumpolar" stars – those that are close enough to the celestial pole to stay permanently above the horizon – appear to travel around the pole. If a sufficiently long exposure is taken, the stars will show up as streaks of light, or star trails. A series of photographs can be taken to demonstrate the different apparent rates at which stars at different distances from the celestial poles cross the sky.

You may want to capture the stars as points of light rather than as trails. On sufficiently short exposures the effect of trailing will be negligible, although these exposure times will vary according to which areas of the sky are being photographed. To obtain pictures that show the stars near the celestial equator as points of light the maximum exposure should be somewhere in the region of 20 to 25 seconds with a standard 50-mm lens. Exposure times can be increased as you move towards the celestial poles. By using a lens with a wider field of view longer exposures are possible without producing star trails. By the same token, long focal-length lenses have the opposite effect: a much narrower field of view produces a dramatic increase in the amount of star trailing.

Exposures can be timed with a wristwatch or a stopwatch. Other more sophisticated methods of timing are available, including countdown timers. These come equipped with an alarm that sounds when the indicated time reaches zero.

Above Astrophotography is taken a stage beyond the simple tripod-mounted camera shown on the opposite page by attaching the camera to a telescope as senn here. The telescope is focused on a bright star located within the same field of view as that of the camera. It is then moved throughout the exposure to keep the star at the centre of the field of view. Eyepieces with cross-hairs are available, which allow precise tracking of the guide star.

For each exposure, various details should be recorded, including type of film, lens size, area or subject being photographed and time and length of exposure. Illumination

Right The three brightest objects in the center of this photograph are, in descending order Saturn Mars, and Alpha Librae. Another feature of this photograph is the light polution from sodium lamps, which is an increasingly common problem facing amateur astronomers.

Below During this exposure, a tripod-mounted unguided cmera was trained on the constellation of Orion. The shutter was then left open to produce the star trails seen here.

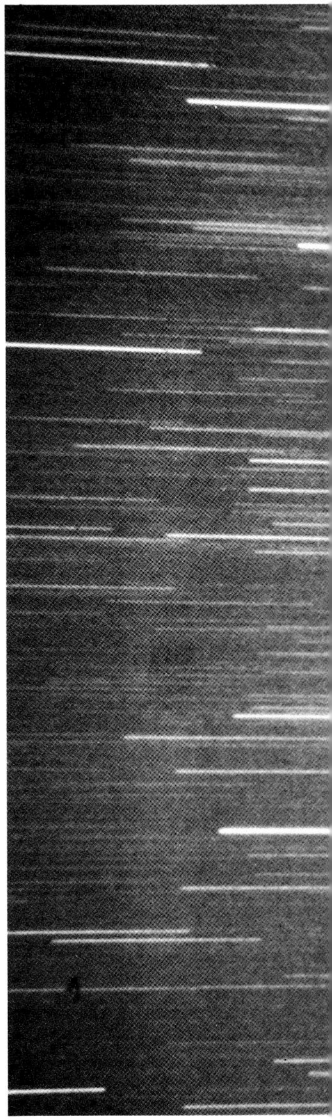

Below This beautiful photograph taken by amateur photographer, John Thomas, shows Venus and Jupiter at twilight. Venus, apart from the Moon, the brightest object in the night sky, makes a perfect target for amateur astrophotographers.

at the observing site should be provided with a red light, the glow from which has least effect on the observer's dark adaptation.

Further projects

So far we have talked about taking pictures using a straightforward unguided camera. Although there are quite a few areas of observation that can be carried out with the basic equipment mentioned above, the use of more sophisticated equipment, such as telephoto lenses, camera guides, filters and so on, greatly increases the scope for the astrophotographer. Instructions for building a simple but effective camera mount are given on page 78-9. This will help to compensate for the Earth's rotation and allow the camera to follow the stars across the sky, enabling much longer exposures to be taken.

Quite different from the techniques described above is the use of a telescope for astrophotography. In some cases the camera can simply be held to the eyepiece and short exposures taken of bright objects such as the Moon. The camera can also be mounted on top of the telescope, which is then used to track the object during the exposure. The camera body, without a lens, may be coupled to the telescope, which takes the place of the lens. If the camera is an SLR, the image can be seen in the viewfinder exactly as it will appear in the final picture.

The possibilities open to the serious astrophotographer are almost endless. Many amateurs are highly specialized and carry out most or all of the work involved, from developing their own films to constructing special cameras.

RECORDING WHAT YOU SEE

Many amateur astronomers keep and constantly update observing notebooks in which they store permanent reminders of what they have seen. These notebooks are more than mere references. The effort to record what is seen in the sky stimulates careful observation. Details that might be missed if you are simply 'looking and moving on' are diligently sought out and recorded. Careful observation of a galaxy, for example, will bring out more than just a faint smudge of light. Its shape will become apparent; so will areas of contrasting brightness, a bright nucleus standing out against the fainter spiral arms. The arms themselves may begin to show detail in the form of dust lanes. Careful observation, spurred on by the need to record, will at last enable you to piece together a detailed image of the galaxy.

One thing to remember is that you should record all that you see: putting down all details will help to keep your records as complete as possible and your stargazing memories fresh in your mind.

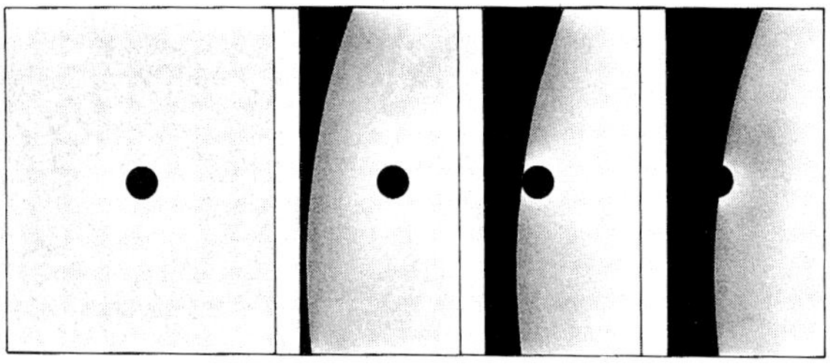

Above A series of drawings made by solar projection showing Mercury passing from the solar disc during the latter stages of the transit of 10 November 1973. Images show Mercury on solar disc at 13.09 UT (A), nearing limb at 13.13 UT (B), touching solar limb at 13h 15m 45s UT (C) and half off disc at 13h 16m 20s UT (D). Seeing was poor throughout. 115mm refractor at 186x magnification.

Where to make your notes

Although individual sheets of paper can be used, some prefer the permanence of notebooks. These can have ruled or blank pages, or a combination of both. Notebooks with pages ruled off in graph form are also available: these are probably the best choice for those who wish not only to make drawings but to plot variable stars' light curves and chart meteor shower activity. Hardbound notebooks are best, as they will stay looking neat over many years. For a general purpose notebook it is probably best to choose a large format, as each spread will have room for several drawings and sets of notes on one theme – perhaps a night-by-night series of meteor shower observations or series of lunar drawings made on consecutive nights.

What to record

There is a certain amount of basic information that should be recorded in your logbook. First and foremost are the date and time of observation, the latter generally being given as Greenwich Mean Time (GMT) or Universal Time (UT). Failing this, make a note of your local standard or daylight saving time, thus ensuring that a conversion to GMT or UT can be made at a later date if required. Record details of the instrument used, including type, aperture, focal length, eyepiece and magnification. As a general rule extended objects, such as comets, star clusters, nebulae and galaxies, benefit from low magnifications and correspondingly wider fields of view. Objects whose light is concentrated into a relatively small area, such as planets, double stars and planetary nebulae, usually demand higher magnifications. In some cases a mixture of magnifications may be beneficial: for example, "the swathes of fluorescence in an emission nebula" may be shown to best effect with a low magnification, whereas higher powers may be needed to bring out the tight knot of stars at the nebula's core that make it shine.

Note also the observing location, together with the seeing conditions. Seeing conditions are best expressed by the well tried scale devised by the planetary observer Eugene Antoniadi:

I Perfect seeing, without a quiver

II Slight undulations, with moments of calm lasting several seconds

III Moderate seeing, with large air tremors

IV Poor seeing, with large air tremors

V Very bad seeing, scarcely allowing the making of a rough sketch

Finally, an indication of the air's transparency should be given. This can be rated on a scale ranging from 0 (cloudy) to 10 (a sky totally free of haze, cloud or water vapour). Making good estimates of seeing conditions and sky transparency

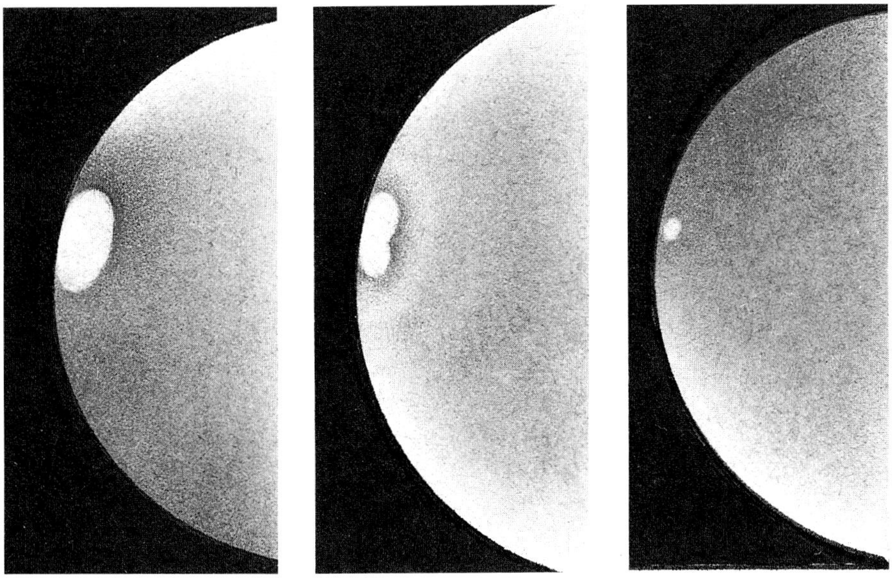

Left A series of drawings showing the retreat of the Martian south polar cap. The first drawing, made on 6/7 August 1988 between 23.15 UT and 24.25 UT, shows a large, bright cap. This has shrunk significantly by 7 September, although it is still quite conspicuous. The last picture, drawn on 28 November, was made well after summer solstice in the Martian southern hemisphere, and shows the cap as a tiny bright speck. No other detail was visible and the cap was difficult to detect. 115-mm (4.5-inch) refractor at 186x magnification.

comes with practice, so don't expect to make correct estimates straight away. If in doubt, call in the help of a more experienced observer, if one is available.

Making astronomical drawings

To assist you in making drawings during an observing session, it is a good idea to prepare circular outlines to represent the field of view. Circles of around 10 cm (4 inches) diameter are about right. After studying, the field of view, carefully mark the positions of stars by dots (the larger the dot the brighter the star). Start by drawing the brightest stars and use these as a framework when you put in fainter ones. Double-check the positions and don't be reluctant to rub out and alter them until you have got things right.

The next stage depends upon what type of object you are drawing. For a star cluster, the central region of stars should be dotted in at the appropriate positions relative to the framework already built up. Then the outlying members of the cluster can be inserted.

For a galaxy or nebula things are different. With a soft pencil (2B or softer), mark in the brightest areas of nebulosity. For a galaxy, these will generally lie in the nucleus.

Working from here, the different regions of brightness are then inserted with correspondingly lighter areas of shading.

Now you will have a picture of the object, but improvements need to be made. The boundaries between the different areas of shading need to be less well defined. Rub the markings gently until they blend in with each other to produce a gradual series of changes from different areas of brightness rather than a series of 'steps' as before.

The orientation of the telescope field should be marked on each sketch. Bearing in mind that using a Cassegrain or refractor with a fixed Newtonian eyepiece gives an inverted image therefore, for northern hemisphere observers, north is at the bottom of the field of view, south at the top, east to the right and west to the left. The situation is reversed for observers in the southern hemisphere, with north at the top, south at the bottom, east to the left and west to the right. If this sounds a little confusing, then remember that stars enter the field of view from the east; a few moments' wait will therefore soon reveal the east point of the field of view.

The angular diameter of the field of view must be noted on the drawing. To obtain this, use the standard 'star drift' method. Select a star close to the celestial equator and measure how long it takes to drift across the field of view. The diameter of the field in arcminutes can then be obtained by multiplying the time (in minutes) by 15. The above description covers the technique of drawing with a pencil, the end result being a 'negative' image of the star cluster, nebula or galaxy. Other techniques are possible including the use of white chalk on black paper. Realistic effects can be obtained if a 'positive' image is produced using your original drawing at the telescope as a reference.

The original basic sketches, together with relevant notes on the object being observed, even enable colour renditions to be put together while the observation is still fresh in the mind. Unlike deep sky objects, many of which appear colourless to all but the experienced observer with a large telescope, many of the planets have distinctive colours. The prime example here is stars, especially doubles, and Mars, its ruddy glow and contrasting surface features presenting a welcoming challenge for the would-be artist. Jupiter also makes an attractive subject. Its Great Red Spot, in recent years ranging from salmon pink to tan, contrasting with the

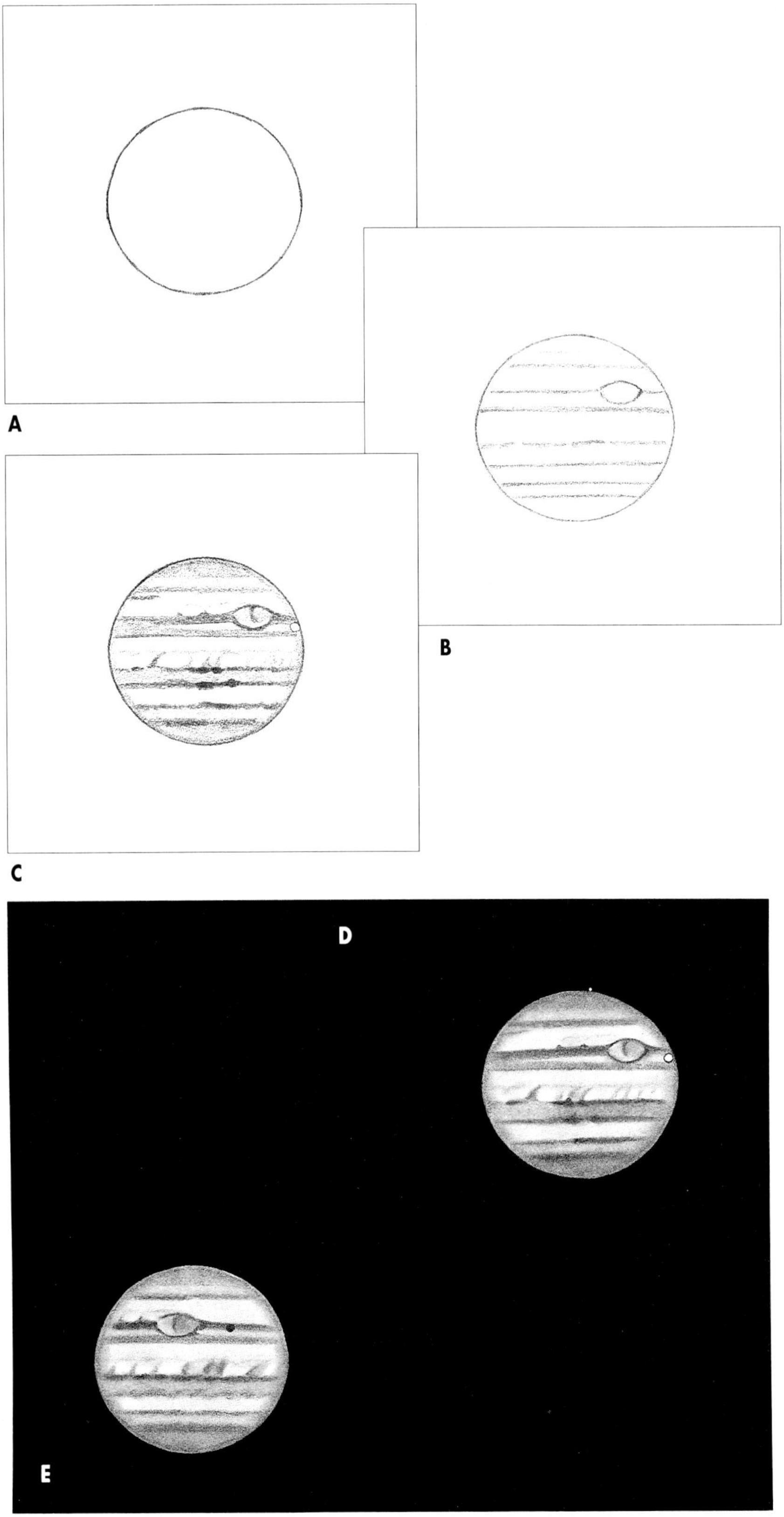

Left A sequence of drawings of Jupiter made using a 152-mm (6 - inch) refractor at f13.on 16 December 1988 between 21.40 UT and 23.30 UT. It shows the various stages in building up the picture. Using a soft pencil and good quality cartridge paper, take a blank outline (A) showing the oblate appearance of the disc and insert the main belts and zones (B). Then include finer details (C), which will become more apparent once you have familiarized yourself with the disc. Be careful not to take more than 15 minutes or so to complete the drawing, as Jupiter spins quite rapidly and some surface features may disappear behind the planet. The final touches can be added away from the telescope. The belts and zones can be blended (D) by 'rubbing in' with cotton wool or similar maertial, and the night sky can be added using black paint. In this sequence the shadow of Io can be seen on the last drawing (E), made roughly an hour after the first to show the effects of Jupiter's rapid rotation. The satellite appears as a bright speck on the limb of Jupiter.

brownish-orange and yellowish belts and zones. These colours become apparent in telescopes of around 200 -mm (8-inches) aperture although they may be glimpsed in smaller instruments.

Whatever objects you decide to record on paper, do not abandon all hope of producing good drawings if your first few attempts are not as good as you would like them to be. Practice makes perfect and you will eventually master the skills required. In the end, it is for the individual observer to decide which materials to use, what techniques to develop and what standard to work for.

Bear in mind too that your notes can be not only records of your observations but also reminders of your journeys through the sky. Jot down a reminder of how tired you were, or of terrestrial events that took place while you were observing (perhaps you heard an owl hooting as you were gazing at the Owl Nebula), or the relief you felt when your neighbour finally turned off his nightlight! By keeping records this way you will recall with even more pleasure the nights you spent gazing at the sky.

Right Although Venus can approach closer than any other planet to the Earth, it offers little in the way of artistic inspiration since it is completely covered in clouds. However, vague cloud features can be seen from time to time. This is a pastel rendering of a black-and-white pencil drawing of Venus as a crescent made on 16 May 1988 at 18.50 UT. It shows irregularities in the terminator. 152-mm (6-inch) refractor at f13 with 166x magnification.

Right A series of drawings of the position of Comet Bradfield made in November 1987 using 7 x 50mm binocluars. The circular misty patch is the open cluster NGC 6633. Drawing 1 shows the comet in Serpens Cauda with the tail 2 long but very faint. The coma is just visible to the naked eye at a magnitude of 4.9. In drawing 2 the comet has moved into Ophiucus and the coma is mostly in front of NGC 6633 so details are uncertain. It is easily visible to the naked eye at a magnitude of 4.6. The third and fourth drawings were done under poor sky conditions the comt still being similar to previous observations.

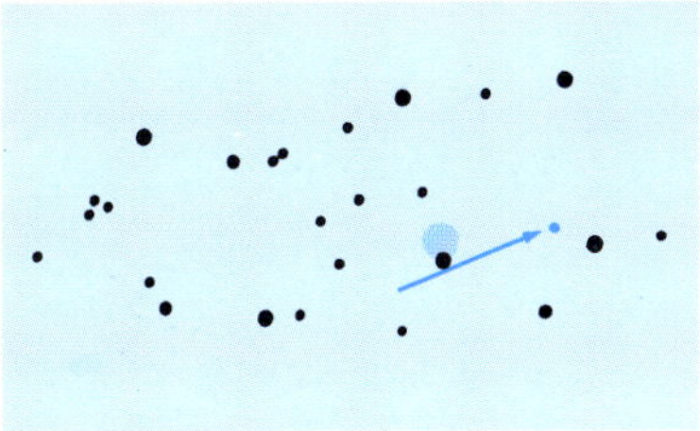

13/14 November 1987
17.55 - 18.10 UT

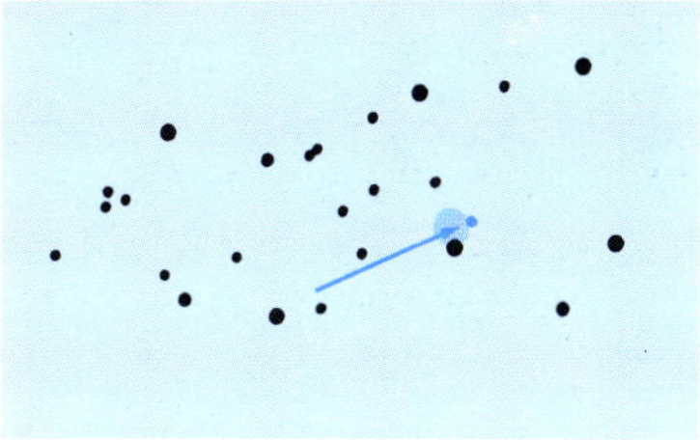

14/15 November 1987
17.50 - 18.00 UT

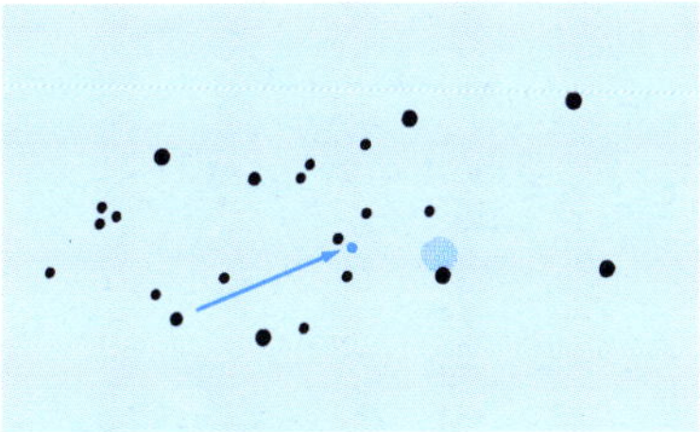

15/16 November 1987
19.05 - 19.05 UT

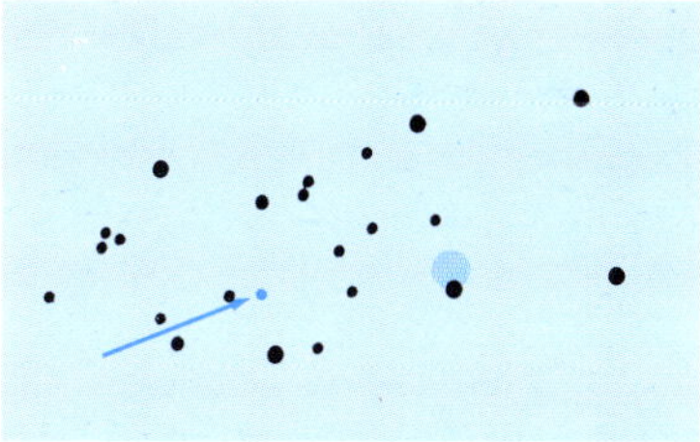

16/17 November 1987
18.00 - 18.10 UT

AMATEUR OBSERVATORIES

Small telescopes are generally portable and easily taken outdoors when needed. Larger instruments, however, cannot be handled so easily. Refractors of 100mm (4 inches) aperture or more, and reflectors of 200mm (8 inches) aperture or more, should be permanently housed in a purpose-built observatory. Repeatedly setting up a large telescope each time it is required may eventually result in damage being caused - to the telescope or its owner!

So how do you go about building an observatory? There are two main possibilities: either you buy one in pre-fabricated form or you set about constructing one yourself from raw materials. If you have a healthy bank balance, the first option seems the best. After all, the less time you spend constructing a home for your telescope, the more time you will have for observing. However, for those of us with limited funds, starting from scratch is the best option.

What type of observatory?

There are three main types of observatory: those with slide-off roofs, those with revolving domes, and the run-off shed type. Each has its advantages and disadvantages: but the more work you put into designing and building the observatory, the more benefits you will get from it.

The most basic type is the run-off shed which, as its name suggests, is nothing more than a housing that protects the telescope from the elements when not in use. When the instrument is required, the shed splits into two parts, each of which is rolled to one side to expose the telescope. A variation is the shed with a removable door or end panel: this is taken off and the whole building pushed to one side. In each case the movable sections are fitted with wheels that run on metal rails set into a concrete base.

The run-off shed has several advantages. One is its low cost. Because it has to be large enough for the telescope only, and not for the observer, its size is kept to a minmum. It is also the easiest of the three types to construct.

However, the run-off shed offers no protection whatever to the hapless observer, who is left exposed to the chill night air! Another disadvantage is that it is less well suited to refractors than reflector; the latter are usually low-slung instruments requiring a correspondingly low building. Refractors are much taller, and a suitably tall building is open to the danger of blowing over in a high wind. Of course, it could be made wide enough to provide increased stability, but this entails rather a lot of work.

Far better than the run-off shed is the building with a removable roof. Although both reflectors and refractors can be housed in this type of observatory, the high walls of the construction mean that the effective horizon for reflectors is somewhat restricted.

Again, there are advantages and disadvantages. One of the main benefits is that the walls offer protection from both wind and stray light. These observatories are relatively easy to build. Like the other two types, they can be made ready for use in a short time. One disadvantage is that as much ground is required at the rear of the building as is taken up by the observatory itself, to accommodate the roof when it is removed.

A revolving dome observatory is difficult to construct. However, it gives almost complete protection to the observer and shields the telescope from virtually all stray light. Any type of telescope can be housed in a dome which also provides room for storage space, shelves., racks and so on. The run-off roof observatory can also be equipped with storage facilities, but the same cannot be said for the run-off shed.

Locating the observatory

Great care must be given to the observatory's location. One option that must be ruled out straightaway is a rooftop. All telescopes must stand on a solid base: An observatory on the roof of a house or other building would suffer excessive vibration. It would also be prone to the effects of high winds. Warm air currents from the building below could create turbulence around the observatory and severely distort the image. This effect can be seen when you look at the severe air turbulence just above a road or roof in hot weather. Imagine trying to carry out observations of faint celestial objects through that!

An isolated site is preferable even if you are not blessed with a long garden. The observatory should be as far as possible from other buildings with a horizon that is as unrestricted as possible. It is at times like this that you realize just how inconveniently placed the surrounding houses, outbuildings, trees and streetlights are, and often you will have to make the best of a bad job.

If possible, northern hemisphere observers should aim for an unobstructed view from the north celestial pole to the southern horizon, while the reverse is true for those in the southern hemisphere. All celestial objects visible from your location will pass through this region of sky at some time or another.

How big (or small)?

The observatory's job is to accommodate the telescope and, in the cases of the run-off roof and revolving dome types, the observer. In order to determine the dimensions, measure the length of the telescope tube from the centre of the mount to the skyward end of the tube. Add the amount of clearance to

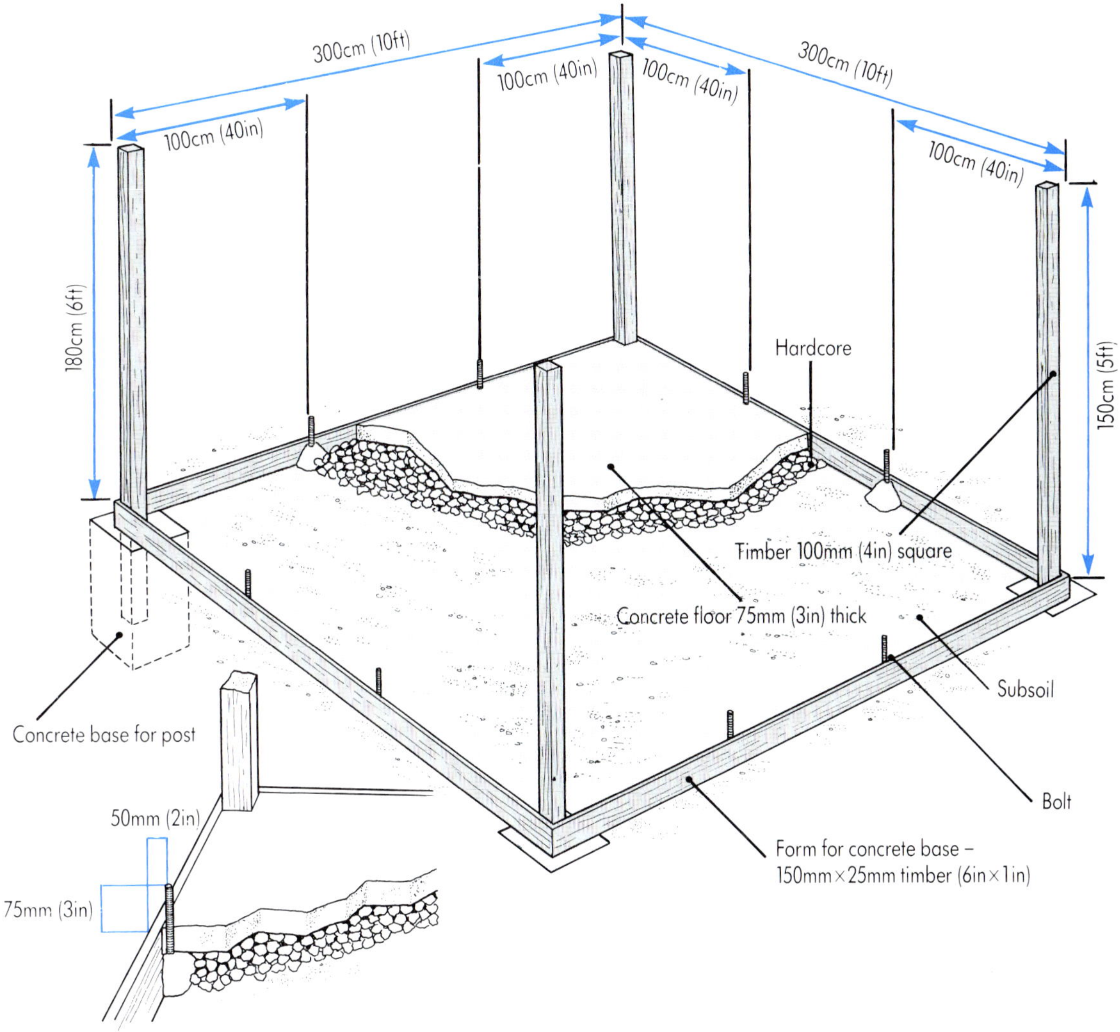

Above The following plans assume internal dimensions of 300cm x 300cm (10 feet x 10 feet) with a height for the lowest wall of 150cm (5feet). Consideration must be given to the angle of inclination of the roof in order that the height of the opposite wall can be determined . A height difference of 30cm (12 inches) will give an inclination of 1 in 10, ensuring that the roof can be pulled on and off quite easily. Put the lowest wall at the southern end of the observatory if possible (at the northern end for southern hemisphere observers), as this will allow maximum sky exposure. Clear and level the ground at the selected site. Given the above dimensions, allow an area of around 360cm x 360cm (12 feet x 12 feet) within which to work. Mark out the site with pegs and string before errecting the four corner posts, which should be made from lengths of 100mm x 100mm (4 inches x 4 inches) timber. These will have to form a square with a distance of 300cm (10 feet) between the outer faces of any two posts. Dig a hole at each corner roughly 300mm (12 inches) square and 450mm (18 inches) deep. The length of each post should be equal to the height of the observatory wall either 150cm (5 feet) or 180cm (6 feet) in this case plus the depth of the hole. Ensure that the whole layout is 'square' and of the correct dimensions. Place the posts in the holes and pour concrete around them so that they are fixed in position. Allow the concrete to set. To make the observatory floor, make a mould into which to pour the concrete. Ensure the top edges of the mould are horizontal. Lay a bed of gravel over the subsoil, hammer down and leave to settle for a period of two to three weeks. Before laying the concrete floor, set two bolts on each side of the observatory floor, each 100cm (40 inches) in from the outer edge of the corner posts. Leaving at least 75mm (3 inches) thick. Once the floor has hardened, the wooden mould can be removed.

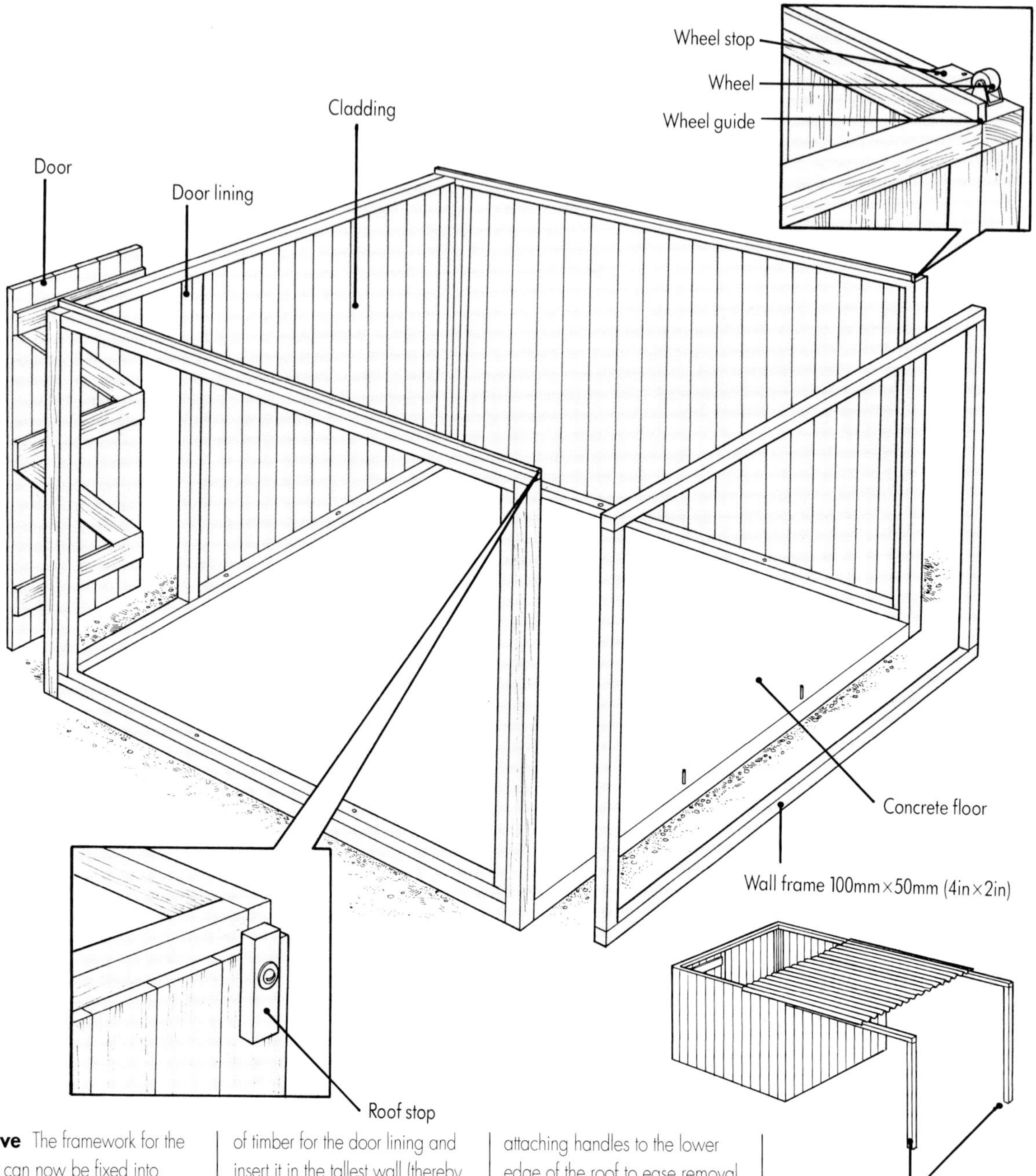

Above The framework for the walls can now be fixed into place. There are a total of four frames, one each for the highest and lowest walls and a matching pair for the sidewalls, constructed from 100mm x 50mm (4 inches x 2 inches) timber. After drilling suitable holes to take the floor bolts, insert the frames between the corner posts and firmly bolt them to the floor. Now cut a piece of timber for the door lining and insert it in the tallest wall (thereby giving maximum headroom). Once the main frame is complete and before assembling the roof a variety of jobs can be done. Fitting roof stops to prevent the roof running back after being closed; fixing hasps and staples, together with suitable padlocks, to clamp the roof down when the observatory is unattended; attaching handles to the lower edge of the roof to ease removal and replacement; and treating the exposed woodwork, either with paint (applied as a final operation) or creosote (best applied to each section as you go along). Finally, erect a couple of upright support posts with guide rails if desired upon which to rest the roof when run off.

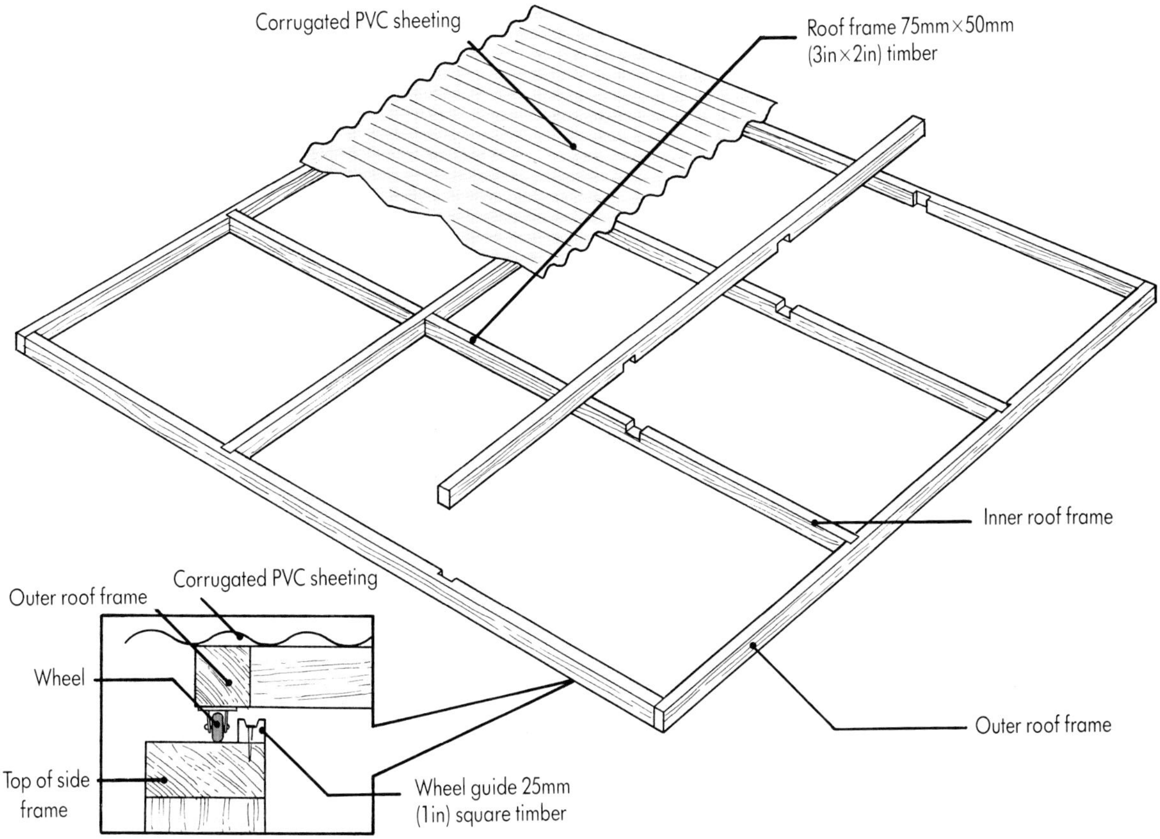

Above The roof is by far the most difficult section to construct. The roof frame should be made from 75mm x 50mm (3 inches x 2 inches) timber cut and jointed as shown. It is useful to clamp together the lengths of timber to be used for the roof before cutting out for the joints. The width of the roof frame should be 75mm (3 inches) less than that of the walls, but the length from the top to bottom should be the same. Fit a pair of small wheels to the underside of the roof frame and fasten wheel guides along the top edges of the sidewall frames. Similarly fit a wheel (upside down) on each sidewall frame. A wheel stop, made from a piece of timber, should also be attached to the wall frame to prevent the two wheels hitting each other when rolling back the roof. Corrugated plastic sheeting is recommended for the final roof covering: its low cost, durability and lightness makes it ideal for the job. Sheets of the material should be fastened across the upper side of the roof frame with a suitable overhang to help keep out the elements. Strips of sponge rubber, treated with a sealant, should be inserted between the sheeting and the top and bottom edges of the roof frame. The overlaps between sheets should also be treated.

determine the distance from the centre of the observatory to the wall (assuming, of course, that the instrument will be situated at the centre of the floor). Doubling this figure will give the total distance from wall to wall of the observatory (or, in the case of a domed observatory, the diameter of the dome itself). At least 30cm (12-inches) clearance should be allowed on all sides of the observatory.

A run-off roof should be high enough to clear the telescope when the latter is stored in its horizontal position. Do not forget to take into consideration attachments such as finders, eyepiece mounts, camera mounts and so on. Other than to reduce the risk of banging your head when first entering the observatory, no more height is required. A domed observatory, of course, has to be high enough to accommodate the observer, Run-off roof observatories should have their lowest wall at the southen end of the building, for northern hemisphere observers, or at the northern end, for those in the southern hemisphere, thereby providing the maximum amount of accessibility to the sky.

One very important thing to bear in mind is that, if you intend to acquire a larger telescope in the future, you must make allowance for it at this stage in construction.

GUIDE TO THE MOON

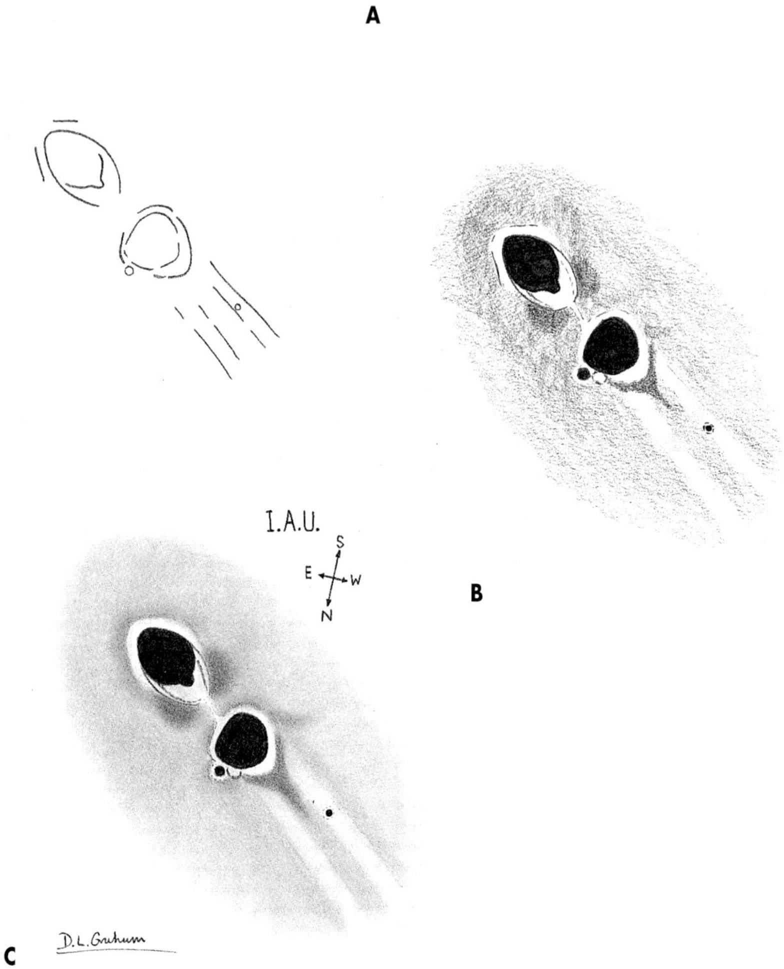

Above Messier and Messier A craters drawn on 21 February 1988 between 19.20 and 19.35 UT using 152-mm (6-inch) refractor at 333x magnification. Seeing I-II. (Messier and Messier A form a double crater in Mare Fecunditatis in the Moon's eastern hemisphere. They lie at the centre of two bright rays that can be seen extending to the west). Prior to making the drawing, study the feature for some time before commencing. Doing this will help you to become familiarized with all the details present. Note the time at which you start. First of all draw an outline containing all the main details in proportion (A). Now use a soft pencil to sketch in the main shading and add finer detail (B). The black crater shadow can be inserted with a felt tip pen. To finish, carefully 'rub in' using soft tissue or cotton wool and insert the cardinal points (C) to show drawing orientation. Make a final check through the eyepiece and note time the drawing was finished. Include with the drawing your name, location, times and details of instrument used, magnification and seeing conditions.

Right The two types of lunar terrain are well displayed in this photograph of the full Moon, the bright cratered upland contrasting with the darker maria. The prominent rayed crater at bottom is Tycho.

Left 6-Day Old Moon. Of interest here is Mare Spumans, seen just to the southeast (lower right) of the circular Mare Crisium near the lunar limb. Copernicus is prominent near the terminator, above centre, while the 100km diameter walled plain Plato is well seen near top of picture located between Mare Frigoris (top) and Mare Imbrium.

Left This picture is dominated by the crater Albategnius, seen here at centre with the disintegrated walled plain Hipparchus just above it to the north. The pair of smaller craters between the two are Halley (left) and Hind. Crater Horrocks can be seen on the northern border of Hipparchus. The crater Triesnecker, with its floor in shadow, can be seen near the top of picture near the eastern border of Sinus Medii, just visible at top left.

Above Prominent on this photograph of the Moon is the circular Mare Crisium at centre right, near the lunar limb with Mare Fecunditatis below it. To the left of Mare Crisium are the twin dark areas Mare Serenitatis (top) and Mare Tranquillitatis. The bright crater Albategnius can be seen on the terminator at centre of picture with the prominent pair of craters Werner (top) and Aliacensis to the south (below).

Left The prominent crater seen here just below centre is Stöfler with Faraday on its southeastern wall. The 'L' - shaped trio of craters just to the south of Stöfler are Licetus (top). Heraclitus and Cuvier, all of which are around 75km in diameter. Considerably disintegrated Heraclitus has a central mountain range. The crater at top of picture is the 136km diameter Albategnius.

Right The most prominent feature here is Sinus Iridium, the great bay visible just to the right of cente on the northwestern border of Mare Imbrium. Two mountain ranges can be seen; the Jura Mountains, bordering the Sinus Iridium and the Carpathian Mountains following the southern border of Mare Imbrium.

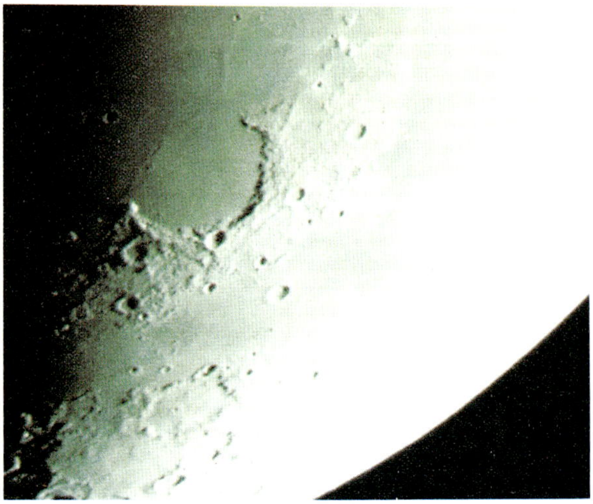

Left The large walled plain Clavius with the chain of craters running across its floor can be seen here to the lower left. On the wall of Clavius are the craters Rutherford, with its floor half in shadow, and above it Porter, with its western wall bathed in sunlight. Above Clavius, just off the left of centre, is the crater Tycho, a prominent 85km diameter feature with huge terraced walls and a central peak over 1,500 metres high. To the upper right of Tycho is the considerably disintegrated walled plan Deslandres with crater Hell prominent near its eastern (left) flank. The southern shores of Mare Nubium can be seen at top of picture.

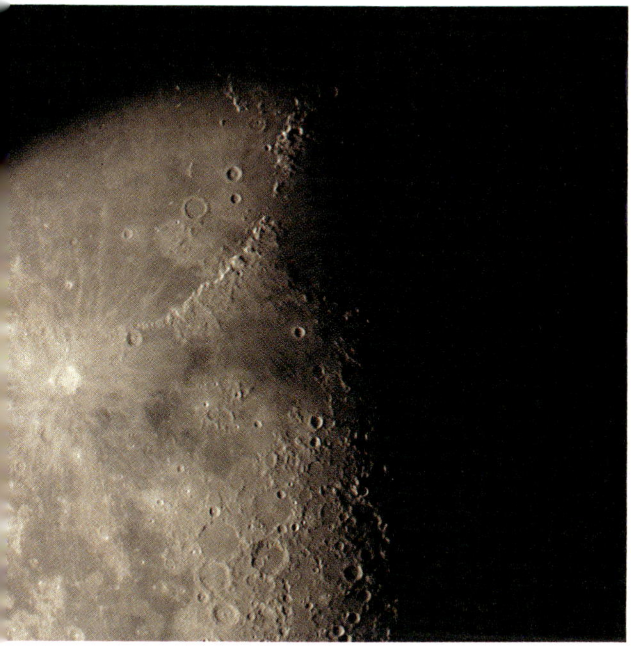

Above The bright rayed crater Copernicus can be seen here to the upper left with Eratosthenes to its upper right. The distinctive arc of the Apennine Mountins sweeps away towards the top of the picture, running along the southeastern border of Mare Imbrium, seen at upper left corner. A number of craters can be seen in the Moon's southern hemisphere including the prominent Albateginus just below centre.

Above The waning Moon, seen shortly after being full, displays the almost circular Mare Imbrium at upper centre with Sinus Iridium flanking its northwestern shore and the bright rayed crater Copernicus to its south. The vast and irregular area of Oceanus Procellarum is seen at left below which is the conspicuous rayed crater Tycho seen towards the Moon's south pole at bottom.

OBSERVING THE SUN

Warning

The Sun is the brightest object in the sky and the most accessible to astronomers. However, its brightness makes it a potential hazard to observers. You must never look directly at the Sun, to do so would almost certainly cause blindness. Whenever you look at the sun.through a telescope or binoculars you must take the careful precautions to protect your eyesight.

Filters are available that can be placed over the end of the telescope to reduce the amount of light entering the instrument. They are in the form of plastic film, which is inexpensive but can give the solar image an unnatural tint. If you are using a filter, follow the manufacturer's instructions carefully when attaching it to the telescope. Take care to ensure that the filter does not become damaged, as even the slightest tear or smallest hole will render it useless.

But the only really safe way to observe the Sun is by projection: using the telescope to focus an image of the Sun onto a white screen. Many new telescopes come complete with a solar projection screen, although there is nothing difficult about constructing your own. When used with a low-power eyepiece the complete solar disc can be seen at once, enlarged views of parts of the disc being obtained with higher-power eyepieces.

For general observing, use a projected image around 15 cm (6 inches) in diameter. This can be obtained by moving the screen away from the eyepiece until the image is of the right size. Then bring it into focus by adjusting the focusing mount. A counterweight will have to be placed at the opposite end of the tube to balance the telescope after the screen has been attached. This can be in the form of a cardboard or hardwood shade, which will keep direct sunlight away from the screen.

Many observers have made special projection boxes, from hard board or thin card. The box fits over the eyepiece, the image being projected onto its back wall. With a projection box, virtually all stray light is cut out, resulting in an even brighter image.

Observing sunspots

Of the different types of solar feature available for study by the amateur, sunspots are the easiest to observe. One useful type of observation is to make a daily count of active areas on the solar disc. This involves counting each sunspot or group of sunspots visible at the time. To count as an individual active area, a sunspot must be at least 10° from its nearest neighbour. However, what may initially be seen as two active areas may eventually approach each other. If they come within 10° of each other, they then count as one area. Some very large groups may have two centres of activity. If

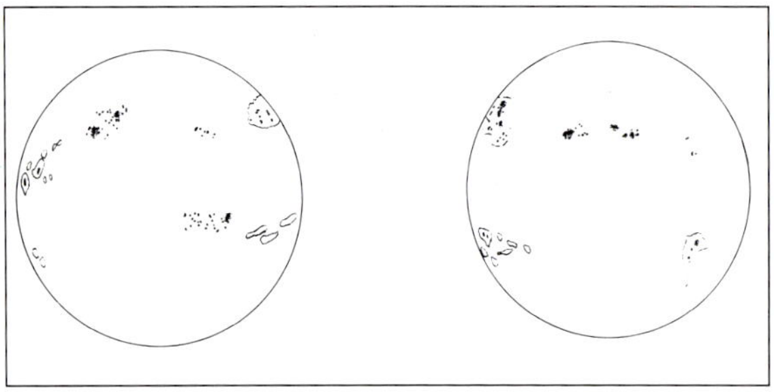

Above Drawings made with a 25-mm (1-inch) refractor at 25x magnification on 24 December 1988 between 12.00 UT and 12.10 UT (left) and 12 February 1989 between 12.20 UT and 12.30 UT. Sunspots are shown with main penumbrae shaded in and with prominent areas of faculae.

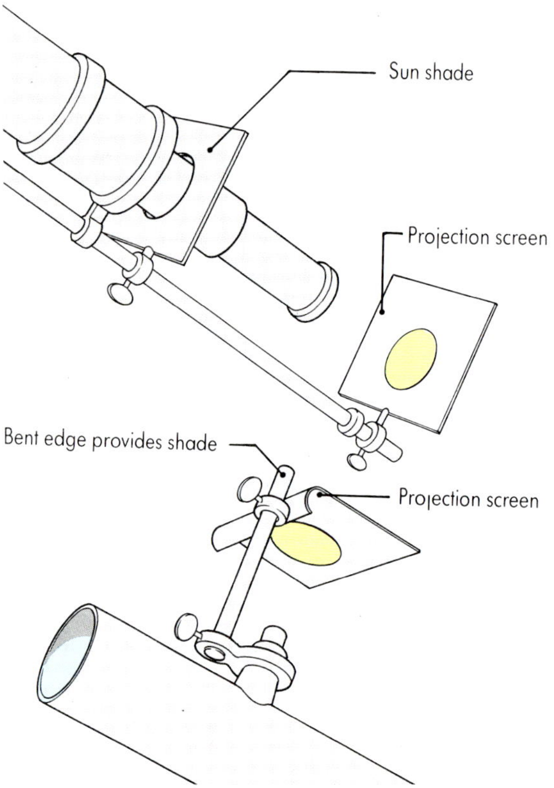

Above Solar projection using a refractor (top) and a reflector (bottom). In each case a white screen is attached to the telescope in such a way that an image of the Sun can be projected onto it. Direct sunlight can be kept away from the image by use of a shade or of a curved edge on the screen, as shown.

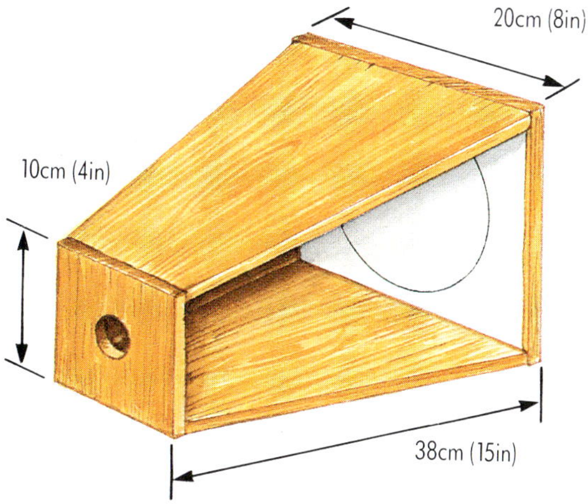

Above A solar projection box, placed over the eyepiece end of the telescope, eliminates most stray sunlight to give a better image with more contrast. Special cards with circles drawn on them to correspond to the size of the solar image can be placed at the back of the box. Any features observ ed can then be drawn on them.

Above The partial solar eclipse of 9 April 1986, photographed from Australia.

these are 10° or more apart they are counted as two areas, although an area with only one active centre counts as a single area regardless of its size. (Estimating the distance between different areas on the solar disc becomes easier with practice.) The total number of active areas is noted for each day, and at the end of each month the total number of areas seen is divided by the number of observing days to obtain what is called a mean daily frequency (MDF) for that month. By doing this over a prolonged period of, say, several years, a graph of solar activity can be drawn up, showing how sunspot numbers vary throughout the solar cycle. On days around minimum activity you may find the Sun totally devoid of spots for several days or even weeks at a time. However, at maximum the solar disc may be swarming with active areas.

The next step is to draw the sunspots you see. You can draw the whole disc or individual spots. Making the drawing directly onto the screen will tend to shake the telescope: the best method is to project the image onto a grid placed on the screen. A drawing of the feature is then made on a similar grid but on a separate sheet of paper. The picture is build up, s, rather like the process used in children's drawing books where a 'squared off' picture (usually of a pig, elephant or other animal rather than a sunspot!) is placed adjacent to a 'blank' grid. The picture is than copied, square by square, onto the blank grid. If the same spot is drawn daily over a period of time, a record of the growth and decline of the area will be built up.

Drawing sunspots is difficult with a telescope not fitted with a drive, as most of your time will be spent keeping the spots lined up with the grid. This is particularly noticeable when higher magnifications, and consequently smaller areas, are being examined, as the Sun's rate of drift across the field of view will be enhanced.

Other solar features

A magnification of between 100x and 120x may bring out granulation on the solar surface, but this is difficult to see unless observing conditions are excellent. Easier to detect is the phenomenon known as limb darkening, an apparent dimming of the photosphere near the limb (the edge of the Sun). This is caused by increased absorption of light from the photosphere near the limb, where we have an oblique view through a greater depth of atmosphere.

Faculae are bright clouds of hydrogen, similar in brightness to the photosphere. They show little contrast when seen near the centre of the solar disc. Near the limb, however, they are far more prominent as their light originates in the chromosphere several hundred kilometres above the photosphere. They tend to appear with sunspot areas. They may also show that an active sunspot group is on the way or has disappeared from the area.

OBSERVING THE TERRESTRIAL PLANETS

Mercury

Mercury is never further than 28° from the Sun and is always seen low down in the sky, either in the west after sunset or the east before sunrise. It can also be observed during daytime and is at its best when viewed telescopically against a bright sky.

However, great care must be taken when attempting to locate Mercury in the daytime. You must not sweep the sky with either telescope or binoculars. Accidentally bringing the Sun into your field of view could result in serious damage to your eyesight.

The correct method is to obtain the coordinates at the time of observation – ephemerides for Mercury and the other planets are available in various publications. Then use a telescope fitted with setting circles to locate it. Use a solar fitter until you have found the planet.

The angular diameter of Mercury varies between 4.5" and 12.9". It is at its smallest apparent size when displaying full phase and situated at the other side of the Sun from the Earth. The largest angular size is seen when Mercury is displaying a thin crescent. Magnifications of around 150 times will show the Mercurian phases, which will be seen to change quickly because of Mercury's rapid orbital motion. This rapid motion also results in Mercury being at or near a favourable elongation for only 7-10 days before it is once more carried in towards the Sun.

Venus

Many amateur astronomers have never seen Mercury, but there must be few who have never caught sight of Venus, the brightest planet in the sky. Venus has a maximum magnitude of -4.4 and an angular diameter that varies between 9.5" at full phase to 65.2" when it is displaying a thin crescent. The

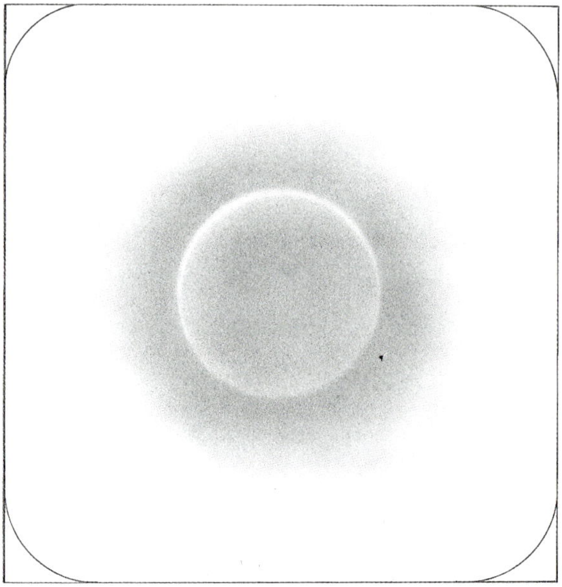

Above Drawing of Venus made on April 2, 1977 at 18.40 UT when the planet was near inferior conjunction. Extensions to the cusps can be clearly seen as can the Ashen Light, a plae glow on the dark side similar to earthshine onthe Moon in appearance but not in cause. 115mm refractor at 186x magnification.

Left Mercury's proximity to the Sun makes observation difficult, but surface markings are sometimes visible. This drawing shows some vague areas of shading on the disc. 152mm refractor at 186x magnification.

phases can be seen quite well with magnifications of only around 50 times.

The surface of Venus is completely hidden from Earth-based observers by the thick cloud-laden atmosphere that enshrouds the planet. Many observers claim to have detected markings in the Venusian atmosphere, although space missions to the planet put the existence of these markings into doubt.

Venus is so bright that any serious observation should be carried out before the sky becomes dark. Any markings seen in the atmosphere are indistinct and difficult to make out at the best of times, and the glare from the planet when seen against a black sky is so great that subtle details can easily be lost to the observer. But one type of observation that can be carried out with the planet seen against a dark sky is that of the 'ashen light'. When the illuminated part of Venus is a thin crescent, the remainder of the disc may be seen to be dimly illuminated. This is very difficult to pick out and such observations may be possible only when the light from the crescent is blocked out.

As with Mercury, observations may be carried out during the day, but great care in locating the planet with the telescope must be taken.

Mars

The angular diameter of Mars can reach 25.7" during favourable oppositions, and the planet is observed to best effect at these times. Even telescopes of only 100 mm (4 inches) aperture may reveal surface markings on Mars. These features are dark in comparison to the surrounding desertlike surface and are composed of material with a lower reflectivity, or albedo. By far the most prominent of these so-called albedo features is Syrtis Major, a distinct V-shaped patch first seen by Christiaan Huygens in 1659.

Prolonged observation may reveal other features, which will occasionally spring into view during moments of good atmospheric transparency. Drawing the features seen will provide a permanent record and will help you to identify them when seen on subsequent occasions. Long-term observations may reveal changes in the structure of some of the albedo features. Such changes have been noted both in Syrtis Major and Meridiani Sinus, another fairly prominent albedo feature.

Occasionally all or part of the Martian surface may be hidden from view for days or even weeks on end as winds whip up dust from the planet's surface to produce a screen that effectively blocks our view of the planet. If such a dust storm is localized, the material borne by the wind may be seen as a yellowish patch above the Martian surface.

Other features that may occasionally be visible include atmospheric clouds, suspended high in the tenuous Martian atmosphere and best seen when near the limb of the planet. Much easier to see are the highly reflective polar ice caps, which wax and wane throughout the changing Martian seasons. The pole facing us will, of course, also be tilted towards the Sun, and will be experiencing summer. Long-term monitoring of the ice will provide a record of its changing size as the Martian summer develops.

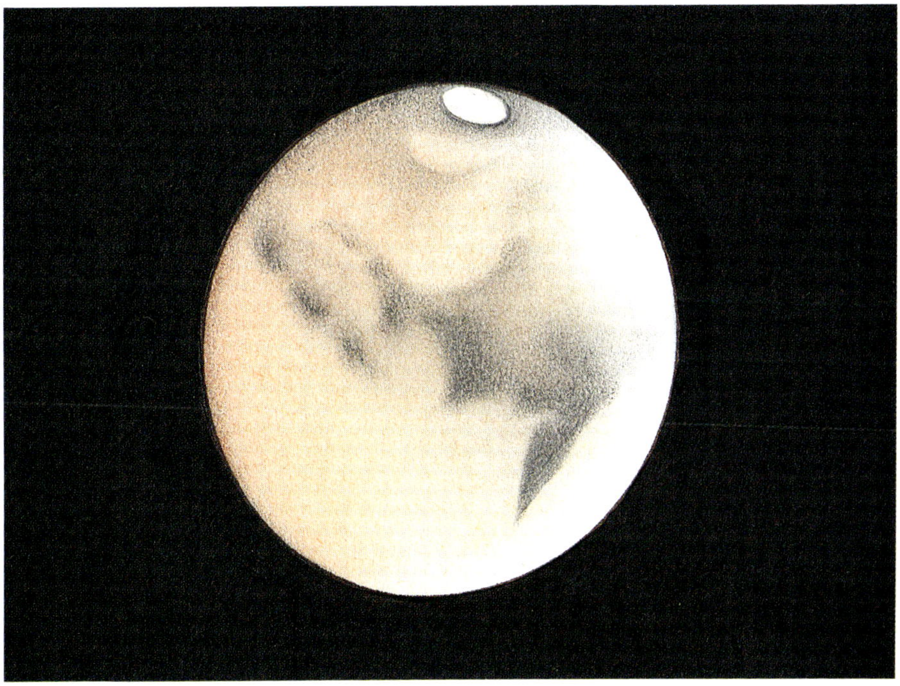

Right Drawing of Mars made on August 15th, 1988 at 23.45 UT. Seeing was II on the Antoniadi scale and the angular diameter of the planet was 19.4". The South Polar Cap is large, bright, elliptical, and touching the limb. A dusky collar is seen aroung the cap. The prominent V-shaped Syrtis Major is well seen. The northern hemisphere is devoid of detail. 115mm refractor at 186x magnification.

OBSERVING THE ASTEROIDS AND OUTER PLANETS

The asteroids and outer planets are considerably fainter than the other planetary members of the Solar System. Of the objects covered here only Uranus and the asteroid Vesta ever become bright enough to be visible to the unaided eye. Even then, exceptional observing conditions are required.

Although it may seem that amateur work relating to these members of the Sun's family is somewhat limited in scope, this is far from being the case. The asteroids in particular are marvellous objects of study for the backyard astronomer.

The Minor Planets

Even through powerful telescopes the minor planets appear as nothing more than points of light – hence their name, which means 'starlike'. When near opposition, the four largest asteroids – Ceres, Pallas, Juno and Vesta – are all bright enough to be tracked easily with good binoculars or a small telescope. Their maximum magnitudes are 7.4, 8.0, 8.6 and 5.3 respectively. In addition there are a number of others whose magnitudes can be brighter than 10 when suitably placed.

To identify an asteroid, details of its position at the time of observation are needed. Many astronomy magazines and publications carry ephemerides of asteroid positions. The predicted path of the asteroid across the sky should be plotted on a star atlas, preferably one that charts stars down to a magnitude fainter than that of the object being sought. Once the path, with the night-to-night positions of the asteroid, has been marked, take a look at the area on the dates indicated. Draw the field observed to complete the first stage of your minor planet identification, and follow up the observation within a couple of nights. If the object has moved against the background of fixed stars, it can be identified as an asteroid. Subsequent observations can then be made to track it over a prolonged period.

The amount of shift depends upon the distance of the asteroid from the Earth and Sun. Asteroids between Mars and Jupiter will move by around 1/2° per day, while others closer in may move anything up to 2° or more in a 24-hour period. Such rates are typical of asteroids with somewhat eccentric orbits that carry them away from the main zone and across the Earth's orbit.

Other work that can be carried out by the amateur includes estimations of magnitudes, which, in the case of asteroids with irregular shapes, can vary as they rotate.

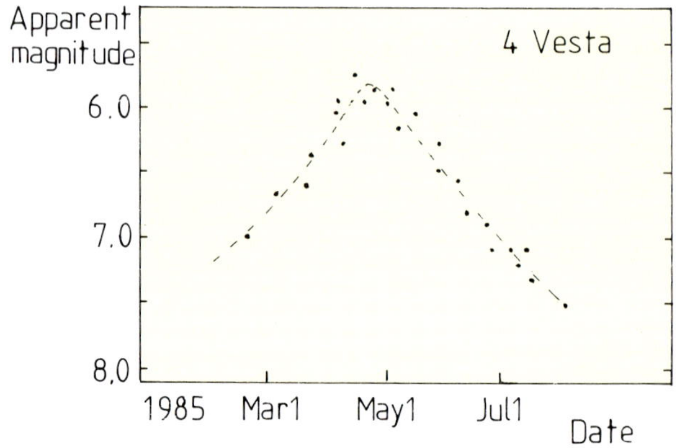

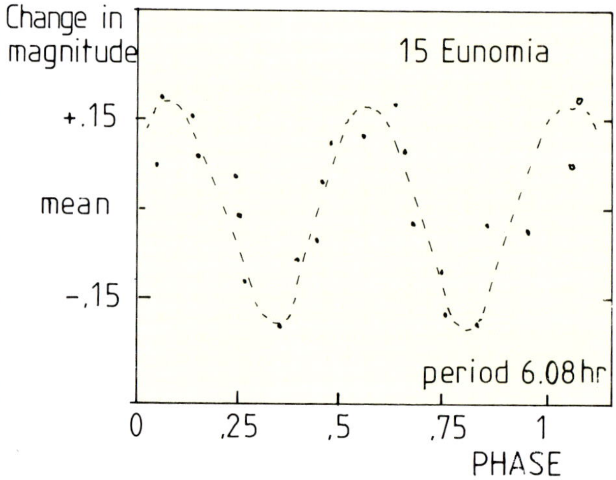

Top Plot of changes in the apparent brightness of asteroid 4 Vesta during the opposition of 1985, made from visual estimates. As can be seen, Vesta was at its brightest (around magnitude 5.8) during late April.

Above Light curve of asteroid 15 Eunomia, obtained in 1981 from visual estimates made during one axial rotation period. Variations of over a tenth of a magnitude above and below mean brightness were recorded.

Unequal surface reflectivity may produce a similar effect. These short-term variations are not to be confused with the long-term increase and decrease in brightness seen as an asteroid moves through opposition.

Estimates of magnitude changes can be made visually, fluctuations of half a magnitude or more being readily visible, although smaller changes can be detected by experienced observers. A prolonged series of observations can reveal a great deal about the asteroid, including details of its rotation period and surface reflectivity. Many asteroids display changes in brightness, some fluctuating by more than a magnitude.

Occultations of stars by asteroids, although rare, offer

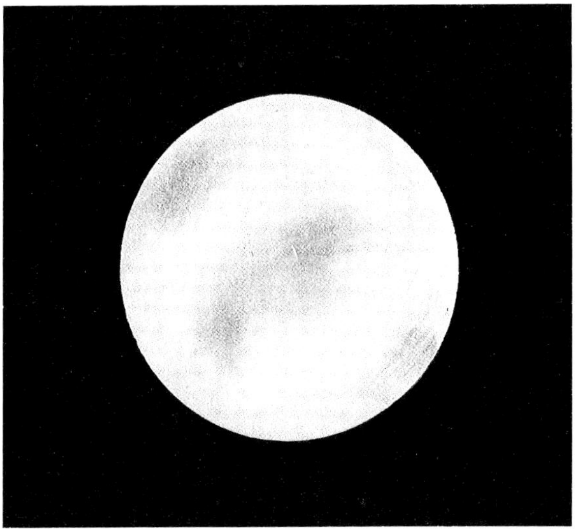

Above Drawing of Uranus made on 8 September 1986 at 19.43 UT with 300-mm (12-inch) reflector at 230x magnification. Seeing was II on the Antoniadi scale. The disc was seen to have a greenish-blue tinge and some features were recorded, although these were quite faint and elusive.

marvellous opportunities for the amateur observer to carry out really useful work. Predictions of occultations are available in a number of the monthly astronomical magazines. These indicate the geographical locations that are likely to fall within the path of occultation. Timing exactly when the star disappears and reappears can tell us a great deal about the diameter and shape of the asteroid.

The outer planets

Detailed charts showing the positions of the outer planets throughout the year appear in many publications, enabling them to be identified and followed. The outer planets move much more slowly across the sky than asteroids do and their motions will not be apparent until several nights have passed. Our knowledge of these far distant worlds is being, and will continue to be, considerably enhanced by the Voyager and Pioneer probes which will be passing by them.

Uranus

The apparent diameter of Uranus varies between 3.1" and 3.7", depending on its distance from Earth. Its brightest magnitude is 5.6. Telescopically it displays a greenish disc upon which various features may be glimpsed by a keen-eyed observer under good seeing conditions. These features are weak, difficult to see and nowhere near as impressive as the swirling cloud belts of Jupiter or even the dusky markings of Saturn. Several observers have reported spots and banding in the Uranian atmosphere, often faint and indistinct. In order to pick up detail of this nature on Uranus, excellent observing conditions are essential, together with a large telescope, an experienced eye and a great deal of patience.

Neptune

Appearing as a bluish disc in telescopes, Neptune has an apparent diameter of between 2.0" and 2.3" making its identification just that bit more difficult than that of Uranus. The planet is also much fainter than Uranus, maximum opposition magnitude being only 7.7.

Generally speaking, Neptune will show no detail on its tiny disc, although a number of astronomers have claimed sightings of features in its clouds. However, these observers were using telescopes that would be generally unavailable to the amateur. Bands, spots, patches and mottling have all been reported in the past, although their existence has been doubted by other astronomers who have failed to detect any form of surface feature. However, in spite of this, it does seem that features in Neptune's clouds can be seen through Earth-based telescopes, although these are even more elusive than those of Uranus. Hovering on the threshold of visibility, they will only be seen by highly experienced observers.

Pluto

Although both Uranus and Neptune can be spotted with either good binoculars or a small telescope, Pluto is considerably fainter and requires the use of large instruments in order to detect its 14th magnitude glow. It can be picked out by its motion through the sky, although the task is considerably harder than for the objects discussed above. Most amateur astronomers have never seen it, and the positive identification of this tiny world can be regarded as a notable achievement in itself.

OBSERVING GAS GIANTS

Observing Jupiter

Jupiter exhibits a disc of 50" at opposition, with a maximum magnitude of -2.6. Even small telescopes will show belts and zones crossing the disc, and the four largest satellites are visible through binoculars.

The belts and zones may display different features, and one job for the amateur is to make timings when these features cross the centre of the disc. For this purpose an imaginary line is put down across the disc, running from north to south, and the times at which features cross this central meridian are noted. If possible, a series of timings are taken, to include the moments at which the leading edge, centre and trailing edge of the feature cross the meridian.

Drawing Jupiter

It will help to have a number of blanks available that will provide a ready-made outline of Jupiter's flattened disc. Because Jupiter rotates so quickly, speed is of great importance when making complete-disc drawings. Once the main belts and zones have been marked on the blank, take note of any features that are about to disappear behind the planet and put them on the drawing. Note which features are visible at the opposite side and take care not to include features that appear during the period of observation. Don't forget to make a note of any colours seen, together with the start and finish times of the observation.

Drawings of individual features can also be made. One obvious candidate for this type of observation is the Great Red Spot, which has been seen to undergo numerous changes since it was first observed over three centuries ago.

Observing the Satellites

The four Galilean satellites are all bright enough to be observable with only moderate optical aid, and their motions are apparent even over fairly short periods.

The satellites can be seen to cross the disc of Jupiter (transit), pass behind it (occultation), or pass into the planet's shadow (eclipse). Prior to opposition, Jupiter's shadow extends to the west of the planet, and a satellite will be eclipsed before being occulted. After opposition eclipses follow occultations.

The shadow of a satellite may fall onto the disc of Jupiter. Prior to opposition the shadow will be seen on the planet before the satellite itself crosses the disc. The reverse is true after opposition. Times of these satellite phenomena are available in various publications.

Observing Saturn and its satellites

Even when best placed, Saturn has an angular diameter less than half that of Jupiter. Higher magnifications are therefore required to bring out a disc of comparable size. All of Saturn's major features (the disc, main rings and Titan, the brightest satellite) can be resolved with telescopes of just 60-mm ($2\frac{1}{2}$-inch) aperture. However, larger instruments are needed for detailed studies of the planet: refractors of at least 100-mm (4-inch) aperture or reflectors of 150-mm (6-inch) aperture.

One particularly interesting area of research open to all observers of Saturn is the examination of the shadow of the globe on the rings and of the rings on the globe. Prior to opposition the width of the globe's shadow on the rings diminishes, only to expand after opposition. Any irregularities in shadow outline should be carefully noted. Look also for the shadow of the rings on the globe, again noting any irregularities.

Left A photograph of Jupiter taken by an amateur astronomer through a 305mm (12 inch) telescope. The major cloud belts and Great Red Spot are clearly visible. This view is similar to that obtained visually through telescopes of around 200mm (8-inches) aperture. The Jovan disc contains a wealth of observable detail, making Jupiter a favourite target for backyard astronomers. Turbulent changes may be seen within the cloud belts and zones. Jupiter's rapid axial rotation period ensures that all features move quickely across the visible disc, presenting a challenge to those attempting to draw the planet.

Above A drawing of Saturn made on 1 August 1988 at 21.15 UT. The magnificent ring system of Saturn makes it an excellent object for the amateur observer. Our view of the rings of Saturn varies over a period of 13.75 year. The rings will be edge on to the Earth in the year 1995.

Observing the disc

The belts and zones of Saturn are subject to occasional disturbances, although these are rare and difficult to discern. The most common are projections from the belts and whitish spots within the zones. If such features are seen they should be searched for on successive nights. Timings should also be made of when the feature crosses the planet's central meridian, to the nearest minute if possible. Regular examination of the disc will increase the chances of seeing any disturbances. Bright areas can also appear on the rings, but care should be taken to ensure that these are not optical effects. Any genuine feature will move with the planet's rotation.

The latitude of a belt, zone or other observed feature can also be estimated. Although these measurements are best carried out with a special micrometer, visual estimates can be very useful. The distance of each belt edge from the centre of the disc, working along the central meridian, should be estimated.

Brightness estimates

One of the main areas of observation is making brightness estimates of the belts, zones and features of the ring system. Brightnesses are estimated according to a scale of 1 to 10, where higher numbers indicate darker areas. There are a couple of standard brightnesses: 1 for the brightness of the outer part of Ring B and 10 for a very dark sky or a region of deep shadow. If a feature is seen to be brighter than 1, this can be recorded as 0 (in exceptional cases), 1/4, 1/2 or 3/4. When it comes to estimating brightnesses in this way, there is nothing better than practice. Particular attention should be paid to observing brightness changes in the polar regions of the planet, as these appear to change according to the inclination of Saturn with respect to the Earth. These observations are best recorded by entering numbers on diagrams of the planet and its rings.

The rings

Observers using small instruments see just the three main components of the ring system, together with the conspicuous Cassini Division. Larger telescopes may help you to pick out Encke's Division (Ring A). The innermost ring (Ring C) is also difficult without a large telescope.

Bright patches are sometimes reported, particularly in Ring B. Radial spokes have also been reported. Another feature worth looking out for is any change in intensity of the rings at different distances from the planet. These so-called ripples, or intensity minima, are exemplified by the Cassini Division, the best and most prominent example. However, excellent seeing conditions are required.

Twice during the 29½-year orbital period of Saturn the rings are edge-on to us and become extremely difficult to see – they may even disappear from view altogether. If you are making observations of the planet at such times, note the dates and times when the rings disappear and reappear.

The satellites

Most of the satellites are beyond the range of amateur telescopes but Titan can be seen through good binoculars. It is fascinating to watch Titan from night to night during its 16-day orbit. Titan can reach a magnitude of 8.4. The next brightest satellite is Rhea, at magnitude 9.7, which can be seen through a 100-mm (4-inch) telescope under excellent observing conditions. Tethys (magnitude 10.3) and Dione (magnitude 10.4) need a 150-mm (6-inch) telescope. Iapetus varies in brightness as it orbits Saturn. When on the western side of the planet Iapetus attains 10th magnitude: this drops to around 12 when on the eastern side.

Occultations

One final and very important thing to watch out for is the occultation of a star by Saturn. These events are very rare and not always predictable. Estimate the variations in brightness and colour of the star as it passes behind the rings, together with the times of the changes. Record also the time that the star disappears behind the planet.

OBSERVING COMETS

Searching for comets

There are many amateurs who dream of discovering a comet and having it named after them. But comet-searching requires a phenomenal amount of patience and dedication.

There are two basic methods of searching for comets. One is to scan particular areas of the sky meticulously each night in an attempt to pick out objects that may wander into the field of view. This method requires an intimate knowledge of the patterns of stars and deep sky objects down to a chosen magnitude in the areas of sky you will be scanning, a knowledge that will be built up only after perhaps hundreds of hours of observing. Ideally, large binoculars or rich-field telescopes should be used for visual comet-searching.

The other, and better, method is to search photographically by taking pictures of the sky on successive nights, developing them as soon as possible, and seeing if any object has moved between the times of the two exposures. The best areas of sky to search are the western sky just after sunset or the eastern sky before sunrise, where comets can often sneak up on the unwary astronomer.

Care must be taken to ensure that a newly detected object is not an asteroid or faint planet. It must be borne in mind that comets are almost always nebulous. Check also that you have not picked up a previously known comet making one of its regular and predicted returns. Finally, if possible, make a visual check through the telescope, in case the object detected is nothing more than a flaw on the film. Quite often a comet will appear as a distinctly diffuse and unstarlike object, thereby giving itself away. But care should be taken here, as cometary tails are not always prominent visually when the comet is a long way from the Sun.

The next thing to do is to determine the right ascension and declination of the comet, preferably by making measurements on a picture of the area around it. Then report your finding to the correct authority. This can be either the recorder of the section of the Association of Lunar and Planetary Observers or the Center for Astronomical Telegrams of the International Astronomical Union in Cambridge, Massachusetts. Before you commence your search make a note of the required telephone numbers, as speed of reporting will be of the essence when a discovery is made: no more than three names may be attached to any new comet discovered.

Observing comets

Of course, searching for new comets is only one (albeit exciting, unpredictable and potentially rewarding) branch of cometary astronomy. The regular visitors to our skies also need monitoring. The work involved includes checking the motion of comets to ensure that any changes in the orbit are detected. The best way of doing this is to photograph the comet on several occasions to show its path against the stars. This can have its problems if the comet is travelling fairly quickly. In these cases the camera should be mounted on top of the telescope which is then used as a guidescope to enable the comet to be followed during the exposure. The final photograph should then contain a good image of the comet, accompanied by star trails. The position of the comet relative to the surrounding stars is then plotted, although work of this kind is normally beyond the scope of the amateur astronomer.

Above Comet West, one of the most spectacular comets of recent years seen in an amateur photograph taken on 9 March 1976. In the same month its nucleus disintegrated.

Above In this amateur photograph of Halley's comet taken from Queenstown, New Zealand, the comet is 64.7 million km (40 million miles) from the Earth. It is seen here, moving towards the Sun, against the background of the Milky Way.

Visual observation of the comet's structure can also be made. Wide-field telescopes will help to bring out details of the tail, which may be quite long and faint. Higher magnifications can be used on the head, which may display various features in and around the coma, including material escaping and forming jets or umbrella-type formations. The more observations of this nature that are carried out the better, as the appearance of a comet can change over remarkably short periods as its distance from the Sun changes.

Estimates of the magnitude of the nucleus, if visible, can also be made by comparing its apparent brightness with that of nearby stars of known magnitude. It is useful to make a note of nearby stars when tracking a comet. Estimating the overall brightness of the comet is another proposition; however, it is very difficult to compare the brightness of a point of light to that of a comet, whose light is spread out. Although the returns of many comets are predictable, their visual appearance is not .In its last apparition in 1986 Halley's comet was faint compared with its previous apparition in 1910 when it reached a magnitude of 0. Such variations in comet brightness are in the main caused by the relative position of the Sun and Earth rather than any change in the constitution of the comet. Thus astronomers consider it likely that the apparation of Halley's comet in 2061 will be brighter than its apparation in 1986. This makes comet observation a very interesting and rewarding area of astronomy, with many objects available to the amateur armed with suitable equipment.

OBSERVING GLOWS IN THE SKY

Below Zodiacal light seen from Tenerife in an exposure of ten minutes.
Left A striking display of the Aurora Borealis with Ursae Major visible above it.

Aurorae

Aurorae are best observed with the naked-eye: the limited field of view of telescopes will reveal no detail whatsoever, and binoculars are also of little use, other than to plot the locations of field stars to determine the position of the display. It is worthwhile to check on the poleward horizon during every clear night, especially near solar maximum.

Observational records of auroral displays should contain a number of details: the date, starting and finishing times of your observations, the location of the observing site (preferably in terms of latitude and longitude) and observing conditions, including any clouds or moonlight.

The aurora itself can be described in full and supplemented with drawings. When drawing an aurora, mark in the positions of any bright stars that will act as a reference for determining its position and extent. The shape and form of the display should be noted, as should the extent of the display and reference to the horizon. Using standard three-digit azimuths (where true north is 000°, east to 090°, south 180° and west 270°), the width from east to west of the display should be noted as two azimuth points: e.g. extending from 330° to 015°'. Measure also the heights in degrees of the upper and lower edges of the display, provided that these can be clearly seen. The heights must be taken from the true, and not from the apparent, horizon. The brightness can be indicated by a comparison with the Milky

Way or moonlit clouds. Note also any colour visible in the display. The most usual colours are white, green and yellow, although red, blue and purple may also be observed. Different areas of the display may take on different colours, and these should be carefully noted.

Aurorae that display little or no change in form are classed as 'quiet' displays, while 'active' displays show changes (often swift) in appearance. These can include anything from irregularities travelling along the lower edge of the display to wholesale changes across the entire aurora. Forms may disappear to be replaced by new ones at different locations.

There is a wide range of different auroral forms, including everything from an ill-defined glow on the poleward horizon to arcs stretching up into the sky. These latter forms can occur singly or in combination. They follow the lines of force of the Earth's magnetic field. Quite often the different forms seen within an auroral display are superimposed on an extensive and uniform veil. Auroral bands may also be seen. These are similar in many ways to arcs, but their lower edges are subject to irregularities. Sometimes only part of an arc or band is visible.

The brightness of the display can change, with variations taking place uniformly within certain areas or sweeping through the display, in the direction away from the pole. Flickering aurorae undergo irregular changes in brightness, rather as if the display were fluttering in the wind.

Aurorae can be rewarding photographically. A 35-mm or 50-mm lens should be used, set wide open. Colour or black-and-white ISO 400 or 1000 film can be used. Make a number of exposures. For faint displays, the shutter should be left open for at least 30 seconds – exposures of a minute or longer may be needed. Really bright displays require exposures of much shorter duration, ranging from around 2 seconds to 15 seconds or so. Remember that aurorae undergoing rapid changes in form and shape will be blurred on exposures of more than a few seconds' duration. Records should always be kept of the exposure times and camera settings.

The glow along the ecliptic

The zodiacal light, zodiacal band and gegenschein are very difficult to see, particularly for those at mid-latitudes. You must observe on a very dark, moonless night, and well removed from any form of light pollution. Naked-eye observation is essential. To pick out the glow of the zodiacal light, let your gaze wander slowly along the horizon around the point at which it meets the ecliptic at the end of astronomical twilight in the evening or before it begins in the morning. If you are lucky enough to spot it, try and estimate its width and height. Plot its position relative to the background stars, making a sketch of its outline.

Once you spot the zodiacal light, follow it away from the horizon as far as you can. In exceptional conditions you may be able to follow the path of the zodiacal band across the sky along the ecliptic, and perhaps even detect the gegenschein.

Capturing the zodiacal light on film is difficult. Fast film is needed, ISO 400 or 1000. A wide-angle lens should be used. The camera should, of course, to tripod-mounted and exposures ranging from 30 seconds to several minutes should be taken.

Noctilucent clouds

Noctilucent clouds are the only clouds whose appearance in the sky is welcomed by the astronomer! They are fascinating to watch and are often the only observable feature during the summer, when – especially at high latitudes – the sky never becomes truly dark.

First record the date, start and finish times of observation, location of observing site and observing conditions, including the presence of other cloud. Then note the azimuthal extent of the display, in terms of the eastern and western extremes of the clouds. Then record the heights above the horizon of the lower edge (if visible) and the upper edge.

Noctilucent clouds can show a number of different features: veils, billows, bands, either parallel or criss-cross, and whirls. The appearance of each of these features should be recorded, with the times at which they appear. The brightness of noctilucent cloud can be expressed as a number: 1 = faint; 2 = medium brightness; 3 = very bright. Numbers can be inserted on a drawing to illustrate the brightnesses of different regions.

OBSERVING METEORS

Amateur astronomers can play a very important role in improving our understanding of meteor streams. Only basic recording equipment is needed, and a willingness to spend prolonged periods lying under the sky, wrapped against the cold and watchful for the occasional streak of light dashing across the sky.

During the course of a year there are many meteor showers, each with its own radiant from which all the meteors in that shower appear to emanate. The showers are named after the constellation in which the radiant lies or after a star located near the radiant point. For example, the Alpha Cygnids appear to radiate from a point near the bright star Deneb (Alpha Cygni) while the Taurids emanate from Taurus.

It is a fairly straightforward job to determine whether a meteor is travelling from a known radiant. Place a straight-edge, such as a ruler, along the observed path of the meteor and trace it back across the sky to see whether the meteor came from a shower radiant.

Equipment

The vigil of the meteor observer can be an uncomfortable task unless adequate preparations are made. It is important to be fully protected against the cold: you will be motionless for most of the time and it is surprising just how cold it can feel even during summer nights. Warm clothing is essential, including a thick anorak (with plenty of pockets for storage), a sweatshirt, pullover and scarf. Don't forget that most body heat is lost through the uncovered head, making a woolly hat essential. Thick trousers, socks, comfortably fitting boots and gloves are also needed.

A sleeping bag is also recommended, used with a reclining chair or sun-lounger. meteor-watching entails constant sky surveillance and the last thing you want is a stiff neck!

Times for the start and finish of the watch need to be accurately determined, so a good timepiece is essential. The time of any particularly bright meteor should be noted. All times should be given in GMT or UT. Illumination should be provided by a red light to preserve dark adaptation (it is sometimes useful to carry spare bulbs). Record observations on paper mounted on a clipboard (a plastic sheet to cover the paper when you are not writing on it will help to stop it getting damp). Use pencils, as pens will quite often cease to function under damp conditions.

Don't forget that other priceless commodity-patience! Time always seems to drag by when all you are doing is lying there, watching and waiting. If you are not fully alert and comfortable, you will not produce useful results.

Before you start your watch, locate the radiants of the currently active showers. Memorize also the brightnesses of a few comparison stars so that you can readily estimate the magnitude of a meteor. Any watch should be as long as possible (weather, fatigue, cloud and other factors permitting), with an absolute minimum of one hour.

Below Meteor watching is an ideal group activity, each member of the group watching an area of the sky. It is very important to be both comfortable and warm since discomfort can produce inaccurate results.

What to record

Record your name, address, observing site (in terms of latitude and longitude or as a grid reference) and the date and duration of the watch. If the watch stretches over midnight, then make sure that this is clearly indicated on the observing records. Note down also any factors that may affect observation, including the presence of moonlight, haze or cloud. If the situation changes during the course of a watch then record this also. Finally, note the limiting magnitude, given by the faintest star visible to the naked eye. Changing conditions may alter the limiting magnitude, so do not forget to make a note when this happens.

Record the magnitude of each meteor (obtained by comparison with stars of known magnitude) and its time of appearance to the nearest minute. Any other details felt to be important should also be recorded, such as whether the meteor left a train (if so, note the length in degrees and time taken ot fade from view), colour, speed and whether the meteor broke up.

Right It is very important when meteor watching to keep accurate records of your sightings At the end of each session transfer your notes to a report form noting the time of each sighting, its magnitude, its type and other points of interest. The keeping of such accurate records is one of the useful pieces of research that amateur astronomers can do.

VISUAL METEOR REPORT

Date 88/8/12-13 Observer ALASTAIR McBEATH

Site MORPETH, NORTHUMBERLAND: 55°10'N, 1°42'W Lim. Mag. +6.3

Conditions BEAUTIFULLY CLEAR.

Watch Times: Start 01.10 U.T. End 02.10 U.T. Length 1h00m

Time	Mag.	Type	Rel.	Train	Notes
01.11 U.T.	3	PERSEID	A		POINT-SOURCE.
01.13	2	PERSEID	A	1 SEC. DURATION	MED. SPEED. SHORT.
01.14	3	δ AQUARID (N)	A		MOD. SWIFT.
01.15	3	SPORADIC	A		MED. SPEED. LONG.
01.17	4	PERSEID	B		SWIFT.
01.22	2	PERSEID	C	0.25 SEC. DUR'N	SWIFT.
01.22	5	PERSEID	A		SWIFT.
01.29	1	SPORADIC	C		MED. SPEED.
01.31	4	PERSEID	A		SLOW. SHORT.
01.33	-1	SPORADIC	C		TWO FLARES. YELLOW. SWIFT. LONG.
01.33	-1	PERSEID	B	0.5 SEC. DURATION	SWIFT. BLUE-WHITE. SECONDS AFTER PREVIOUS METEOR.
01.34	4	PERSEID	B		SWIFT.
01.35	2	PERSEID	B		SWIFT. CROSSED CAMERA FIELD.
01.35	3	α AURIGID	B	0.25 SEC. DUR'N	SWIFT.
01.41	-1?	PERSEID	C	1 SEC. DURATION	V. SWIFT. BLUE-WHITE. FLARE. START IN CAMERA FIELD?
01.42	2	PERSEID	A	0.25 SEC. DUR'N	V. SWIFT.
01.43	1	PERSEID	C		V. SWIFT. YELLOW.
01.43	0	PERSEID	B		V. SWIFT.
01.47	0	PERSEID	A	0.5 SEC. DUR'N	V. SWIFT. BLUE-WHITE.
01.49	3	PERSEID	A	0.25 SEC. DUR'N	SWIFT.
01.50	4	SPORADIC	A		MOD. SWIFT.
01.52	-3	PERSEID	C		YELLOW. SWIFT.
01.53	-2	SPORADIC	C		SLOW. YELLOW. FLARING.
01.53	3	SPORADIC	A		SLOW.
01.54	3	α CYGNID	A		MOD. SWIFT. SHORT.
01.54	0?	PERSEID	C		SWIFT. BLUE-WHITE.
01.55	0	PERSEID	A	2.5 SEC. DUR'N	V. SHORT – NEAR RADIANT. MED. SPEED. BLUE-WHITE.
01.55	1?	PERSEID	C		SWIFT. LONG.
01.58	-2	PERSEID	B	2 SEC. DURATION	SWIFT. BLUE-WHITE. FLARE. CROSSED CAMERA FIELD.
02.02	3	PERSEID	B		SWIFT.
02.06	3	SPORADIC	B		SHORT. MED. SPEED.
02.07	3	PERSEID	A		SWIFT.
02.08	-1?	PERSEID	C	3 SEC. DURATION	SWIFT. YELLOW.

Watching as a group

A number of observers can get together to carry out a group watch. The entire sky can be observed, each member of the watch being allocated a particular segment. There is the added benefit of having someone to talk to during the watch, making it easier to stay awake!

The standard procedure is for all but one of the participants to lie in a ring, facing outwards, each watching a particular part of the sky. The final member of the group records the details of meteors seen by those watching. In this way the entire sky can be monitored continuously. It is recommended that the recorder be replaced occasionally to prevent boredom setting in!

If you see a fireball...

A meteor of magnitude -5 or brighter is classed as a fireball. Objects that produce fireballs are generally much larger than those that end their lives as meteors. The brighter the fireball, the larger the object. In many cases the particle may be large enough to partially survive the fall to Earth. If enough reliable reports of a fireball are collected, the location of its fall may be determined and it may be recovered. It is important that the location be determined as quickly as possible, so fireball reports should be submitted at the earliest opportunity. It can be difficult to assess the magnitudes of very bright objects because there is little to compare them with. The brightest 'comparison object' (apart from the Moon) is Venus, which iS magnitude -4.4 at best. If you are in any doubt as to the magnitude of a fireball, make this clear on your report. Other details to record are the same as those made on standard naked-eye meteor reports. Particular care should be taken with assessing the track of the fireball, the start and finish points being given in terms of right ascension and declination.

OBSERVING DEEP SKY OBJECTS

Find your way around

The first priority for any would-be stargazer is to become familiar with the night sky. By convention, every object in the sky has been assigned to some constellation, and an ideal start is to identify the different star patterns. Starting with some of the better-known groups, such as Cassiopeia (in the northern sky) or Crux (in the southern), set yourself the target of identifying a different group each clear night. Many constellations make good pointers to other groups. Good examples are the Belt of Orion, the line of which can be followed to find both Sirius in Canis Major and Aldebaran in Taurus, and the two stars Merak and Dubhe in Ursa Major, which point the way to Polaris in nearby Ursa Minor. Many of the smaller and somewhat obscure groups can be picked out in this way. Memorize the basic outline and main stars of different constellations and it won't be long before you gain a reasonably thorough working knowledge of the night sky.

The next thing is to learn a little about the stars you have seen. Why do Aldebaran and Arcturus have such distinctive orange-red tints? Why is Sirius so conspicuous? Is it really especially bright or does it just happen to lie close by? How big are the stars? Once you learn some basic facts, you will gain a closer affinity with the stars and come to regard them as more than just points of light in the sky.

Looking into deep space

Star clusters, nebulae and galaxies present some of the most interesting (and popular) targets for amateur astronomers. Many thousands of these objects are within the grasp of small to medium-sized telescopes, although locating them can often be a problem.

One way is to use the 'drift' method. Bring into the field of view a star that lies a little to the west of the object being sought. From a star catalogue note the distance that the object is to the east of the star, leave the telescope stationary and allow the sky to drift across the field of view for the corresponding time, until the object appears. This method, calls for some patience and a convenient star.

Setting circles can also be used, although these should be reserved for instruments that are permanently mounted. If they are used with portable telescopes, too much time may be spent setting up the telescope mounting and, unless the alignment is precise, the object may still not appear in the field of view.

Star-hopping is one of the best methods for locating deep-sky objects. Once a fairly bright nearby star has been

Above The open cluster M46 in Puppis is a popular object for amateur astronomers to observe. It can be viewed with binoculars but a small telescope will reveal much greater detail.

located, the observer can track the object down by hopping from one star to another until the target is reached. Once it has been observed several times, it becomes much easier to relocate the object without having to resort to star charts. A good finder, essential for locating deep-sky objects, can be invaluable when using the star-hopping method.

Techniques

Before you start to look for deep-sky objects such as those mentioned above, it is important to get your eyes dark-adapted. Also, clear, moonless nights are greatly to be preferred. Should a particular search prove fruitless, trying again the next night may bring better results.

Generally speaking, low magnification and a wide field of view are essential for deep-sky observing. Quite often the object being observed is large or faint, or both, and in many cases high magnifications bring out only the central regions. The visual effect that low magnifications and wider fields of view provide is lost.

Open clusters can make good targets for small telescopes, and even binoculars can reveal many objects of this type to good effect. A favourite for many observers, either beginners or those with more experience, is the Pleiades open cluster (M45) in Taurus. This is an object well worth repeated observation. Experienced observers may be able to pick out

Above M39 in Cygnus, set against the background of the rich starfields of the Milky Way, makes a fascinating sight for the amateur astronomer.

traces of the nebulosity that surrounds the stars in the Pleiades, a sight that is generally denied to those who are not used to looking at the night sky. Because the stars in open clusters are spread out, a wide field of view is essential. This is even more important when it comes to trying to pick out an open cluster against a bright starry background.

Globular clusters, although containing more stars, are much more compact, generally appearing as faint, diffuse objects. When observing globulars, experiment with different magnifications and fields of view. Higher magnifications may bring out the brightest stars in the cluster.

Some diffuse nebulae and galaxies can be observed with either high or low magnification. However, many are large

Above The famous double-double Episilon Lyrae. Plotting the motions of variable stars is just one of the activities that the amateur astonomer can undertake.

and faint, offering little contrast with the surrounding sky, making low power and a moonless sky essential. Sweeping the telescope back and forth across the area of sky around the nebula may help you to pick it out. This technique can help to enhance contrast between nebula and sky. Higher magnifications may be needed to exclude the glare from nearby bright stars when seeking out certain nebulae. An example is the Horsehead Nebula, which can be swamped in the glow of nearby Zeta Orionis.

Low to medium magnifications can be used with planetary nebulae, which are generally small and relatively distinct. With very low powers, certain planetaries can appear distinctly starlike, making initial identification difficult. Planetary nebulae are extremely interesting targets and within their ranks are many unusually shaped examples. These include the famous Dumbbell Nebula (M27) in Vulpecula and the Butterfly Nebula (M76) in Perseus.

A growing problem for deep-sky observers is that of light pollution. It can be alleviated by using special filters, often referred to as nebula filters. Different types of deep-sky object require different filters, their purpose being to enhance contrast between the object and the background sky. They block out certain light-polluted regions of the spectrum while at the same time allowing the light from the nebula to pass through to the eye.

OBSERVING VARIABLE STARS

Location and observation of a variable star are carried out with the help of a 'comparison chart'. This shows the area of sky around the variable and includes not only the variable itself (usually represented by a small circle with a dot at the centre) but a number of other stars' known magnitude in the same area of sky.

There are two methods of estimating a variable throughout its cycle: the fractional method and the Pogson method. The fractional method is the one recommended for those who are only just becoming involved with variable-star observation.

The Fractional Method

The fractional method requires the use of a pair of comparison stars (let's call them A and B), preferably one brighter and one fainter than the variable at the time of observation. If possible, the difference in magnitude between them should be only around 0.5, although their actual magnitudes need not be known at this stage and may be looked up after the observation has been made. Their difference in magnitude should be mentally divided into parts, or fractions (for example, into fifths.) The variable's brightness is 'placed' between the two comparison stars – say, as one part fainter than A and four parts brighter than B. This would be recorded as A (1) V (4) B.

Suppose it is then found from the magnitude list attached to the chart that the two comparison stars were, for example, of magnitudes 3.5 (star A) and 4.0 (star B). This would give the variable a magnitude of 3.6 at the time the estimate was made.

The Pogson Method

This method relies on the observer being able to estimate the brightness of a star to within a tenth of a magnitude, a skill that requires a great deal of practice.

The variable under scrutiny is compared with as many

Below The long-period variable Chi Cygni, photographed when near maximum brightness. Also shown is the constellation Lyra, towards the right. Albireo (Beta Cygni) is at bottom left.

comparison stars of similar magnitude as possible; the greater the number of comparisons that are made the better. Using the example given above, in which the variable is 0.1 magnitude fainter than star A and 0.4 magnitude brighter than star B, the observation would be recorded as A-1, B+4. The - sign indicates that the variable is fainter than one comparison star, and the + that it is brighter than the other comparison star.

In this example the magnitude estimates taken from each of the two comparison stars agreed at magnitude 3.6, but there will be occasions when this is not the case. When this happens, the calculated magnitudes should be averaged and the result should be rounded off to one decimal place. For example, a mean figure of 7.34 would be rounded off to 7.3, while 6.28 would be rounded off to 6.3. Where the last figure is a 5 round off towards the fainter value: thus, 5.25 rounds off to 5.3.

Points to watch out for

• Always position yourself comfortably when observing. Discomfort and tiredness will tend to produce unreliable estimates.

• Always double-check that the variable and comparison stars have been correctly identified. Take care that other objects not normally in the field of view, such as a minor planet or comet, do not cause confusion.

• Bring the comparison star as close as possible to the centre of the field of view. It can sometimes be helpful to defocus the variable star and its comparison stars to aid the process of comparison. Stars at the edge of the field may be slightly out of focus, making estimates of brightness more difficult.

• Avoid bias – try to forget previous brightness estimates.

Recording observations

The estimates made at the telescope should be entered initially into a log book, but if you are intending to submit your results to one of the observing sections of an astronomical organization, it is desirable that these should be transferred to the variable-star recording form of the organization as soon as possible while the information is still fresh in the observer's mind..

Records of observations should include: the star name; date and time of observation either in local time or in UT; location from which the observation was made; the instrument used, telescope, binoculars or naked eye; the method by which the estimate was obtained - whether by the fractional or Pogson method: and the estimated accuracy of the observation.

Observations taken by practised astronomers under good observing conditions may be considered accurate to within +/- 0.2 magnitude.

How often to make observations

Eclipsing binaries, such as Algol or Delta Librae, only need observing during an actual eclipse, predictions of which are readily available in many astronomical magazines. Irregular variables, such as U Antliae or Beta Pegasi, should be observed once or twice a week, as should the semirregular variables, such as Mira and R Andromedae, which should be observed at least once a week.

Variables with shorter periods, such as the cepheids, should be observed every clear night. Other variables that should be observed as frequently as possible include the Beta Lyrae and W Virginis types, which fluctuate in brightness over periods of several days or so making regular observation essential..

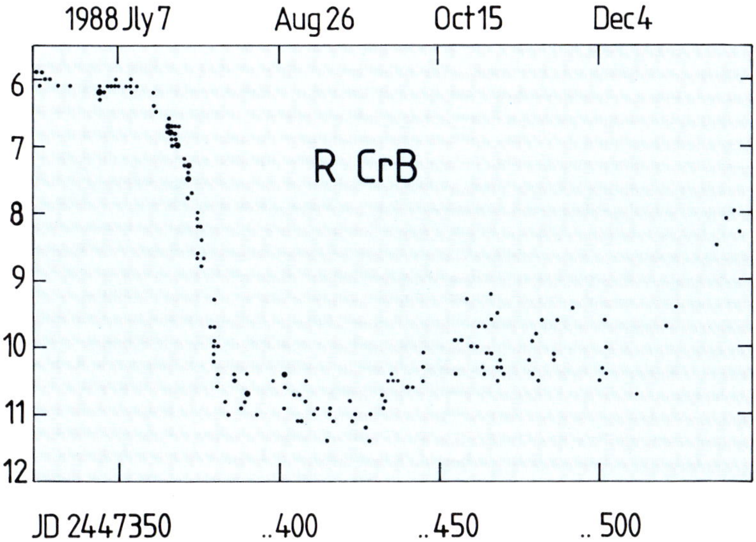

Left Light curve of the variable star R Coronae Borealis, based on estimates made between July and December 1988. Small dots indicate a single estimate, larger dots two or more estimates. Variables of this type are subject to unpredictable fadings in brightness, spending most of their time pulsating slowly near maximum.

OBSERVING ARTIFICIAL SATELLITES

We see satellites because they reflect sunlight. Because of their high altitudes, they remain illuminated long after the Sun has set. Quite often a satellite will suddenly disappear as it travels into the Earth's shadow. The best times to locate satellites are just after sunset or just before sunrise. A satellite may display a constant brightness, but irregularly shaped satellites can appear to blink on and off as they tumble in orbit.

The lower a satellite is, the faster it moves across the sky, objects at around 200 km (125 miles) altitude taking some 90 minutes to orbit the Earth. They remain within the naked eye field of view for perhaps a couple of minutes. Satellites at altitudes of a few thousand kilometres are much slower. Their orbital periods are of the order of several hours and they take anywhere up to a quarter of an hour to cross the sky. Together with its altitude, the size, shape, orientation and surface finish of a satellite dictate how bright it appears. Generally speaking, satellites of magnitude 3 or brighter can be observed with the naked eye; binoculars are required for fainter satellites, down to magnitude 7 or 8. Anything yet fainter requires the use of a telescope.

Timing Observations

Although artificial satellite observation can be carried out with the naked eye, binoculars or a telescope, it is best to start by making a number of timings of naked-eye objects. Keep an eye open for random satellite appearances and practice taking measurements of them. Get used to estimating satellite positions with reference to nearby stars. Observation requires the timing of a satellite's passage close to a convenient star or across an imaginary line joining two stars. Alternatively, timings can be taken of the moment when the satellite crosses an imaginary line running vertically from the star to the apparent horizon. Although this sounds easy, correctly assessing the position of a satellite relative to the background stars and operating the stopwatch at the correct time requires skill, and the ability to make precise observations will be achieved only through experience and constant repetition.

Predictions of satellite appearances are given in various journals and in some daily newspapers. However, the times stated are not highly accurate, and a search for the satellite should commence a few moments before the predicted time. Predictions will normally give rising and setting times of the satellite, its direction of travel and the highest altitude it will reach.

Start a stopwatch before observation begins, synchronised with a radio time signal or the telephone speaking clock. The second method is preferred because the watch can be set a short time before the observations are made. When the satellite appears, follow it across the sky and stop the watch at the precise moment it passes close to a known star or crosses an imaginary line, as detailed above. By adding the time shown on the watch to the time against which it was set, you can determine the exact time at which the satellite was at the reference point chosen. For example, if you started the watch at 21h 12m 30s and stopped it with a reading of 2m 42.5s, the timing of the satellite is 21h 15m 12.5s.

Alternatively, start the watch at the time of observation and later stop it as you hear a time signal. By subtracting the time shown from the time indicated by the signal you obtain the time of observation.

Identifying field stars

You must, of course, be careful to identify correctly the stars you use. For naked-eye observation, *Norton's Star Atlas* is one of the best available. For binocular observation, remember to use an atlas that shows stars down to the magnitude of those selected for the observation. It is no use choosing reference stars that are too faint to appear on the atlas, and consequently cannot be identified! One of the best atlases available is *Sky Atlas 2000*, which plots stars down to magnitude 8.0.

The time of observation and corresponding position of the satellite should be noted together with the time of observation. The position can be marked on a star chart and the subsequent path of the satellite plotted if desired.

Photographing artificial satellites

Only basic equipment is needed to capture artificial satellites on film. A standard 50-mm lens set at its widest aperture will give a wide field of view. Exposures of up to 30 seconds should be taken and 400 ISO film, colour or black-and-white, should be used.

If possible, open the shutter before the satellite enters the field of view and measure how long it takes to cross the field. After closing the shutter, note down details of lens and exposure time, film used, times of entry and exit from the field of view and geographical location of the observing site. Once stars on the photograph have been identified you will have a highly accurate record of the satellite and its track. This will enable you to identify the satellite (if you do not already know what it is).

Above An Echo satellite betrays its presence as a photographic trail on this image of the Milky Way in Sagittarious, looking towards the centre of the Galaxy.

Right Satellite predictions contain a wide range of information which helps the astronomer plt the course of satellites.
Location from where the satellite can be seen at the times stipulated. Rising and setting times for satellites can difer with changes in latitude as can be seen here.
Satellite (generally naked-eye objects) for which the predictions have been made.
Times between which the satellite can be seen in the sky.
Elevation maximum in degrees of arc, attained by the satelite during its passage across the sky.
Cardinal Points at which the satellite appears (rises) and disappears (sets).
Date for which predictions are made.
Time system used (in satellite predictions intended for the general public, the time system currently in operation is generally used, this not necessarily being UT/GMT.
The satellite leaves *Eclipse*, or is eclipsed, when it emerges from or enters the shadow of either the Earth or Moon.

Satellite predictions

LONDON

	From	To	Max Elev	Rises/Sets
Seasat 1	22.08	22.16	30NW	NNE/WSW
Erbs	01.38	01.43	55NE	WNW/*ENE
	22.27	22.34	50N	W/NE

MANCHESTER

	From	To	Max Elev	Rises/Sets
Seasat 1	05.07	05.16	60NE	SE/NNW
	22.07	22.16	40NW	NNE/WSW
Erbs	01.37	01.43	70N	WNW/*E
	03.18	03.19	25W	WNW/*W
	22.27	22.34	65NNE	WSW/ENE

* Leaves or enters eclipse. Predictions are for tomorrow, times are BST.
● Weather information supplied by the Meteorological Office.
Road information supplied by the Department of Transport.
Satellite predictions by the Royal Greenwich Observatory.

INTRODUCTION TO STAR SEARCH

Sky search

The charts on the following pages include two that are centred on the celestial poles and 12 that show the sky as it appears at mid-evening during each month of the year. The monthly charts are centred on a right ascension corresponding to the observer's meridian (the imaginary line passing through the north and south celestial poles and the observer's zenith) at these times. They show the sky between declinations 60°N and 60°S, and each covers a total of 5 hours in right ascension. The stars shown are those seen by either an observer in the northern hemisphere looking towards the south or a southern hemisphere observer looking towards the north. A number of stars depicted on each chart will be invisible to an observer situated at locations away from the Earth's equator. Only someone within 30° latitude of the equator will see all the stars plotted on the monthly charts. The two circumpolar maps show the stars to a distance of 50° from each pole.

Stars down to 6th magnitude are shown. The selection presented does not pretend to offer complete sky coverage. There are many objects not shown here that would have been included had space permitted.

The stars depicted on the charts can be identified in a number of different ways. The brightest may be accompanied by their proper names (Betelgeuse, Rigel, Castor, etc.), others by Greek letters only ('gamma', 'mu' etc.) Variable stars are identified mainly by their official catalogue numbers (R Trianguli, S Sculptoris, etc.), although some are identified by their proper names, such as, Mira (Omicron Ceti).

Deep-sky objects are mainly identified either by their number in Messier's Catalogue (M1, M55, etc.) or by their designation in the New General Catalogue of J L E Dreyer, first published in 1888. Certain individual objects may be accompanied by their popular names: these include the Orion Nebula (M42), the Pleiades (M45) in Taurus, and the Double Cluster (NGC 869 and NGC 884) in Perseus.

Accompanying the sky charts are various finder charts. The finder charts offer a guide to the location of deep-sky objects, providing the surrounding field of view that would be seen through binoculars or a telescope finder. Each contains a reasonably prominent guide star common to both this and the main sky chart. To locate a particular object, such as a star cluster or galaxy, when observing the sky, first of all identify the general area of sky, and the guide star, on the main chart; now pick up the guide star in the field of view and 'star hop' to the object being sought (see 'Observing deep sky objects' pp 116-7 above). Remember that binoculars give an upright image, while a finder presents an inverted one. This should not present any problems, but it explains why some of the finder charts give what appears to be a wrongly oriented view. The order in which the stars are followed to the object being sought will remain unchanged in such charts.

Drawings and photographs (many taken by amateur astronomers) accompany the main charts. In many cases, and in particular with the drawings, the images give a fair indication of how the object will appear through the telescope. Beginners in particular are often disappointed that the sight presented through the binoculars or telescope does not match the photographs, taken with giant telescopes, which often accompany deep-sky guides. One of the secrets of enjoyable stargazing is not to expect too much by way of 'visual splendour' in the early stages. You have to learn to observe and appreciate the objects in the skies.

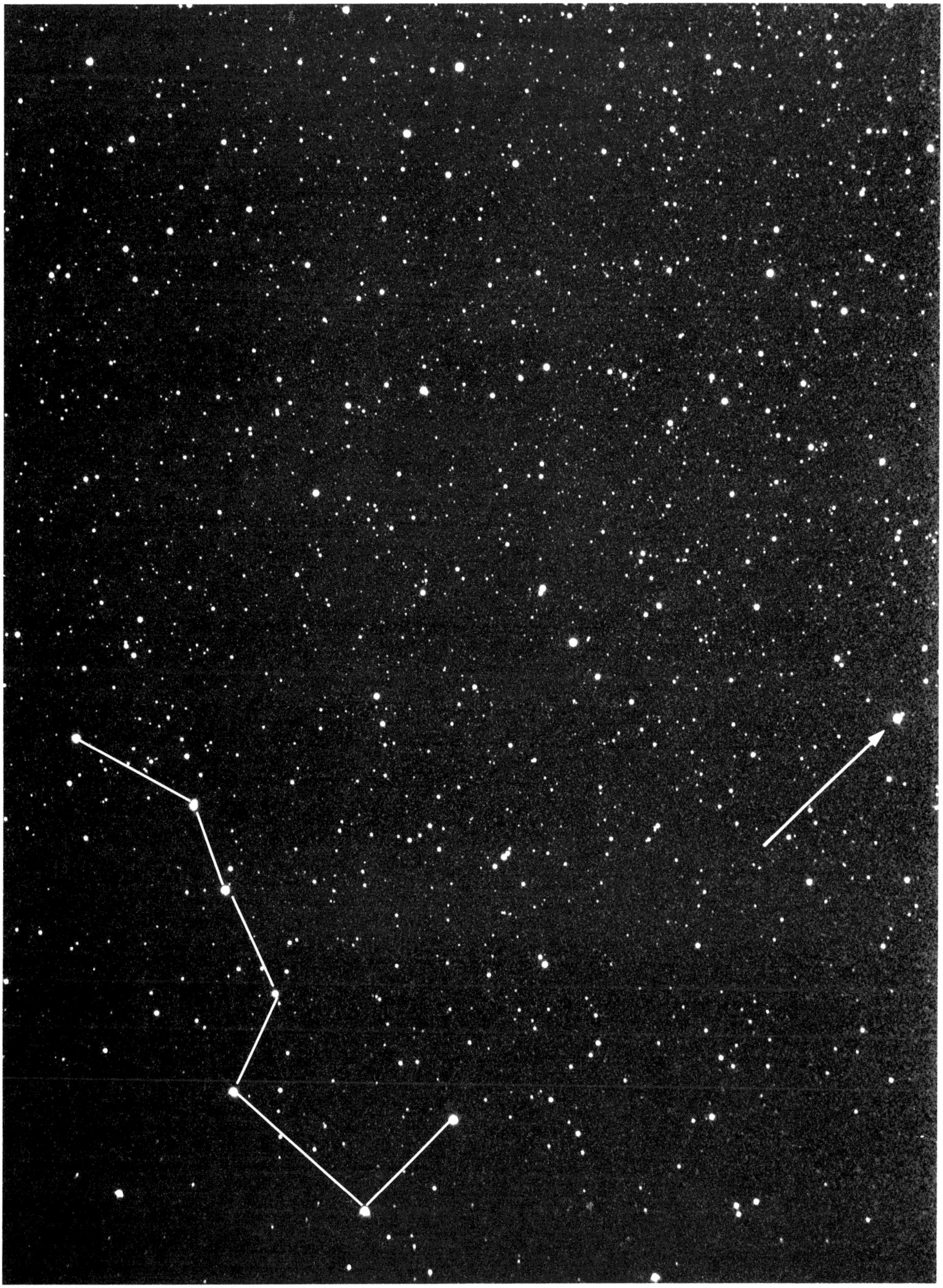

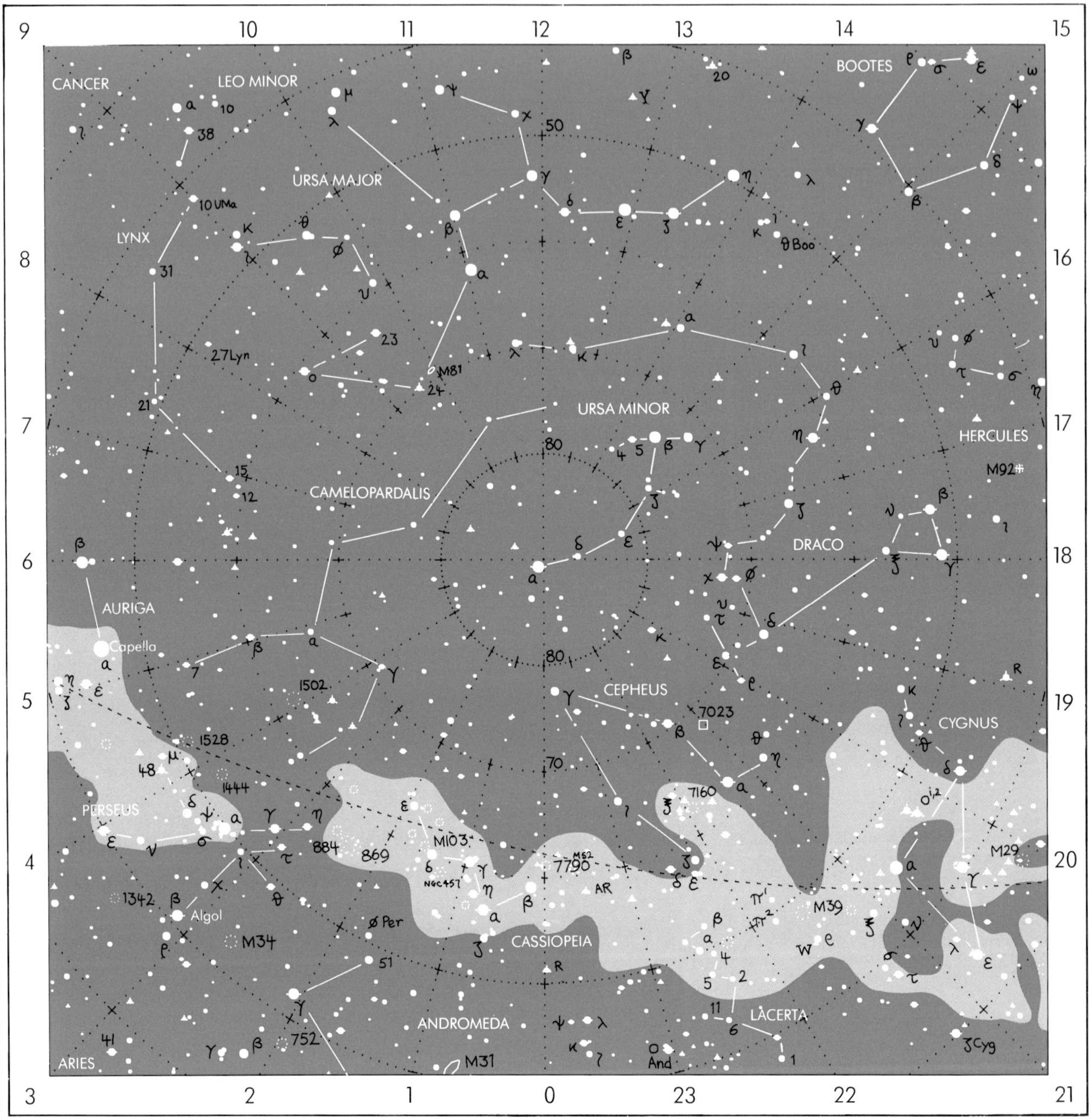
9
10
11
12
13
14
15
CANCER
LEO MINOR
BOOTES
URSA MAJOR
LYNX
10 UMa
27Lyn
M81
URSA MINOR
CAMELOPARDALIS
HERCULES
M92
DRACO
AURIGA
Capella
CEPHEUS
7023
CYGNUS
1502
1528
1444
PERSEUS
7160
M103
884
869
NGC457
7790
M52
M29
M39
Algol
1342
M34
φ Per
CASSIOPEIA
ANDROMEDA
752
LACERTA
ζ Cyg
ARIES
M31
And
50
70
80
8
16
7
17
6
18
5
19
4
20
3
2
1
0
23
22
21

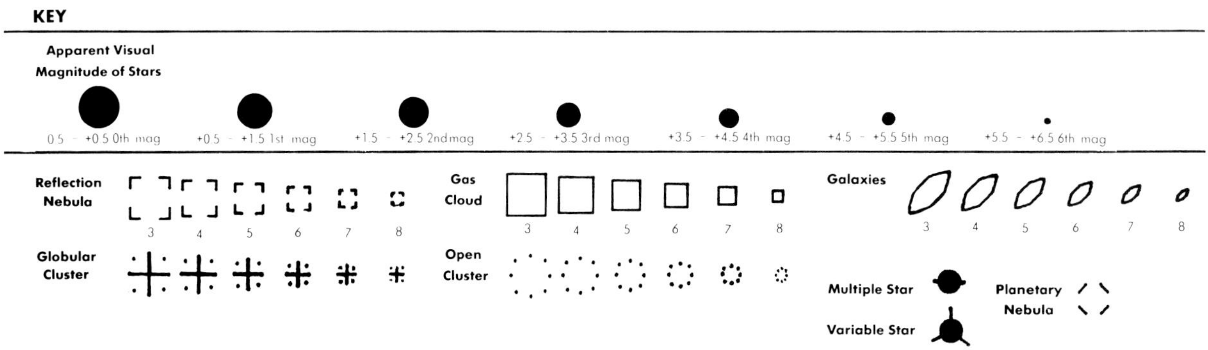
KEY
Apparent Visual
Magnitude of Stars
0.5 – +0.5 0th mag
+0.5 – +1.5 1st mag
+1.5 – +2.5 2nd mag
+2.5 – +3.5 3rd mag
+3.5 – +4.5 4th mag
+4.5 – +5.5 5th mag
+5.5 – +6.5 6th mag
Reflection Nebula
3 4 5 6 7 8
Gas Cloud
3 4 5 6 7 8
Galaxies
3 4 5 6 7 8
Globular Cluster
Open Cluster
Multiple Star
Planetary Nebula
Variable Star

NORTHERN CIRCUMPOLAR STARS

Alcor and Mizar

The second star from the end of the Plough Handle is Zeta Ursae Majoris, or Mizar, which together with Alcor forms a naked-eye double.Mizar is itself a double: it was the first double star to be discovered telescopically, by Giovanni Riccioli around 1650. The two components, A (magnitude 2.3) and B (magnitude 4.0), lie 14.4" apart and are thought to orbit each other.

As well as being the first telescopic double to be discovered, Mizar was also the first double to be photographed, by George Bond in 1857. In 1889 the brighter component, Mizar A, became the first spectroscopic binary to be detected. The two components of Mizar A orbit each other every 20.54 days. Subsequent observations showed that Mizar B is also a spectroscopic binary, so Mizar is actually a quadruple star system.

Clusters in Cassiopeia

The rich star fields of Cassiopeia are home to a number of open star clusters. One of these is NGC 457 which is a fairly young and well populated cluster, situated at a distance of over 9,000 light years. At magnitude 6.4 it is easily picked up next to Phi Cassiopeiae. Binoculars will show NGC 457 as a fuzzy patch of light, although even a 75 mm (3-inch) telescope will bring out well over a dozen individual cluster members.

Other clusters worth looking at in Cassiopeia include M52 and M103. M52, discovered by Charles Messier in 1774, glows at magnitude 6.9 and can be located by following the line from Eta to Beta and then continuing to 4 Cassiopeiae. The cluster can then be seen just to the south of 4 Cassiopeiae. M52 covers an area of sky around a third that of a full Moon and small telescopes will reveal many of its member stars.

M81 and M82 galaxies

Ursa Major contains a number of deep-sky objects well worth seeking out, among the best of which are the galaxy M81 and the nearby M82. These can be found by following a line drawn from Merak (Beta) through Dubhe(Alpha). In the same telescopic field, although not shown on the photograph, may be glimpsed the galaxy NGC 3077. Both M81 and M82 were discovered by Johann Bode in 1774 and, together with NGC 3077 and several other fainter galaxies, form the M81 Group, a neighbour to the Local Group situated almost 10 million light years away.

The M81 Group extends into the adjoining constellation of Camelopardalis and is often referred to as the Ursa Major–Camelopardalis Group. M81 and M82 can be seen even through small telescopes, and their shapes are quite evident in slightly larger instruments with apertures of 4 inches or more. The spiral form of M81 contrasts with M82. M82 is almost certainly a spiral galaxy, seen edge-on, that has suffered gravitational disturbances at the hands of the neighbouring, and much more massive, M81.

M 81 and M 82 galaxies.

Finder chart for M 52 open cluster in Cassiopeia.

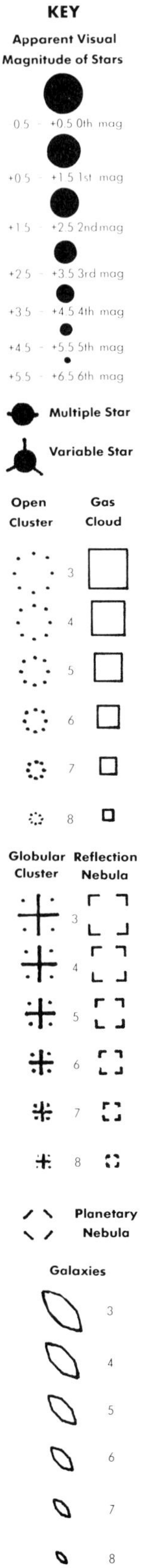
KEY
Apparent Visual Magnitude of Stars
-0.5 – +0.5 0th mag
+0.5 – +1.5 1st mag
+1.5 – +2.5 2nd mag
+2.5 – +3.5 3rd mag
+3.5 – +4.5 4th mag
+4.5 – +5.5 5th mag
+5.5 – +6.5 6th mag
Multiple Star
Variable Star
Open Cluster
Gas Cloud
3
4
5
6
7
8
Globular Cluster
Reflection Nebula
Planetary Nebula
Galaxies

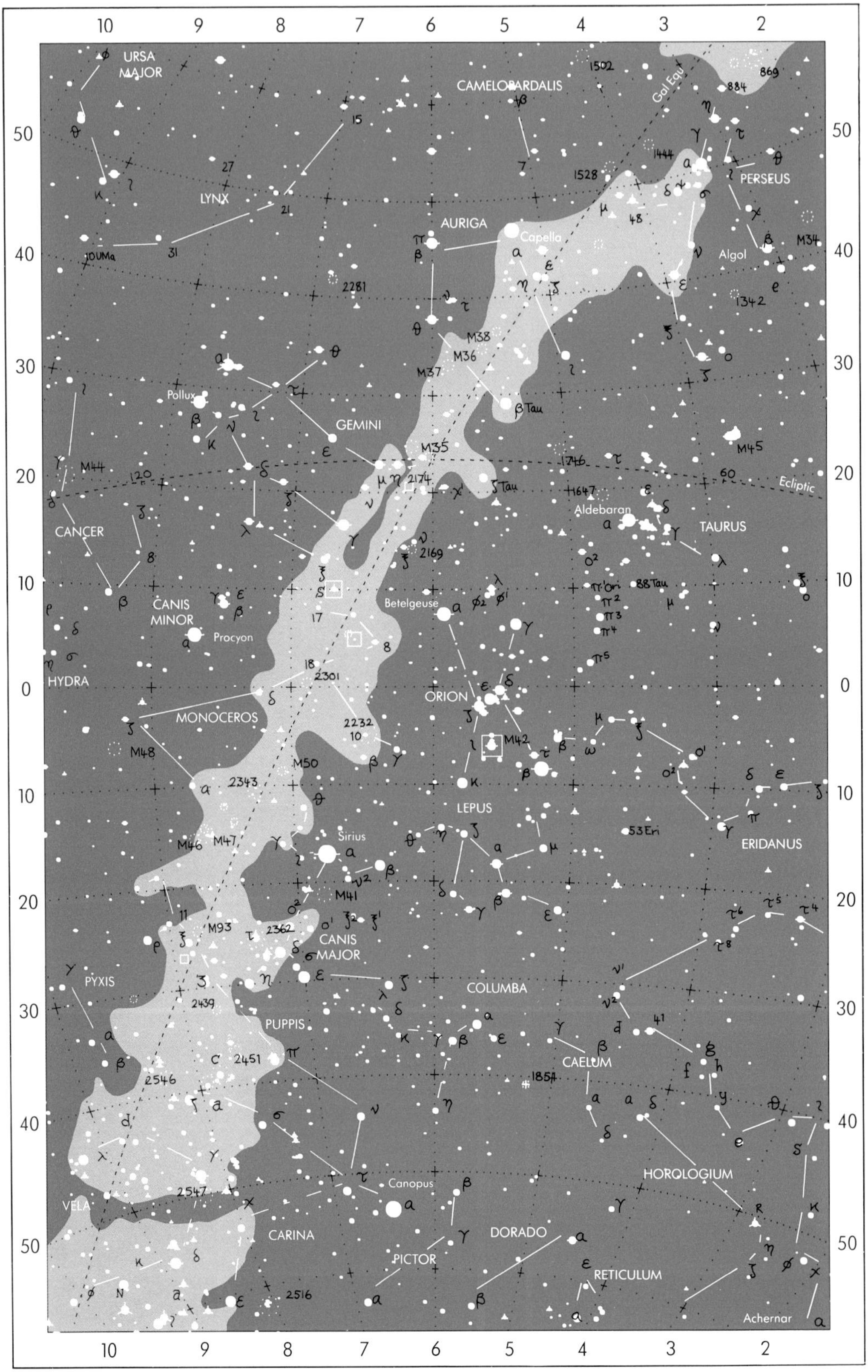
10 9 8 7 6 5 4 3 2
50
40
30
20
10
0
URSA MAJOR
CAMELOPARDALIS
Gal Equ
PERSEUS
LYNX
AURIGA
Capella
Algol
M34
M45
M38
M36
M37
M35
M44
GEMINI
Pollux
CANCER
Ecliptic
Aldebaran
TAURUS
CANIS MINOR
Procyon
Betelgeuse
HYDRA
ORION
MONOCEROS
M42
M48
M50
LEPUS
M46
M47
Sirius
ERIDANUS
M41
M93
CANIS MAJOR
PYXIS
COLUMBA
PUPPIS
CAELUM
HOROLOGIUM
Canopus
VELA
CARINA
DORADO
PICTOR
RETICULUM
Achernar

STAR CHART – JANUARY

The Orion Nebula

The constellation of Orion straddles the celestial equator and consequently can be seen from all inhabited parts of the world, being best placed for observation during northern winter/southern summer. Prominent is the ruddy glow of the famous red giant star Betelgeuse. Marking the Hunter's shoulder at the north-eastern corner of Orion, Betelgeuse is one of the largest stars known to astronomers. Its brightness varies slightly over a period of 2,110 days, these variations being due to expansions and contractions within the star itself.

Contrasting sharply with Betelgeuse is the brilliant white supergiant Rigel, marking Orion's foot and situated at the south-western corner of the group. Rigel lies at a distance of around 900 light years and has a luminosity almost 60,000 times that of the Sun.

The Belt of Orion comprises the three stars Alnitak, Alnilam and Mintaka, while the line of faint stars marking the Sword can be seen a few degrees to the south. The Orion Nebula (M42) can be seen as a hazy patch of light surrounding the group of stars at the southern end of the sword. This gigantic cloud of glowing gas is situated at a distance of over 1,600 light years and shines as a result of the vast energy output of the young, hot stars which are embedded within it.

A Trio of Open Star Clusters

The brightest star in Auriga is Capella, the closest first-magnitude star to the north celestial pole and the sixth brightest star in the sky. Capella, whose name means little she-goat, is a yellow star lying at a distance of 45 light years. Its luminosity is around 80 times that of the Sun. The small triangle of stars seen just below Capella are; Epsilon, Eta and Zeta Aurigae. Epsilon is a famous eclipsing binary, of which the dark secondary star orbits the primary once every 9,892 days. Once during each revolution the visible star is eclipsed by its companion, during which time the magnitude of Epsilon decreases from 2.9 to 3.8. The entire eclipse sequence takes around two years to complete.

Auriga contains a number of interesting open star clusters, the three brightest of which are M36 (NGC 1960), M37 (NGC 2099) and M38 (NGC 1912). These straddle a line between Theta Aurigae and Beta Tauri. All three are below naked-eye visibility, although a careful sweep with binoculars should reveal all three as small diffuse patches of light, with a few of the individual members of each visible. M36 contains around 60 stars, and a telescope should bring out some colour contrasts between them. M37 contains 150 stars and is acknowledged as one of the most beautiful star clusters in the sky. The faintest of the three, M38, is again a pretty sight, especially in a low power, wide-field telescope. All three of these stellar gatherings are located between 4,000 and 5,000 light years away, making them very distant objects indeed.

M 37 open cluster in Auriga

The constellation of Auriga

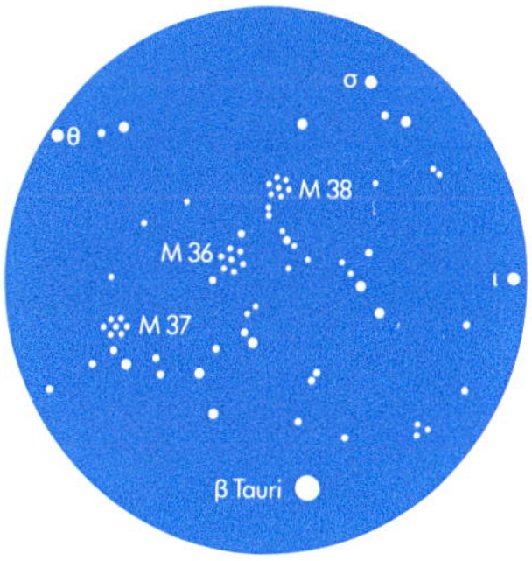

Finder chart for M 36, M 37 and M 38 open clusters.

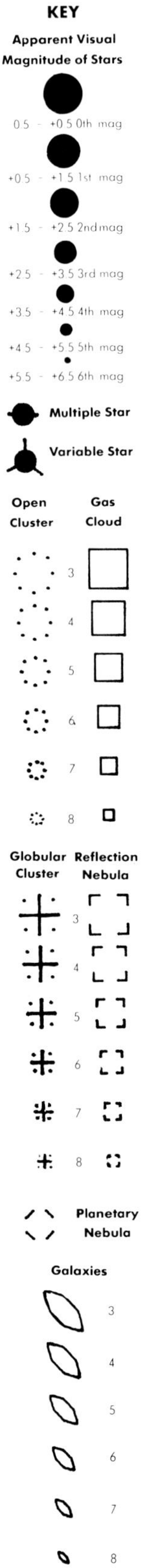
KEY
Apparent Visual Magnitude of Stars
0.5 - +0.5 0th mag
+0.5 - +1.5 1st mag
+1.5 - +2.5 2nd mag
+2.5 - +3.5 3rd mag
+3.5 - +4.5 4th mag
+4.5 - +5.5 5th mag
+5.5 - +6.5 6th mag
Multiple Star
Variable Star
Open Cluster
Gas Cloud
3
4
5
6
7
8
Globular Cluster
Reflection Nebula
3
4
5
6
7
8
Planetary Nebula
Galaxies
3
4
5
6
7
8

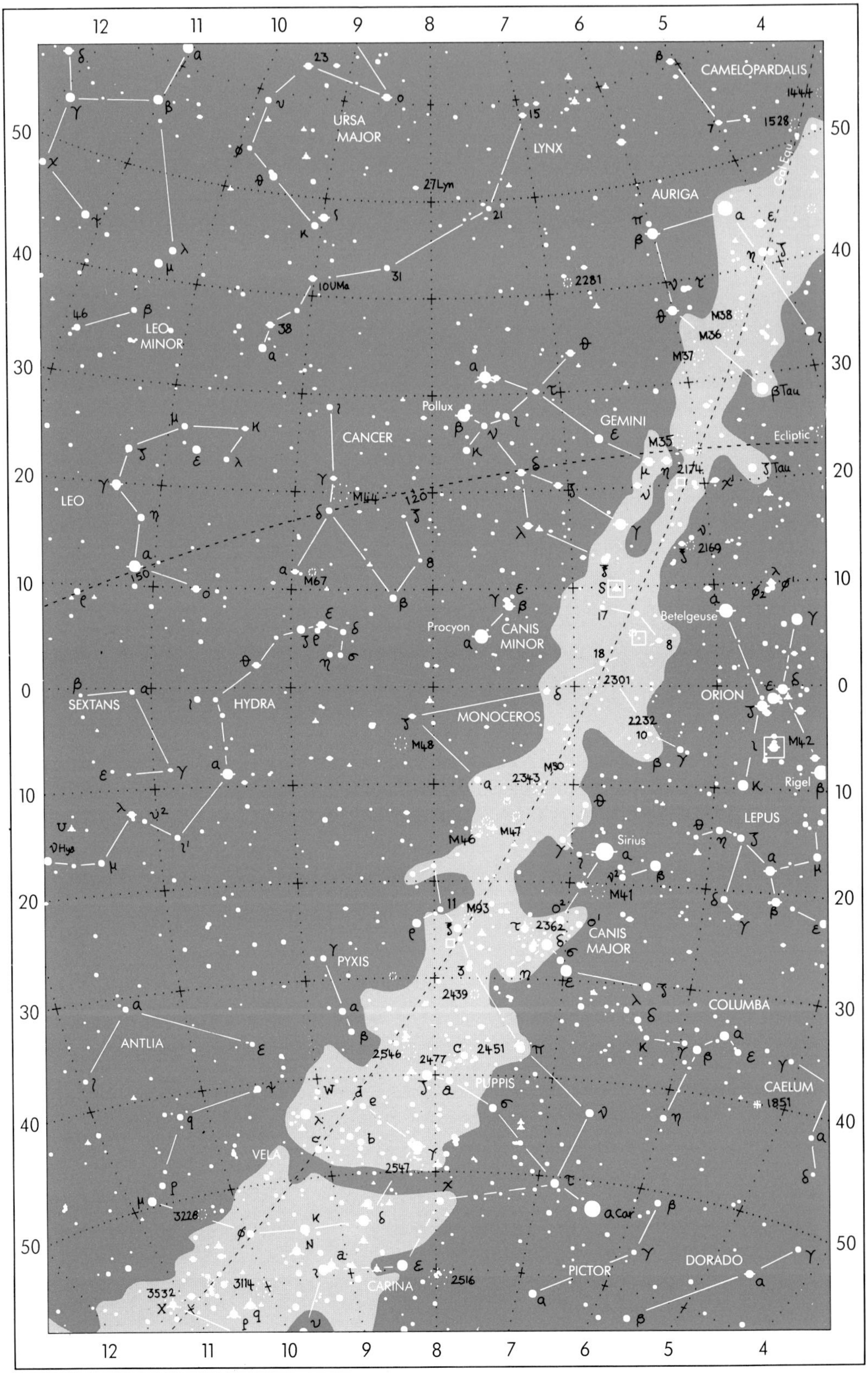
12 11 10 9 8 7 6 5 4
50 40 30 20 10 0 10 20 30 40 50
CAMELOPARDALIS
URSA MAJOR
LYNX
AURIGA
LEO MINOR
Pollux
GEMINI
Ecliptic
CANCER
LEO
M44
M67
Procyon
CANIS MINOR
Betelgeuse
ORION
SEXTANS
HYDRA
MONOCEROS
M48
M42
Rigel
LEPUS
M46
M47
M50
Sirius
M41
M93
CANIS MAJOR
PYXIS
COLUMBA
ANTLIA
PUPPIS
CAELUM
VELA
PICTOR
DORADO
CARINA
M35
M36
M37
M38
βTau
ζTau
αCar
27Lyn
10UMa
1444
1528
2281
2174
2169
2301
2232
2343
2362
2439
2451
2477
2546
2547
3228
3114
3532
2516
1851
12 11 10 9 8 7 6 5 4

STAR CHART - FEBRUARY

Clusters in Gemini

Gemini lies in one of the richest areas of the Milky Way and contains a number of interesting deep-sky objects. Several open star clusters lie close to Mu and Eta Geminorum, notable among which is the conspicuous M35 (NGC 2168). Lying at a distance of 2,200 light years, M35 contains over 200 stars within a radius of about 30 light years. Excellent seeing conditions may render this 5th-magnitude cluster visible to the unaided eye, and 10 x 50 binoculars will resolve some of its outlying stars.

Visible within the same wide-field view as M35 is the fainter cluster NGC 2158, situated a little to the south-west. The 11th-magnitude object has been found to lie at a distance of around 16,000 light years. It appears as a misty patch of light in binoculars and in small telescopes.

A bright cluster in Hydra

Following a line south-east from Procyon in Canis Minor will bring you to a small triangle of faint stars, consisting of 27, 28 and Zeta Monocerotis. Continue the line a little farther to locate the 6th-magnitude open cluster M48 (NGC 2548), a collection of around 80 stars located at a distance of 1,600 light years at the western edge of Hydra. M48 was discovered by Charles Messier in 1771. Its true diameter is 20 light years, giving an apparent visual diameter of some 30'. A wide-field instrument is therefore preferable for viewing the object.

Clusters of northern Puppis

Two prominent open clusters can be seen at the northern end of Puppis: M46 (NGC 2437) and M47 (NGC 2422). They can be located by following a line from Sirius, through Gamma Canis Majoris and on for a further 10° or so. Midway between Gamma Canis Majoris and the two clusters is a small triangle of faint stars, at the western point of which can be seen another open cluster, NGC 2360, a pretty collection of around 50 stars contained within an area of diameter 10'.

M46 and M47 are located within the same wide field of view, being separated by just 1.5° on a roughly east-west line. Messier discovered both clusters in 1771. Sixth-magnitude M46 is a beautiful rich collection of stars located at a distance of around 5,000 light years. Its visual diameter is almost half a degree, corresponding to a true diameter of around 30 light years. M47 is somewhat brighter than M46, with an overall magnitude of 4.4. It contains around 45 stars, as compared with the 100 or so members of M46. The cluster is spread out over half a degree of sky and just over 1,500 light years from us, roughly a third the distance of M46. The diameter of M47 is around 17 light years.

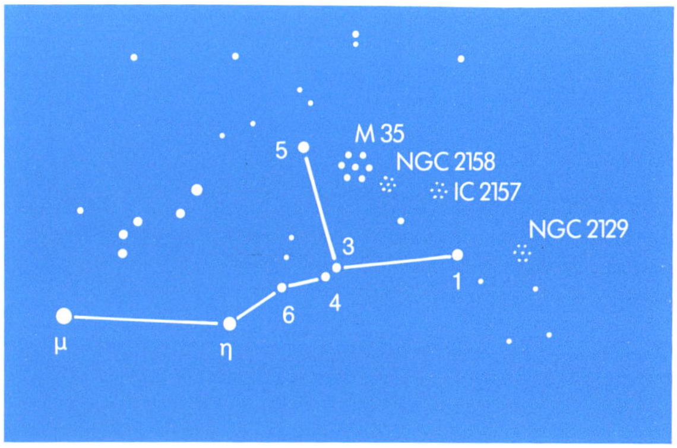

Finder chart for M35 open cluster.

M35 and NGC 2158 in Gemini

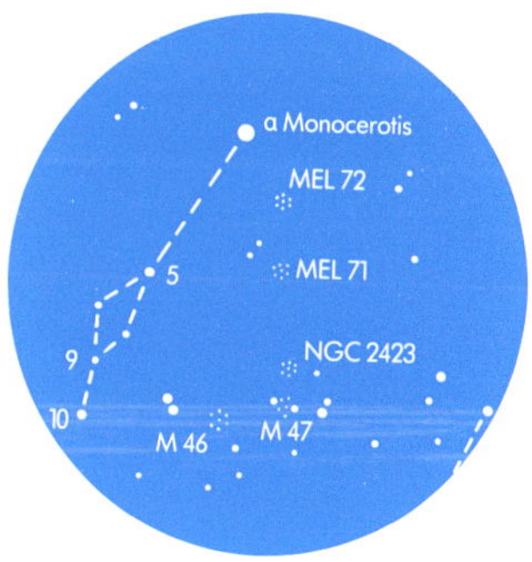

Finder chart for M 46 and M 47 open clusters.

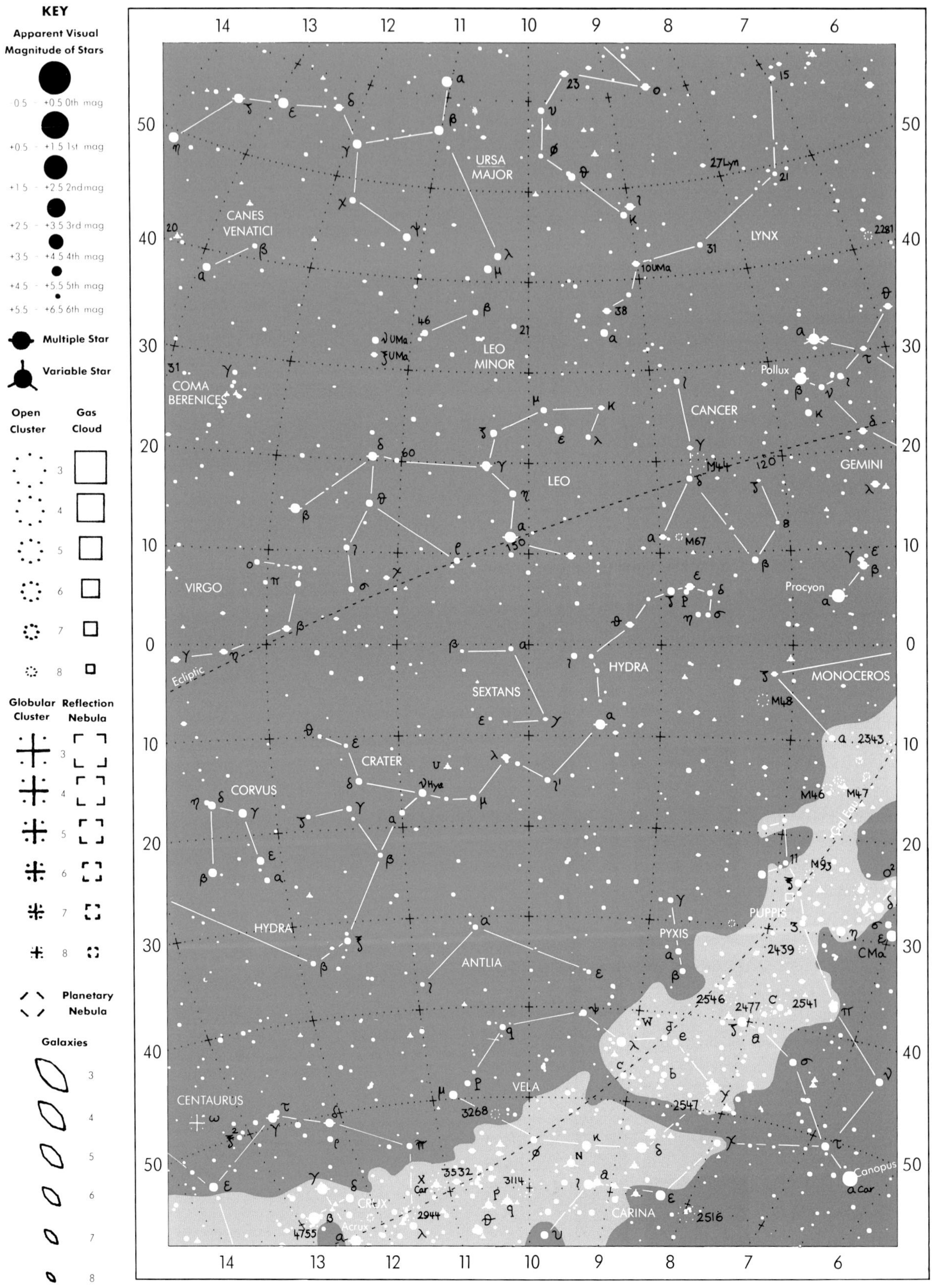
KEY
Apparent Visual Magnitude of Stars
-0.5 - +0.5 0th mag
+0.5 - +1.5 1st mag
+1.5 - +2.5 2nd mag
+2.5 - +3.5 3rd mag
+3.5 - +4.5 4th mag
+4.5 - +5.5 5th mag
+5.5 - +6.5 6th mag
Multiple Star
Variable Star
Open Cluster
Gas Cloud
Globular Cluster
Reflection Nebula
Planetary Nebula
Galaxies
14 13 12 11 10 9 8 7 6
URSA MAJOR
CANES VENATICI
LYNX
LEO MINOR
COMA BERENICES
CANCER
Pollux
LEO
GEMINI
M44
M67
VIRGO
Procyon
Ecliptic
HYDRA
SEXTANS
MONOCEROS
M48
CRATER
CORVUS
M46
M47
M93
PUPPIS
PYXIS
ANTLIA
CMa
VELA
CENTAURUS
CARINA
CRUX
Acrux
Canopus
Col Eau
2343
2439
2546
2477
2541
2547
3268
3532
3114
2944
4755
2516
2281

STAR CHART – MARCH

A Trio of Galaxies in Leo

Lying within one telescopic wide field are the three galaxies M65 (NGC 3623), M66 (NGC 3627) and NGC 3628. This trio of systems is located some 2.5° south-south-east of Theta Leonis, roughly halfway between that star and 78 Leonis. A good pair of binoculars will pick out M65 and M66 on a really dark, clear night. With a magnitude of 9.7, M66 is the brighter of the two, M65 being somewhat fainter at magnitude 10.2. These galaxies, both discovered by Pierre Mechain in 1780, lie at a distance of around 30 million light years. The diameter of M65 is 60,000 light years and that of M66 is 50,000 light years.

Leo plays host to a number of other galaxies and, given good observing conditions, well rewards time spent surveying it with a wide-field telescope or powerful binoculars.

The southern Milky Way

The region of the Milky Way running through Crux, Centaurus, Vela, Musca and Carina.contains the Eta Carinae Nebula (NGC 3372). This nebula is one of the Milky Way's most luminous HII (ionized hydrogen) regions.

This area abounds with open star clusters. The Jewel Box cluster (NGC 4755) in Crux can be seen close to Beta Crucis, as can the edge of the dark Coal Sack Nebula just below it. The magnitude 5.1 open cluster NGC 3766 in Centaurus lies on a line from Lambda to Omicron 1 and 2 Centauri. This fine object is well scattered and offers a splendid view even through small telescopes, with a number of colour contrasts visible between its member stars.

Wreaths of bright nebulosity can be seen surrounding the stars of the open cluster IC 2948, near Lambda Centauri. Just as prominent is the bright open cluster NGC 3532 in Carina, host to around 150 stars, which are spread out over almost a full degree of sky. Its magnitude of 3.0 makes it an easy target for binoculars or a small telescope, either of which will bring out individual members of the cluster.

Surrounding the magnitude 2.8 star Theta Carinae is IC 2602, also known as the Theta Carinae cluster. It has a total magnitude of 1.9, spans 50' of sky and is very prominent, even through binoculars. It is also quite close, at a distance of just under 500 light years.

Towards the right of the chart is the magnitude 4.2 open cluster NGC 3114, a bright, sizable gathering of several dozen stars, many of which can be resolved in small telescopes. Also worthy of note is NGC 3293, a magnitude 4.7 cluster located near the Eta Carinae Nebula, containing around 50 stars. NGC 3293 lies at a distance of around 8,400 light years.

Also worthy of note is NGC 3293, a magnitude 4.7 cluster located near the Eta Carinae Nebula, containing around 50 stars. NGC 3293 lies at a distance of around 8,400 light years.

M65 and M66 in Leo.

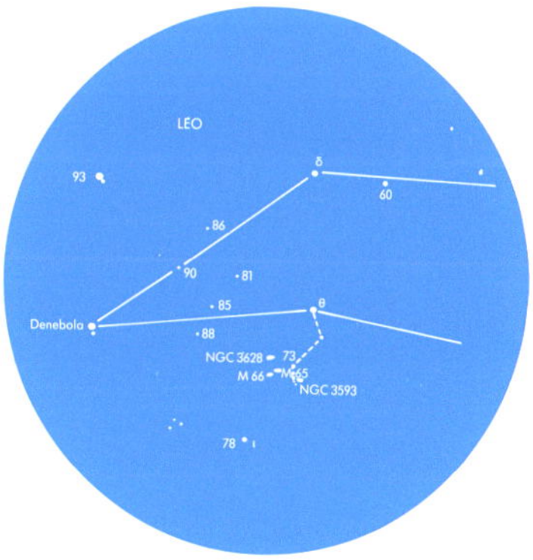

Finder chart for M 65 and M 66 galaxies.

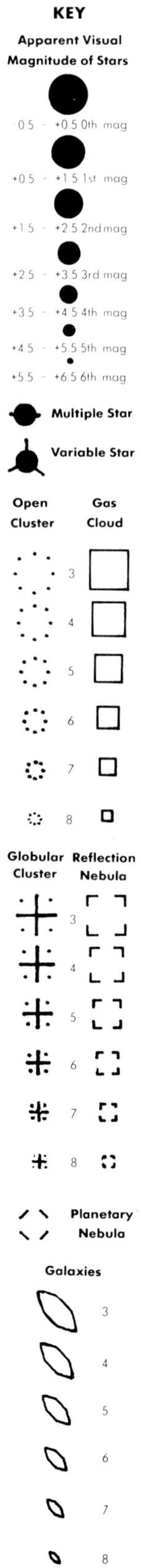
KEY
Apparent Visual Magnitude of Stars
-0.5 - +0.5 0th mag
+0.5 - +1.5 1st mag
+1.5 - +2.5 2nd mag
+2.5 - +3.5 3rd mag
+3.5 - +4.5 4th mag
+4.5 - +5.5 5th mag
+5.5 - +6.5 6th mag
Multiple Star
Variable Star
Open Cluster
Gas Cloud
Globular Cluster
Reflection Nebula
Planetary Nebula
Galaxies

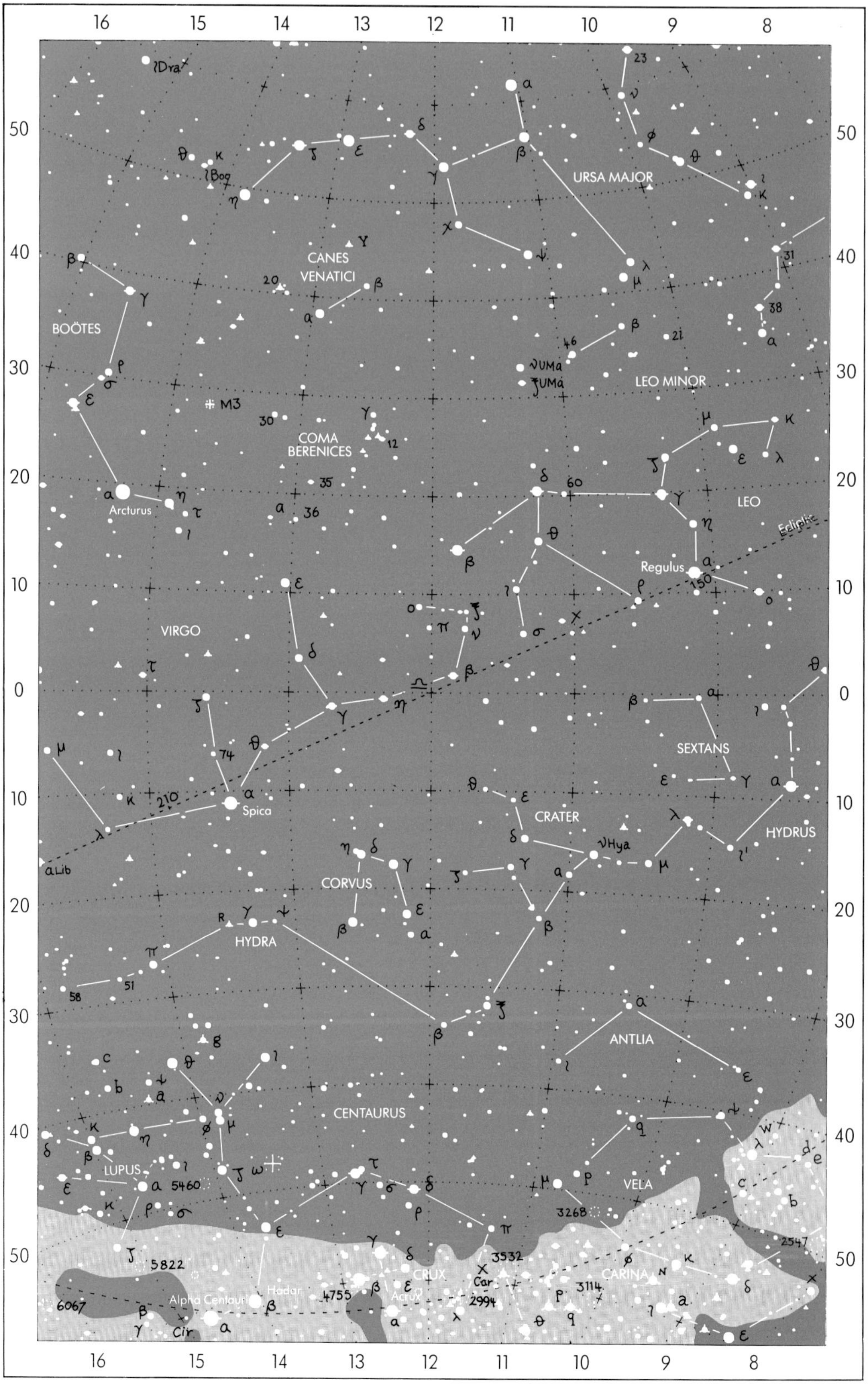
16
15
14
13
12
11
10
9
8
URSA MAJOR
CANES VENATICI
BOÖTES
LEO MINOR
M3
COMA BERENICES
Arcturus
LEO
Regulus
Ecliptic
VIRGO
SEXTANS
CRATER
HYDRUS
Spica
CORVUS
HYDRA
ANTLIA
CENTAURUS
LUPUS
VELA
CRUX
CARINA
Alpha Centauri
Hadar
Acrux

STAR CHART – APRIL

Jewels of Berenice's Hair

The constellation Coma Berenices, or Berenice's Hair, may appear at first sight to be a somewhat barren region of sky. But the area contains a number of galaxies, many of which are outlying members of the Virgo Cluster, whose central regions are found in neighbouring Virgo, to the south.

One of the brightest galaxies is M64 (NGC 4826), the Black Eye Galaxy, discovered by Johann Bode in 1779. In fact it is one of the brightest spiral galaxies in the sky. Found about 1° to the east-north-east of the star 35 Comae Berenicis, as shown on the chart, M64 is so bright that membership of the Virgo Cluster is in some doubt. If it is a member, it must be much closer than its companions.

Several degrees to the south-east of M64, and 1° to the north-east of Alpha Comae Berenicis, lies the bright globular cluster M53 (NGC 5024). This 8th-magnitude object is easily picked up in binoculars, although telescopes of at least 152 mm (6 inches) aperture are needed to resolve any of its stars. Discovered by Johann Bode in 1775, M53 lies at a distance of around 65,000 light years and is regarded as one of the finest objects of its type in the sky.

Sights of Centaurus

Centaurus is a bright and prominent constellation, lying on the borders of the Milky Way and containing a wealth of objects of interest to the backyard astronomer. Of particular note is Alpha Centauri, a double star with magnitude 0.0 and 1.3 components, which orbit each other every 79.9 years. A third star, 11th magnitude Proxima Centauri, can be seen nearby. Proxima is the closest star to our solar system. This triple system is a marvellous sight in 152-mm (6-inch) telescopes, the yellow of the primary contrasting with the orange and red of its companions.

Moving further north we come to Omega Centauri (NGC 5139), found by extending a line from Beta through Epsilon and on almost as far again. Omega Centauri has been described as the most magnificent globular cluster in the heavens. It is a prominent naked-eye object with a magnitude of 3.7.

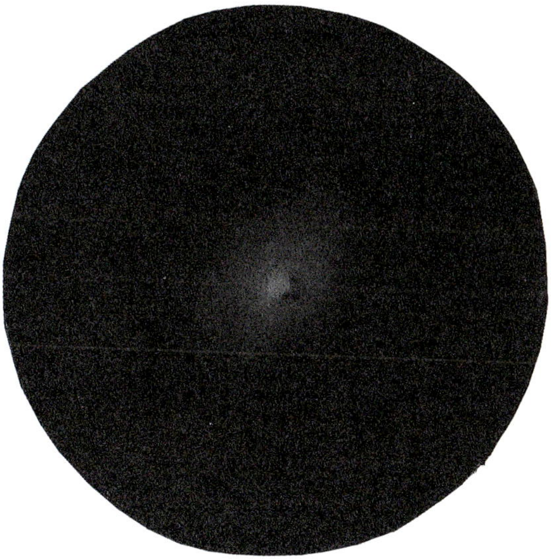

Sketch of M 64, the Black Eye Galaxy by D L Graham.

Omega Centauri (NGC 5139)

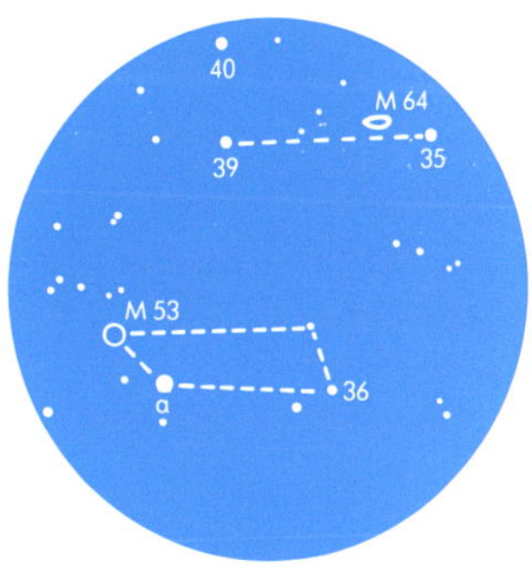

Finder chart for M 53 and M 64.

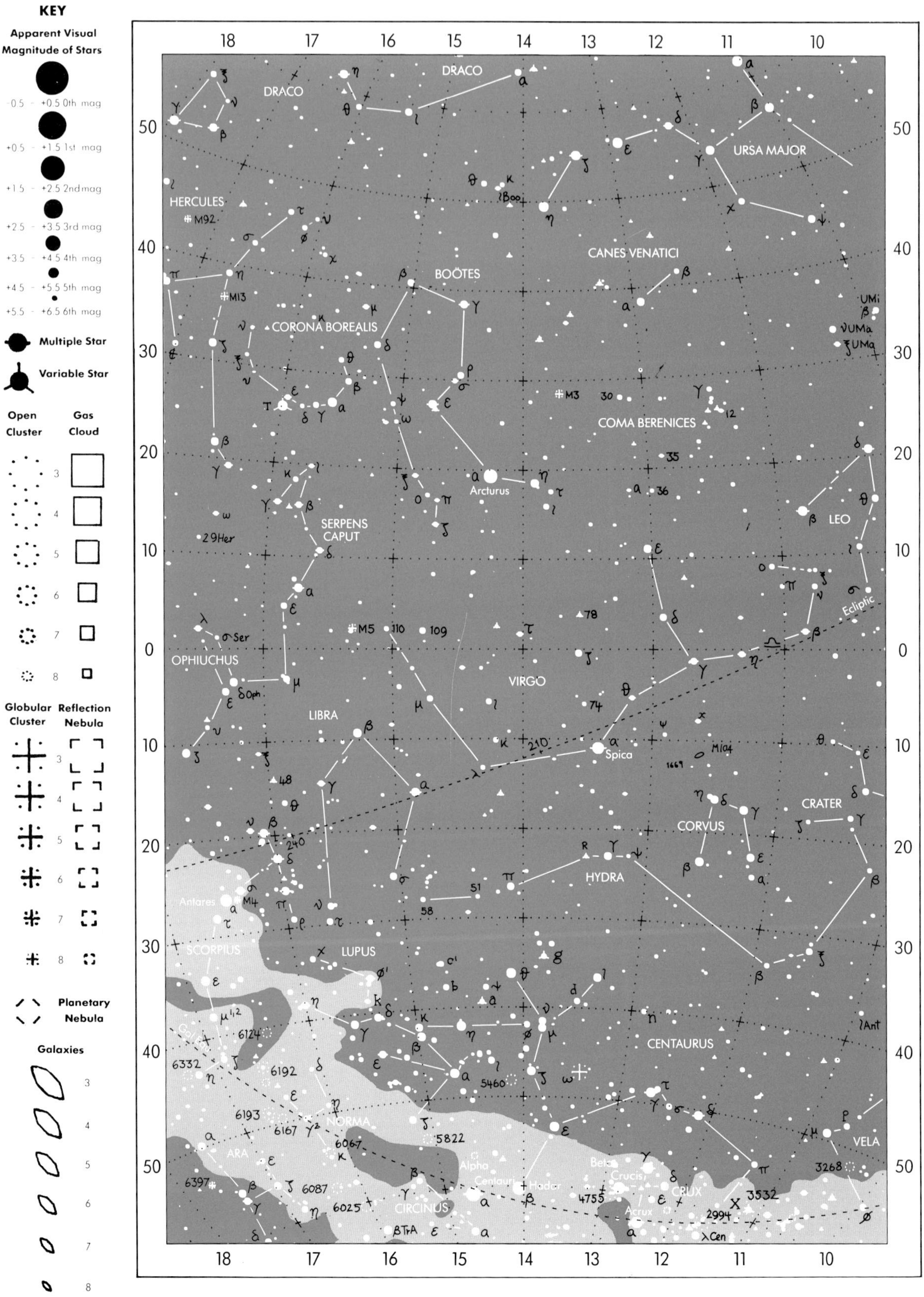
KEY
Apparent Visual Magnitude of Stars
-0.5 – +0.5 0th mag
+0.5 – +1.5 1st mag
+1.5 – +2.5 2nd mag
+2.5 – +3.5 3rd mag
+3.5 – +4.5 4th mag
+4.5 – +5.5 5th mag
+5.5 – +6.5 6th mag
Multiple Star
Variable Star
Open Cluster
Gas Cloud
Globular Cluster
Reflection Nebula
Planetary Nebula
Galaxies
18 17 16 15 14 13 12 11 10
DRACO
URSA MAJOR
HERCULES
M92
CANES VENATICI
BOÖTES
M13
CORONA BOREALIS
UMi
M3
COMA BERENICES
Arcturus
SERPENS CAPUT
LEO
29Her
Ecliptic
M5
OPHIUCHUS
VIRGO
LIBRA
Spica
M104
CRATER
CORVUS
HYDRA
Antares
M4
SCORPIUS
LUPUS
CENTAURUS
NORMA
ARA
VELA
Alpha Centauri
Hadar
Beta Crucis
CRUX
Acrux
CIRCINUS
λCen
βTrA
6124
6332
6192
6193
6167
6067
5822
5460
6397
6087
6025
4755
3532
2994
3268

STAR CHART – MAY

Two of Virgo's galaxies

The constellation of Virgo lies well away from the main plane of the Galaxy and contains no open clusters or nebulae. However, the area is swarming with galaxies. M104 (NGC 4594) is an edge-on spiral galaxy, and one of the few such systems to display a dust lane visible through amateur telescopes. Locating M104 is straightforward: the galaxy lies close to one side of a triangle formed from Psi and Chi Virginis and Sigma 1669 in the neighbouring constellation of Corvus. Telescopically, M104 is seen to lie in a pretty field of stars.

Otherwise known as the Sombrero Galaxy, M104 was discovered by Pierre Mechain in 1781. It is an 8th-magnitude object, easily detectable in small telescopes and presenting a marvellous sight in instruments of 200 mm (8 inches) aperture or larger. This huge system, measuring well in excess of 100,000 light years across, lies at a distance of around 40 million light years.

Located on the northern side of the line from Psi to Chi is the 10th-magnitude spiral galaxy NGC 4699, which may be picked up as an elongated patch of light through telescopes of 152 mm (6 inches) aperture under reasonable seeing conditions.

Sigma 1669 in Corvus is a triple star with two main components of magnitudes 6.0 and 6.1 separated by 5.4", easily resolvable in small telescopes. A third component of magnitude 10.5 can be seen 59" away.

Musca

The constellation Musca is a small fairly prominent group. The area shown also includes parts of the surrounding constellations Chamaeleon, Apus, Circinus and Crux. Alpha Crucis, or Acrux, is the bright star seen at upper left with part of the dark Coal Sack nebula seen just below it.

The photograph shows a number of interesting deep-sky objects, including the variable stars R and S Muscae. Both are cepheid variables, S varying between magnitudes 6.4 to 7.2 over 9.66 days.

The 8th-magnitude globular cluster NGC 4372, 16,000 light years from us, can be seen near Gamma Muscae. Another globular, NGC 4833, is seen close to Delta. This magnitude 7.3 system is located at a distance of around 18,000 light years. Telescopes of 75 mm (3 inches) aperture will resolve one or two individual members of each cluster.

Spiral galaxy M104, Sombrero Galaxy

Area of the sky around Musca

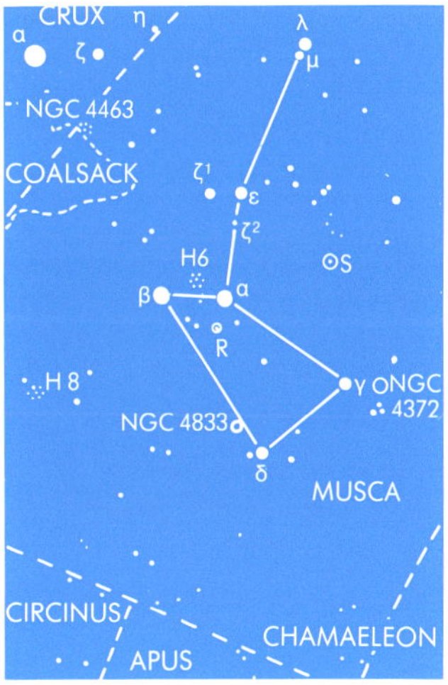

Comparison chart for photograph of Musca.

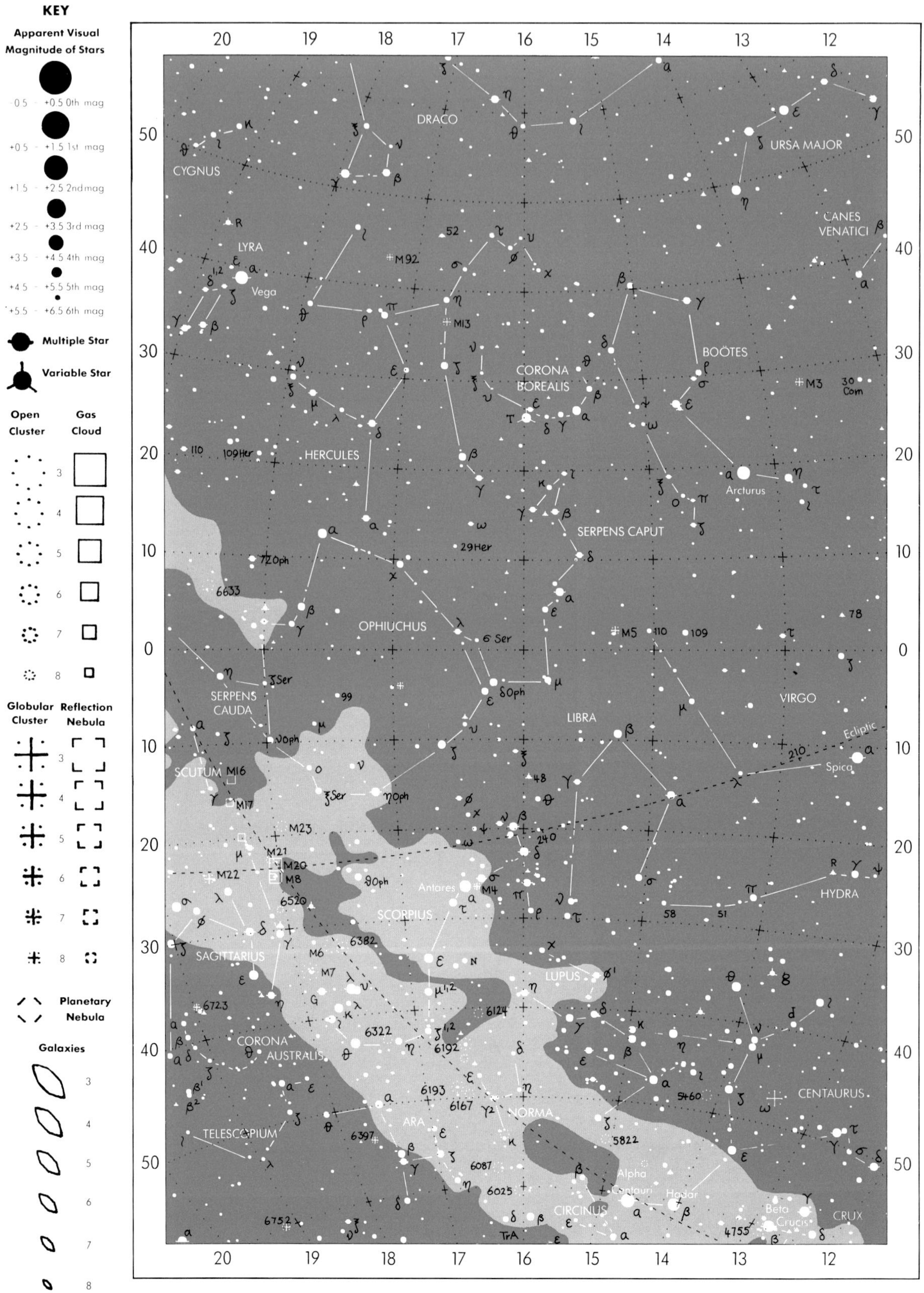
KEY
Apparent Visual Magnitude of Stars
-0.5 – +0.5 0th mag
+0.5 – +1.5 1st mag
+1.5 – +2.5 2nd mag
+2.5 – +3.5 3rd mag
+3.5 – +4.5 4th mag
+4.5 – +5.5 5th mag
+5.5 – +6.5 6th mag
Multiple Star
Variable Star
Open Cluster
Gas Cloud
Globular Cluster
Reflection Nebula
Planetary Nebula
Galaxies
DRACO
CYGNUS
URSA MAJOR
LYRA
Vega
CANES VENATICI
HERCULES
CORONA BOREALIS
BOÖTES
Arcturus
SERPENS CAPUT
OPHIUCHUS
SERPENS CAUDA
VIRGO
LIBRA
Ecliptic
Spica
SCUTUM
Antares
SCORPIUS
HYDRA
SAGITTARIUS
LUPUS
CORONA AUSTRALIS
CENTAURUS
NORMA
ARA
TELESCOPIUM
Alpha Centauri
Hadar
CIRCINUS
Beta Crucis
CRUX
TrA

STAR CHART – JUNE

The Clusters of Hercules

Hercules contains the most frequently observed globular cluster in the northern hemisphere. Lying roughly a third of the way from Eta to Zeta, M13 (NGC 6205) hovers on the border of naked-eye visibility, although excellent sky-darkness and transparency conditions are needed. Any binoculars will bring it out quite well, but a telescope of at least 10 cm (4 inches) is required to resolve any individual stars. M13 lies at a distance of around 22,000 light years. Its diameter exceeds 160 light years. Telescopes of 15 cm (6 inches) aperture or larger may reveal the 11th-magnitude galaxy MGC 6207, lying a little to the north-east of M13.

Lying further to the north-east, forming a small triangle with Iota and 74 Herculis, is the globular cluster M92 (NGC 6341), discovered by Johann Bode in 1777. M92 is a little less impressive than M13 and lies further away, at a distance of around 35,000 light years. Small telescopes will resolve some individual stars around the outer edges of the cluster; binoculars will show it as a small, circular a diffused patch of light.

Other objects worth seeking out in Hercules include the variable star 68 Herculis, an eclipsing binary whose magnitude drops from 4.6 to 5.3 every 2.05 days. 95 and 100 Herculis are both double stars, resolvable in small telescopes. 95 Herculis is notable for its contrasting colours, described by William Smyth as light apple-green and cherry-red. Kappa Herculis is another double star, with components of magnitudes 5.3 and 6.5 separated by 28.4". The components are yellow and red.

Scorpion's Tail

Scorpius occupies one of the richest regions of the night sky and contains a wealth of deep-sky objects. Notable among these are the two open star clusters M6 (NGC 6405) and M7 (NGC 6475), both of which are best seen with low powers and wide fields of view. M6 has an overall magnitude of 4.2, making it visible to the naked eye under good conditions. Its overall diameter is around 20 light years and it contains about 80 stars arranged in a conspicuous formation that has led to the group being nicknamed the Butterfly Cluster.

Lying some 31/2° to the south-east of M6 is M7, another prominent open cluster with an overall magnitude of 3.3. Brighter than its neighbour, M7 is probably the most conspicuous deep-sky object in Scorpius and is the southernmost object in Messier's catalogue. It contains over 80 stars and lies at a distance of around 800 light years.

M13 globular cluster in Hercules

M6 open cluster in Hercules

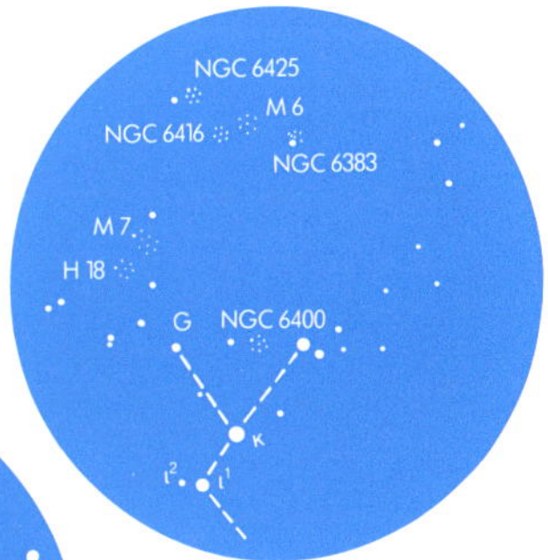

Finder chart for M 6 and M 7 open clusters.

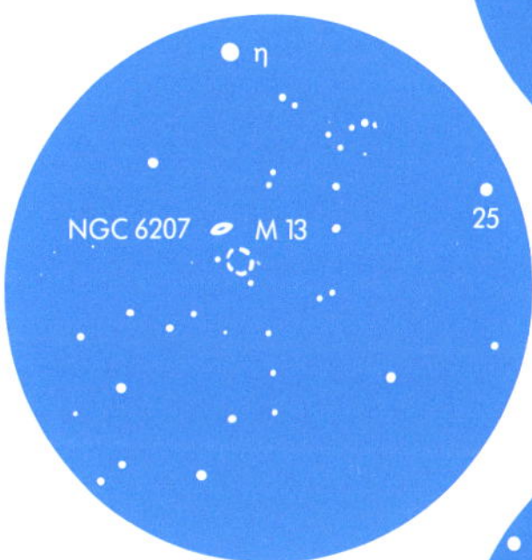

Finder chart for M 13 globular cluster

Finder chart for M 92 globular cluster

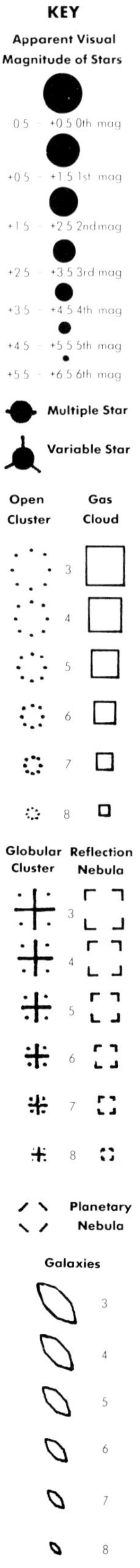
KEY
Apparent Visual Magnitude of Stars
-0.5 – +0.5 0th mag
+0.5 – +1.5 1st mag
+1.5 – +2.5 2nd mag
+2.5 – +3.5 3rd mag
+3.5 – +4.5 4th mag
+4.5 – +5.5 5th mag
+5.5 – +6.5 6th mag
Multiple Star
Variable Star
Open Cluster
Gas Cloud
3
4
5
6
7
8
Globular Cluster
Reflection Nebula
3
4
5
6
7
8
Planetary Nebula
Galaxies
3
4
5
6
7
8

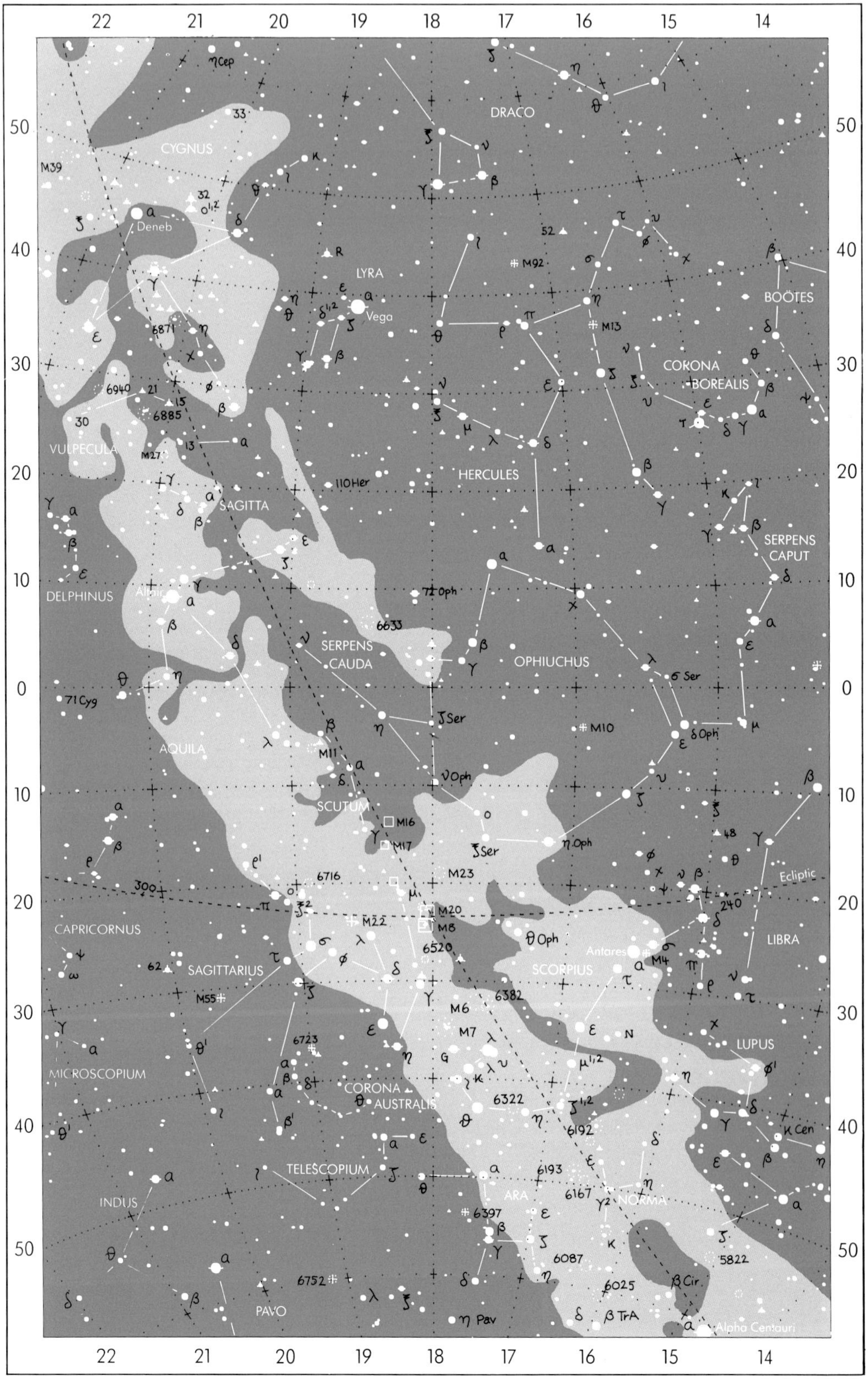
22
21
20
19
18
17
16
15
14
50
40
30
20
10
0
10
20
30
40
50
DRACO
CYGNUS
Deneb
LYRA
Vega
BOÖTES
CORONA BOREALIS
HERCULES
VULPECULA
SAGITTA
SERPENS CAPUT
DELPHINUS
SERPENS CAUDA
OPHIUCHUS
AQUILA
SCUTUM
Ecliptic
CAPRICORNUS
LIBRA
Antares
SCORPIUS
SAGITTARIUS
LUPUS
MICROSCOPIUM
CORONA AUSTRALIS
TELESCOPIUM
INDUS
ARA
NORMA
PAVO
Alpha Centauri

STAR CHART – JULY

Milky Way in Sagittarius

The photograph, which has north to the top, shows the Milky Way in the region of Sagittarius. Mu (the brightest here), 15 and 16 Sagittarii are visible as a small triangle just above left centre. When we view Sagittarius we are looking in towards the centre of the Milky Way Galaxy. Little wonder, therefore, that here we have the richest concentration of star clouds and interstellar material in the entire sky. This is a truly marvellous area for the deep-sky observer.

Prominent here is the Lagoon Nebula (M8), at lower right, with the smaller but equally magnificent Trifid Nebula (M20) just to its north-north-west (upper right). The 6th-magnitude open cluster M21 (NGC 6531) can be seen just above the Trifid Nebula.

Discovered by Messier in 1764, M21 is a stunning sight in telescopes of 100 mm (4 inches) aperture, which will show it quite well with low-power eyepieces. It contains around 70 stars, a number of which can be resolved with binoculars.

Near the right-hand margin, just above the centre of the picture, is the open cluster M23 (NGC 6494). Containing some 150 stars, M23 has a magnitude of 5.5, making it an easy target for binoculars or a small telescope. This is also believed to have been discovered by Messier in 1764 and lies at a distance of around 2,000 light years. The stars of M23 are spread out over a 25' diameter of sky, corresponding to a true diameter of 15 light years for the group.

M24, otherwise known as the Small Sagittarius Star Cloud, is visible to the upper left. M24 is not a true cluster but simply a brightening of the Milky Way silhouetted against the surrounding dark clouds. Here is one of the richest areas of sky for the owners of wide-angle telescopes, and time spent sweeping this field will be well rewarded.

Ara

This small group of stars was included by Ptolemy in his list of 48 constellations. Situated in the Milky Way to the south of Scorpius, Ara contains several open star clusters, notable among which is NGC 6193, a magnitude 5.2 collection of around 30 stars situated at a distance of over 4,000 light years. These stars are fairly loosely spread over an area of sky some 15' across, making it a candidate for wide-field telescopes or binoculars.

Ara also contains three globular clusters, the best example being NGC 6397, located on a line from Beta to Theta Arae. With a magnitude of 5.6, this is a fairly bright object and easily picked up in binoculars. It may be the closest globular cluster to us, measurements indicating a distance of around 8,000 light years. NGC 6397 has a rather loose structure and can be resolved into stars with only moderate telescopes.

Gamma Arae is a triple star, with two main components of magnitudes 3.3 and 10.3 separated by 17.9". A third companion of magnitude 11.8 can be seen 41.6" from the brightest star.

Telescopes of at least 127 mm (5 inches) aperture are required to resolve all three stars. It is not known with certainty whether these three stars are physically connected.

The Algol-type variable R Arae is shown in the chart, along with suitable comparison stars. Its magnitude varies between 6.0 and 7.0 over a period of 4.425 days. The chart also shows part of the neighbouring constellation Norma, which contains a number of interesting open star clusters. NGC 6067 has a magnitude of 5.6 and some 100 member stars, while NGC 6087 is slightly brighter at magnitude 5.4. This group contains around 40 stars. Both objects can be viewed effectively with small telescopes and low-power eyepieces. CR 299 is somewhat fainter than its two neighbours and poorer in stars, but is still worth seeking out.

Milky Way in the region of Sagittarius

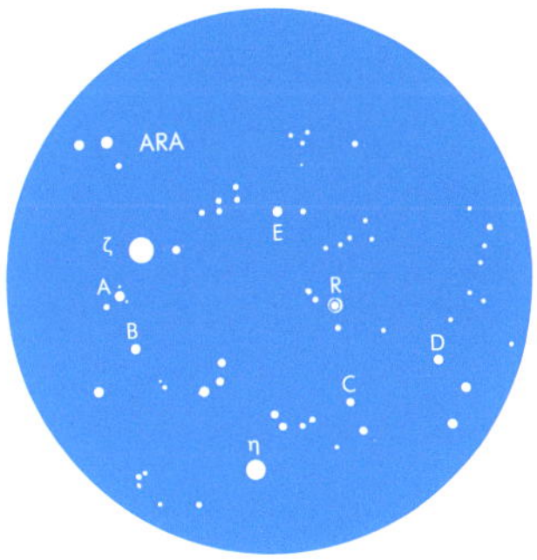

Comparison chart for variable star R Arae.

Comparison Stars

A	6.5
B	6.0
C	7.3
D	6.9
E	6.6

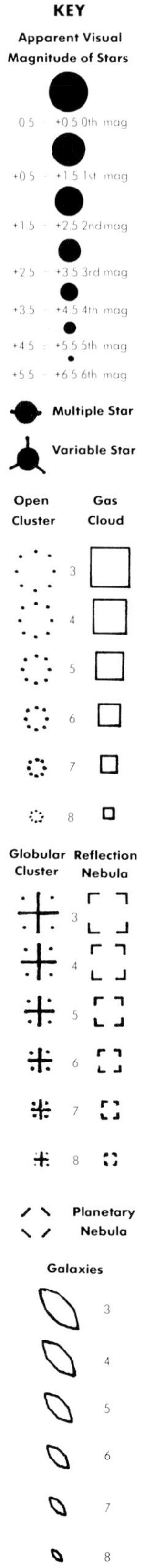
KEY
Apparent Visual Magnitude of Stars
-0.5 - +0.5 0th mag
+0.5 - +1.5 1st mag
+1.5 - +2.5 2nd mag
+2.5 - +3.5 3rd mag
+3.5 - +4.5 4th mag
+4.5 - +5.5 5th mag
+5.5 - +6.5 6th mag
Multiple Star
Variable Star
Open Cluster
Gas Cloud
Globular Cluster
Reflection Nebula
Planetary Nebula
Galaxies

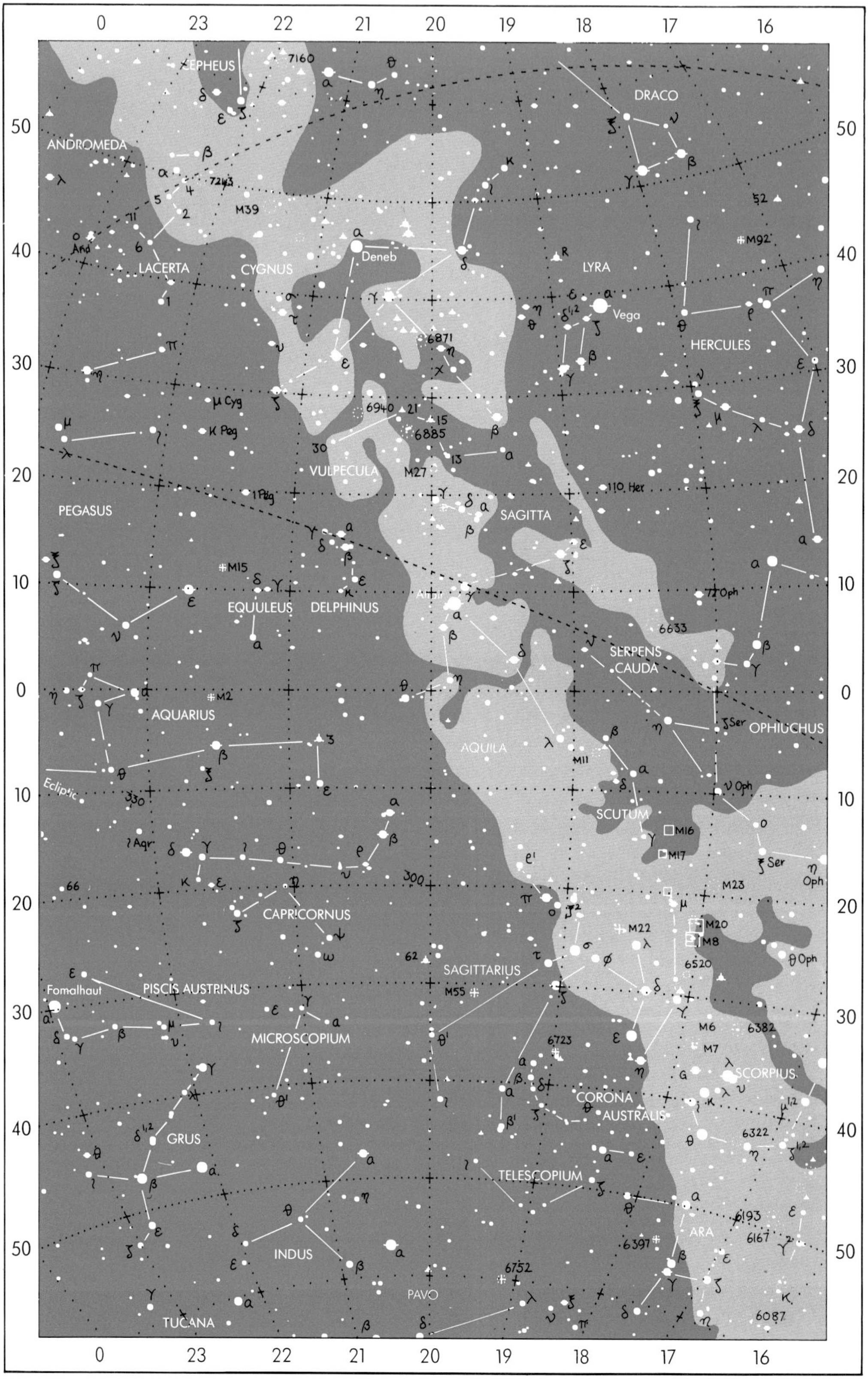
0
23
22
21
20
19
18
17
16
50
40
30
20
10
0
10
20
30
40
50
CEPHEUS
ANDROMEDA
DRACO
LACERTA
CYGNUS
Deneb
LYRA
Vega
HERCULES
VULPECULA
PEGASUS
SAGITTA
EQUULEUS
DELPHINUS
Altair
SERPENS CAUDA
OPHIUCHUS
AQUARIUS
AQUILA
SCUTUM
Ecliptic
CAPRICORNUS
SAGITTARIUS
Fomalhaut
PISCIS AUSTRINUS
MICROSCOPIUM
SCORPIUS
CORONA AUSTRALIS
GRUS
TELESCOPIUM
ARA
INDUS
PAVO
TUCANA
M39
M92
M27
M15
M2
M11
M16
M17
M23
M22
M20
M8
M55
M6
M7
7160
7243
6871
6940
6885
6633
6520
6723
6382
6322
6193
6167
6397
6752
6087

STAR CHART – AUGUST

Cygnus

Dominating the northern night sky of summer, the constellation of Cygnus is spread across the Milky Way and contains a large number of interesting deep-sky objects. One of these is the open cluster M39 (NGC 7092), a large, loose gathering of stars situated to the ENE of Deneb. M39 forms a neat triangle with Rho and Pi^{2}. It contains around 30 stars and lies at a distance of about 800 light years. This object is scattered over an area of sky a little larger than a full Moon, its large apparent diameter making it best suited for observation through binoculars or a rich-field telescope.

Another open cluster in Cygnus is M29 (NGC 6913), a 7th-magnitude object whose light has taken over 7000 years to reach us. This large distance, coupled with the fact that M29 is seen through a heavily obscured region of the Milky Way, ensures that the cluster is nowhere near as striking as it would be if located away from the Milky Way. A 150-mm (6-inch) telescope will show it well.

Chi Cygni is a long-period variable whose magnitude varies between 3.3 and 14.2 over a period of 406.9 days. Nearby is the beautiful double star Albireo, the yellow and blue components of which offer a beautiful contrast in even the smallest telescopes. Also worth seeking out is the double star 61 Cygni, both components of which are red dwarf stars, displaying yellowish-orange tints to the obsever. This object has great historical significance, for it was the first star to have its distance determined by trigonometric parallax. Another of the many double stars in Cygnus is Psi Cygni, the 5th- and 7th-magnitude components of which are resolvable in 75-mm (3-inch) telescopes.

Star clusters in Sagitta

The tiny but conspicuously-shaped constellation of Sagitta contains two interesting clusters: the globular M71 (NGC 6838) and the nearby sparse open cluster Harvard 20, seen a little to its south-west. Lying just to the south of the line joining Gamma and Delta Sagittae, 8th-magnitude M71 is visible as a bright and compact group of stars through a 75-mm (3-inch) telescope, larger instruments bringing out many individual members. There has been much debate over the years as to whether M71 is an open or globular cluster, although opinion now seems to favour the latter. The cluster lies at a distance of around 18,000 light years and is some 30 light years in diameter.

Lying nearby, in the neighbouring constellation of Vulpecula, is the open cluster Collinder 399, better known as the Coathanger. Distinguishable with the naked eye and easily visible in binoculars, this delightful little gathering of stars takes its name from its fancied resemblance to a tiny celestial coathanger. The 4th-magnitude group contains around 40 stars and lies at a distance of just over 400 light years. The sudden appearance of Collinder 399 in the field of view when this area of sky is being swept with binoculars or a low-power telescope never fails to bring delight to the observer who sees it for the first time.

Alpha Capricorni

Alpha Capricorni is a very wide double, easily resolved with the naked eye or binoculars. The two stars are not physically related to each other, Alpha^{2} lying at a distance of only 120 light years, whereas Alpha^{1} is estimated to be at a distance of over 1500 light years. After observing the wide, naked-eye pair, try taking a closer look at each star in turn. Both will be seen to have a number of companion stars, although these are all quite faint and will require telescopes to resolve them.

Lying some 2½° to the south of Alpha is Beta Capricorni, a wide double star shining from a distance of around 150 light years and with a separation of some 3½'. The magnitude 3.4 and 6.2 components are resolvable in binoculars of 10 x magnification, and even small telescopes will show their white and blue tints.

Sagitta and open cluster, Collinder 399, the Coathanger.

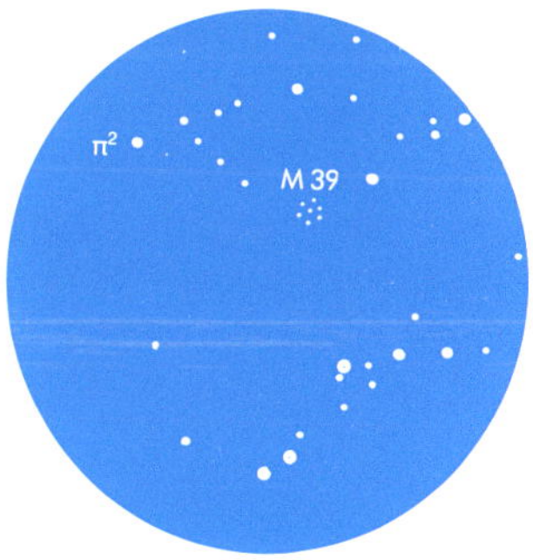

Finder chart for M 39 open cluster.

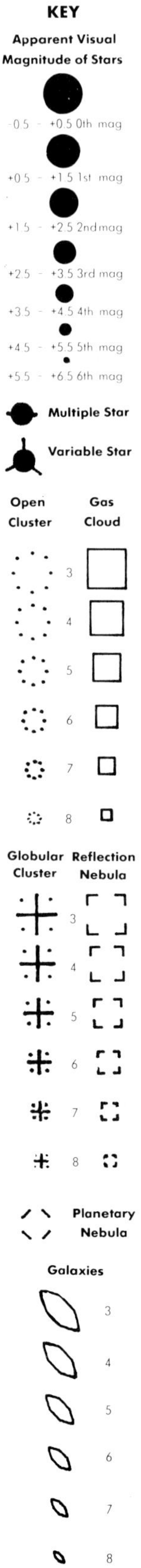
KEY
Apparent Visual Magnitude of Stars
-0.5 – +0.5 0th mag
+0.5 – +1.5 1st mag
+1.5 – +2.5 2nd mag
+2.5 – +3.5 3rd mag
+3.5 – +4.5 4th mag
+4.5 – +5.5 5th mag
+5.5 – +6.5 6th mag
Multiple Star
Variable Star
Open Cluster
Gas Cloud
3
4
5
6
7
8
Globular Cluster
Reflection Nebula
Planetary Nebula
Galaxies

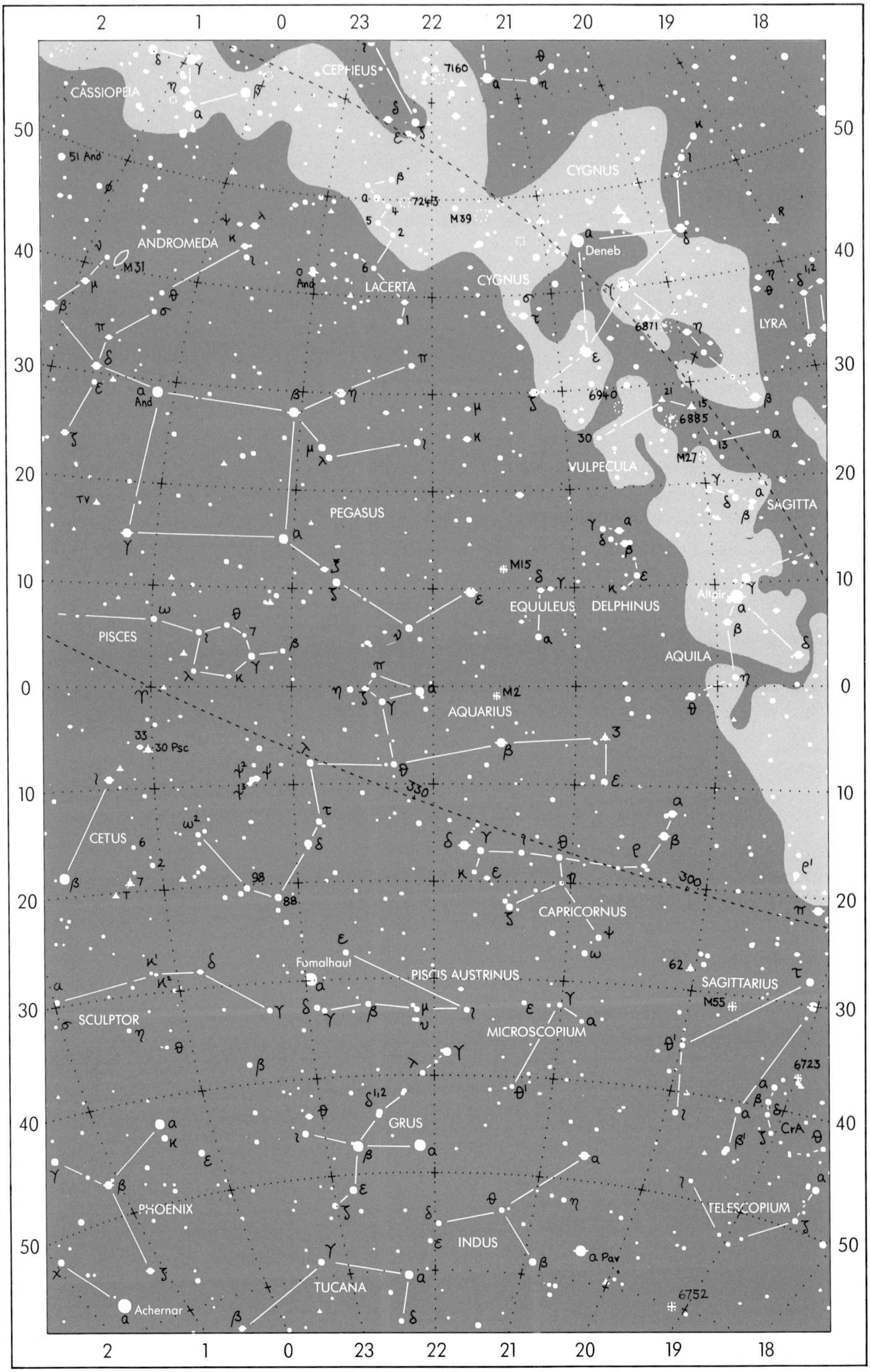
2
1
0
23
22
21
20
19
18
50
40
30
20
10
0
CASSIOPEIA
CEPHEUS
7160
51 And
CYGNUS
ANDROMEDA
M31
LACERTA
7243
M39
Deneb
LYRA
6871
6940
6885
VULPECULA
M27
SAGITTA
PEGASUS
M15
EQUULEUS
DELPHINUS
Altair
PISCES
AQUILA
M2
AQUARIUS
30 Psc
CETUS
CAPRICORNUS
Fomalhaut
PISCIS AUSTRINUS
SAGITTARIUS
M55
SCULPTOR
MICROSCOPIUM
6723
GRUS
CrA
PHOENIX
TELESCOPIUM
INDUS
TUCANA
α Pav
Achernar
6752

STAR CHART – SEPTEMBER

Sights of Pegasus

Although star charts give the impression that Pegasus, the Winged Horse, is a rather conspicuous group, the four stars that form the Square of Pegasus are not very bright. Once located, it becomes clear that this area of sky is rather barren. It is an interesting exercise to see how many stars you can count with the naked eye within the Square. If you get into double figures you have done well, although 20 or more can be seen under excellent seeing conditions with the eyes fully dark-adapted.

The chart shows the area around the globular cluster M15 (NGC 7078), a magnitude 7.3 object situated to the north-west of Epsilon Pegasi, or Enif. M15 is regarded as one of the finest globular clusters in the sky. It can be seen as a fuzzy starlike object through binoculars or a small telescope. Apertures of at least 75 mm (3 inches) are needed to bring out individual members of the cluster, which has been found to lie at a distance of almost 40,000 light years. Its diameter is in the region of 130 light years.

Epsilon Pegasi is a triple star, although the three components are not physically related to each other. The primary has a magnitude of 2.31, and has a magnitude 11.2 companion situated 81.1" away. A third component, of magnitude 9.4, is 142.5" from the primary. Telescopes of at least 100 mm (4 inches) aperture are needed to resolve all three stars.

Another multiple star is Beta Pegasi, or Scheat, marking the north-west corner of the Square. The primary is an irregular variable whose magnitude varies between 2.3 and 2.8. There are two faint companions: one of magnitude 11.6 at 108.5" distance and one of 9.4 at 253.1".

Piscis Austrinus and Grus

The photograph (which has north to the top) shows the region of sky containing the Southern Fish and the Crane. The bright star to the upper left of the Crane is Fomalhaut, a name derived from the Arabic *Fum al Hut*, the Mouth of the Fish. Also known as the Solitary One, owing to its location in a somewhat barren region of sky, Fomalhaut is the 18th-brightest star in the heavens. Its magnitude is 1.17 and it liesat a distance of 23 light years.

Just below Fomalhaut are two pairs of stars. The lower, and more widely spaced, of these pairs comprises Delta and Gamma Piscis Auistrini. Examination with telescopes of 75 mm (3 inches) aperture or larger will show that each of these stars is actually double. Delta, on the left, has components of magnitudes 4.2 and 9.2 separated by 5.0". Gamma comprises magnitude 4.5 and 8.0 stars with a separation of 4.2".

M15, globular cluster in Pegasus

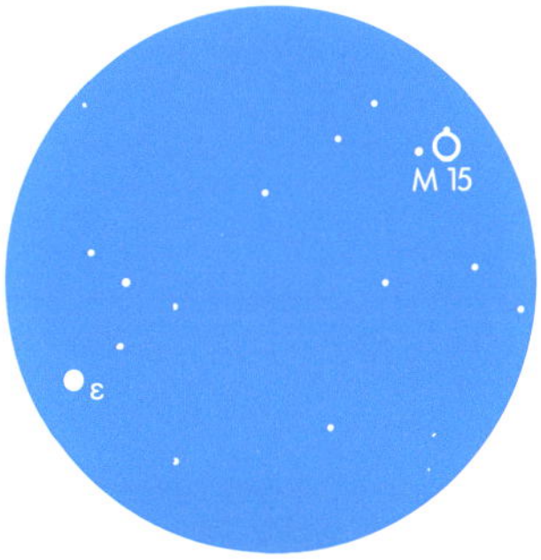

Finder chart for M 15 globular cluster.

Area of Picis Austrinus and Grus

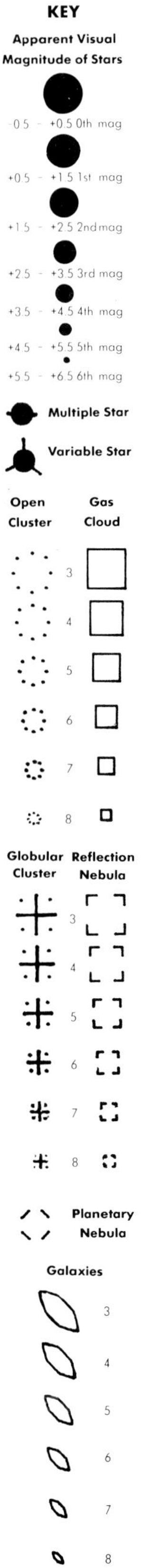
KEY
Apparent Visual Magnitude of Stars
-0.5 - +0.5 0th mag
+0.5 - +1.5 1st mag
+1.5 - +2.5 2nd mag
+2.5 - +3.5 3rd mag
+3.5 - +4.5 4th mag
+4.5 - +5.5 5th mag
+5.5 - +6.5 6th mag
Multiple Star
Variable Star
Open Cluster
Gas Cloud
Globular Cluster
Reflection Nebula
Planetary Nebula
Galaxies

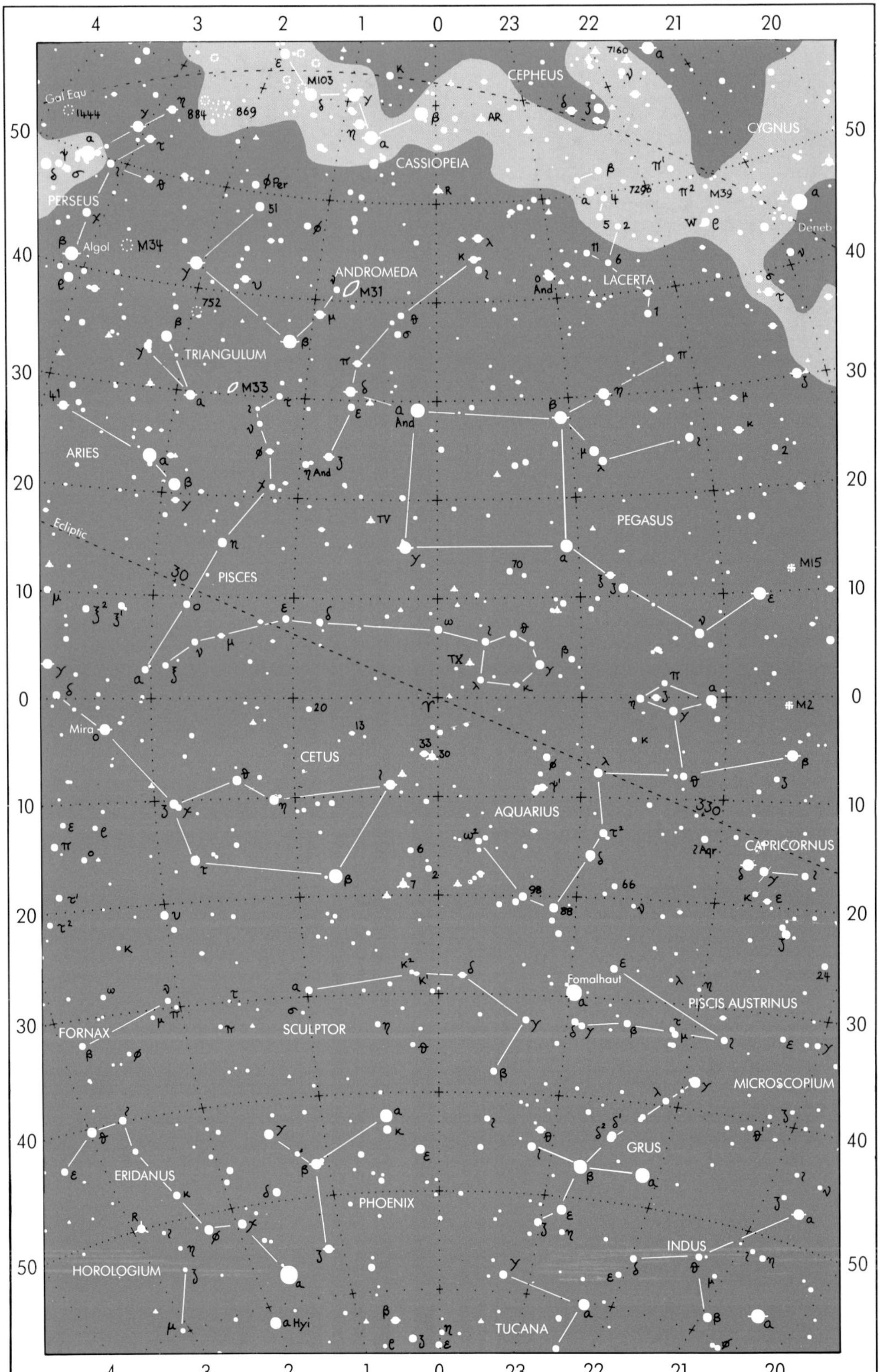
4 3 2 1 0 23 22 21 20
50
40
30
20
10
0
10
20
30
40
50
CEPHEUS
CYGNUS
CASSIOPEIA
PERSEUS
Gal Equ
Algol
M34
M103
884
869
1444
ANDROMEDA
M31
LACERTA
Deneb
M39
TRIANGULUM
M33
ARIES
PEGASUS
Ecliptic
PISCES
M15
M2
Mira
CETUS
AQUARIUS
CAPRICORNUS
Fomalhaut
PISCIS AUSTRINUS
FORNAX
SCULPTOR
MICROSCOPIUM
GRUS
ERIDANUS
PHOENIX
INDUS
HOROLOGIUM
TUCANA
α Hyi
4 3 2 1 0 23 22 21 20

STAR CHART – OCTOBER

Andromeda

The Great Andromeda Galaxy, or M31, located at a distance of 2.2 million light years, is the largest member of the Local Group and can be found about 1° to the west of Nu Andromedae. The naked eye reveals M31 as an elongated, diffused patch of light of magnitude 3.5. Binoculars will enable it to be traced out to a length of around 4° under good seeing conditions.

M31 contains around 300 billion stars and has a diameter of 180,000 light years, making it a truly colossal system and larger by far than our own Milky Way. The bright core can be seen in binoculars, which will reveal it as an elongated patch of light. The surrounding disc is much more difficult to see, however, and a telescope of at least 250 mm (10 inches) aperture is required to detect any hint of the structure.

A 152-mm (6-inch) telescope with a low-power eyepiece will reveal two smaller patches of light close to M31. These are two of the Andromeda spiral's satellite galaxies, M32 (NGC 221) and M110 (NGC 205). The larger of these is M110, which has a magnitude of 8.0 and is located just over 1/2° to the north-west of the M31 central region. M32 has a magnitude of 8.2 and lies just under 1/2° to the south of M31. Both objects are elliptical galaxies.

Other objects of note in Andromeda include the pretty double star Gamma Andromedae, which has yellow and blue-white components of magnitudes 3.0 and 5.0 separated by 9.4". Pi Andromedae has components of magnitude 4.4 and 8.6, 35.9" apart. 59 Andromedae is another double, with yellow and blue stars of magnitudes 6.0 and 6.7 at 16.7". R Andromedae is a Mira-type variable star whose brightness varies between 5.8 and 14.9 over a period of 409.3 days.

Sights of Sculptor

Sculptor is a faint constellation to the east of Fomalhaut in Piscis Austrinus and below Beta Ceti. However, although containing no bright stars and to the naked eye appearing empty, it plays host to several galaxies, the brightest of which is shown in the photograph.

The accompanying chart shows the position of the spiral galaxy NGC 253 and the nearby globular cluster NGC 288, situated around 2° to the south-east of NGC 253. NGC 253 appears as an elongated sliver of light slightly less than 1/2° in extent. With a magnitude of 7.1, NGC 253 is tilted just 12° from an edge-on position. It has a fairly high surface brightness and much detail can be made out if the right equipment is used. A low-power eyepiece on a 152-mm (6-inch) telescope will reveal the distinctive shape of the galaxy, while higher powers will bring out the nucleus and some structure in the spiral arms. NGC 253 is the leading member of the Sculptor Group of galaxies, situated at a distance of about 10 million light years.

NGC 288 is a conspicuous magnitude 8.1 object, detectable in binoculars as a spherical patch of diffused light. Telescopes of 75-mm (3-inch) aperture will bring out some individual stars in the cluster. NGC 288 has a visual diameter of almost 14' and is located at a distance of around 27,000 light years.

Delta Sculptoris is a double star with components of magnitudes 4.5 and 11.5, just 3.9" apart. This pair is difficult and a large telescope is required to resolve them. However, a third component of magnitude 9.3 situated 74.3" from the brighter member of the system may prove easier to resolve.

To the south-east of Delta is the Mira-type variable S Sculptoris. The magnitude of this star varies between 5.5 and 13.6 over a period of 365.3 days – almost exactly a year.

Galaxy NGC253 in area of Sculptor

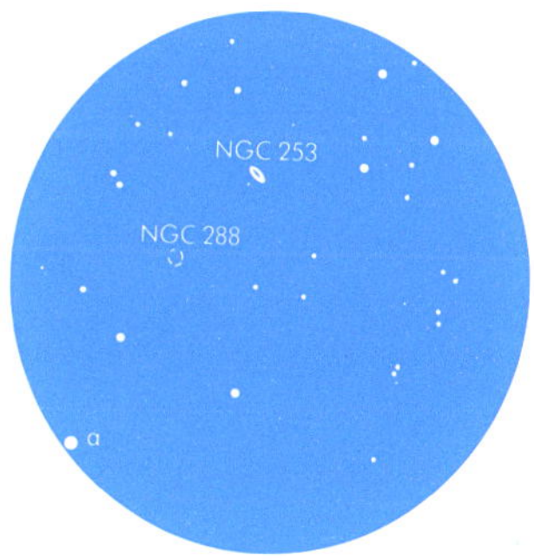

Finder chart for NGC 253 spiral galaxy and NGC 288 globular cluster.

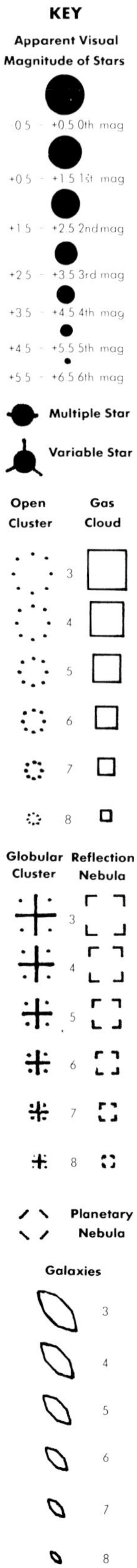
KEY
Apparent Visual Magnitude of Stars
0.5 – +0.5 0th mag
+0.5 – +1.5 1st mag
+1.5 – +2.5 2nd mag
+2.5 – +3.5 3rd mag
+3.5 – +4.5 4th mag
+4.5 – +5.5 5th mag
+5.5 – +6.5 6th mag
Multiple Star
Variable Star
Open Cluster
Gas Cloud
Globular Cluster
Reflection Nebula
Planetary Nebula
Galaxies

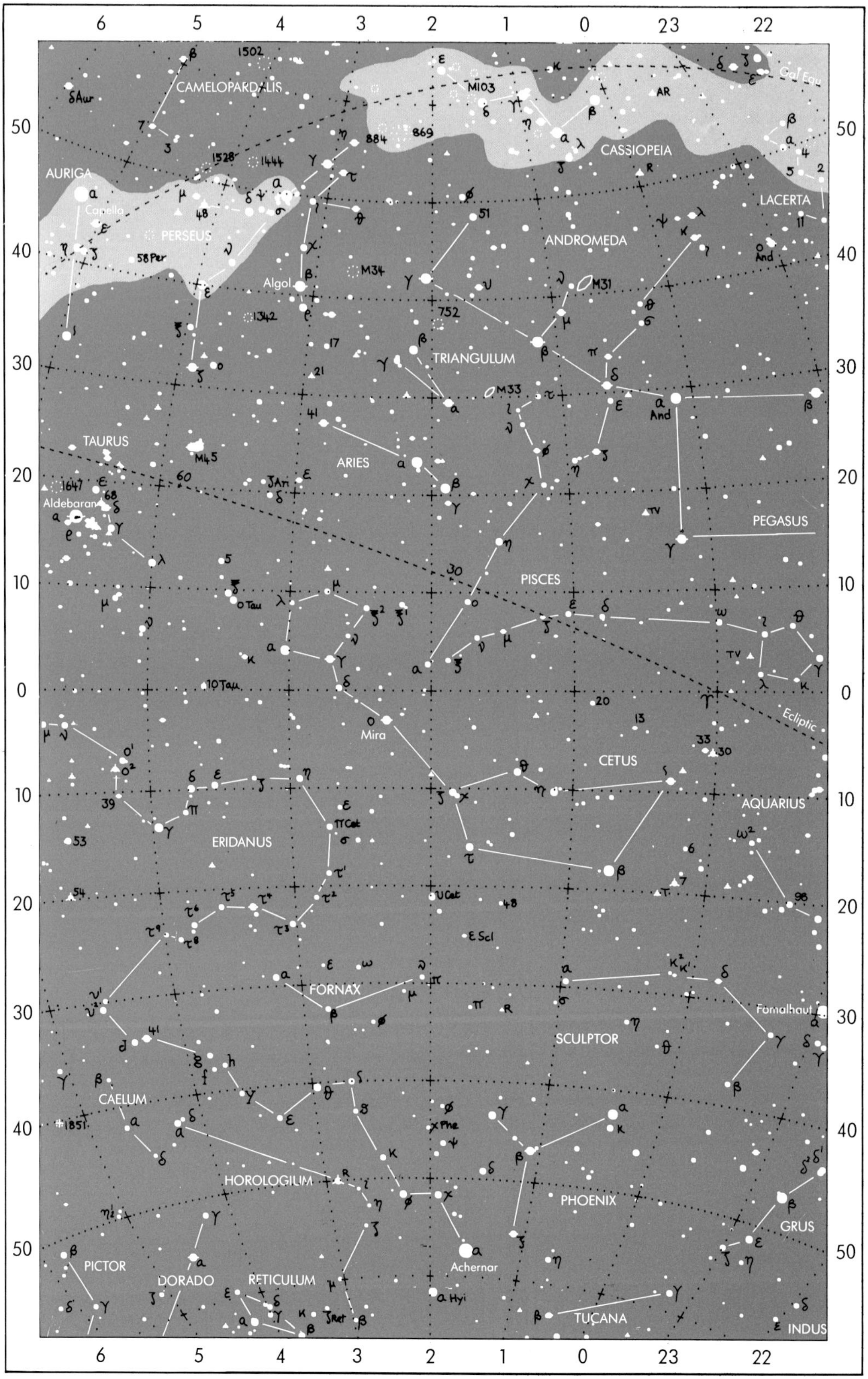
CAMELOPARDALIS
CASSIOPEIA
AURIGA
Capella
PERSEUS
Algol
LACERTA
ANDROMEDA
M31
TRIANGULUM
M33
TAURUS
M45
Aldebaran
ARIES
PEGASUS
PISCES
Ecliptic
Mira
CETUS
AQUARIUS
ERIDANUS
FORNAX
SCULPTOR
Fomalhaut
CAELUM
HOROLOGIUM
PHOENIX
GRUS
PICTOR
DORADO
RETICULUM
Achernar
TUCANA
INDUS

STAR CHART – NOVEMBER

The Triangulum Spiral

The Triangulum spiral galaxy (M33) is one of the brightest members of the Local Group and is best seen in wide-field instruments. Large binoculars are ideal for this object, which is spread out over a comparatively large area of sky and has a low surface brightness. Remember to look for a glow some 1/2° across, similar in size to the full Moon. (Large telescopes enable detail to be seen out to a diameter of a degree or more.)

Finding the area in which the galaxy lies and then slowly sweeping with binoculars will probably give the best chance of locating this object. Some observers have glimpsed M33 with the unaided eye, but experience coupled with exceptionally dark skies are essential for this feat to be emulated.

When Messier discovered this galaxy in 1764 he described it as a 'whitish light of almost even brightness', a description that ties in quite well with the view obtained through small telescopes and binoculars. M33 lies at a distance of around 2.3 million light years, only a little more distant than the Andromeda Galaxy. Large telescopes reveal copious amounts of detail in M33, including individual stars, star clouds and nebulae, all of which are contained within a loose spiral structure emanating from a bright nucleus.

R Trianguli is a Mira-type variable whose magnitude varies between 5.4 and 12.6 over a period of slightly more than 266 days. Telescopes are needed to follow the complete cycle. A short way to the south of Triangulum can be found the small constellation Aries, containing the double star Gamma Arietis, which is visible as a matched pair of white magnitude 4.8 stars 7.8" apart.

Mira

Mira, or Omicron Ceti, is the best-known long-period variable and the first star of its type to be discovered. First catalogued as Omicron Ceti by Bayer in 1603, Mira was not recognized as a variable until several years later. Like the other 4,000-plus long-period variables that have been catalogued, Mira is a red giant star, varying from around 3rd to 10th magnitude and back again over a period of 331 days. However, as with other long-period variables, the values of maximum and minimum are not constant. Mira has reached 2nd magnitude on several occasions, on one of these attaining almost 1st magnitude. Mira is an ideal object of study for the amateur. Observations should be made at least once a week, comparisons being made with the stars shown in the accompanying chart. Because Mira never falls below 9th magnitude throughout its cycle, only moderate optical aid is required, in the form of binoculars or a small telescope.

The double star Gamma Ceti, has pale yellow and blue components which are separated by 2.8", making it an object for telescopes of at least 75 mm (3 inches) aperture.

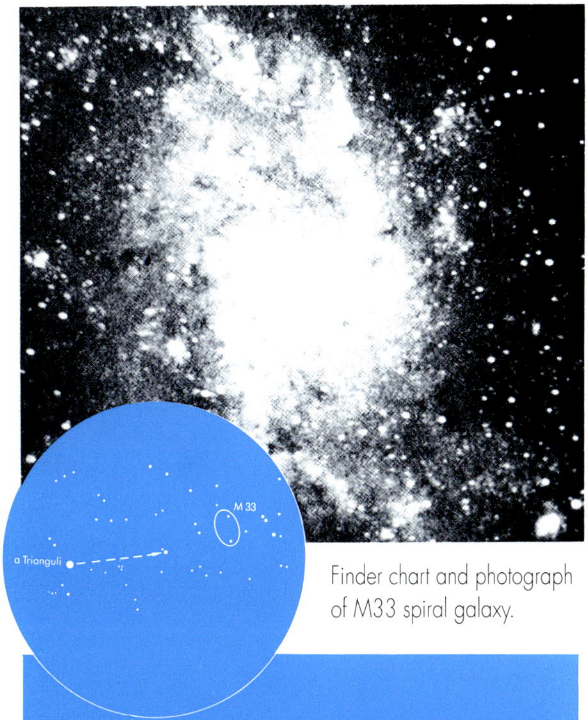

Finder chart and photograph of M33 spiral galaxy.

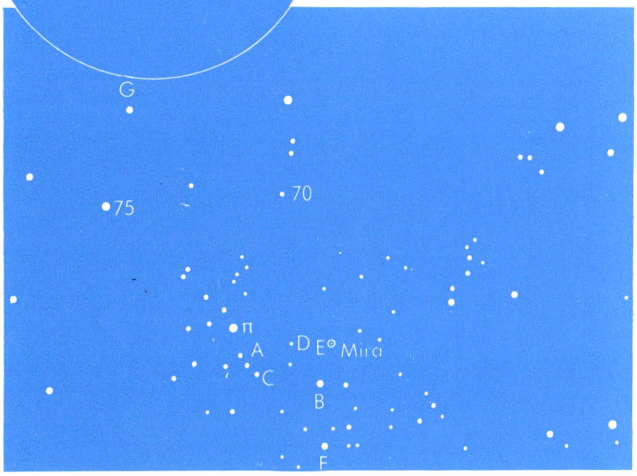

Comparison chart for variable star Mira (Omicron Ceti).

Comparison stars

Beta Ceti	2.00	71 Ceti	6.40
Alpha Ceti	2.52	F	6.49
Mu Ceti	4.26	A	7.19
Nu Ceti	4.87	B	8.00
75 Ceti	5.34	C	8.60
70 Ceti	5.41	D	8.80
G	6.00	E	9.20

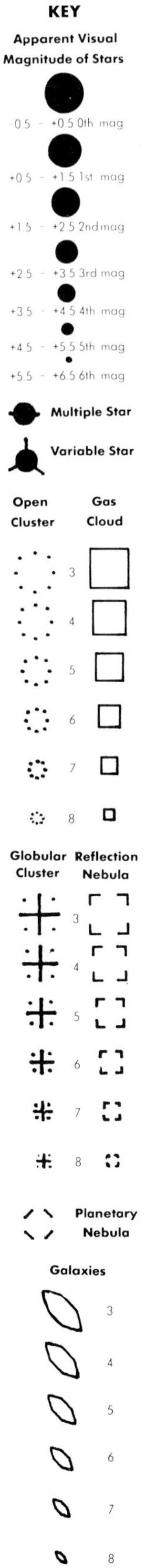
KEY
Apparent Visual Magnitude of Stars
-0.5 - +0.5 0th mag
+0.5 - +1.5 1st mag
+1.5 - +2.5 2nd mag
+2.5 - +3.5 3rd mag
+3.5 - +4.5 4th mag
+4.5 - +5.5 5th mag
+5.5 - +6.5 6th mag
Multiple Star
Variable Star
Open Cluster
Gas Cloud
3
4
5
6
7
8
Globular Cluster
Reflection Nebula
3
4
5
6
7
8
Planetary Nebula
Galaxies
3
4
5
6
7
8

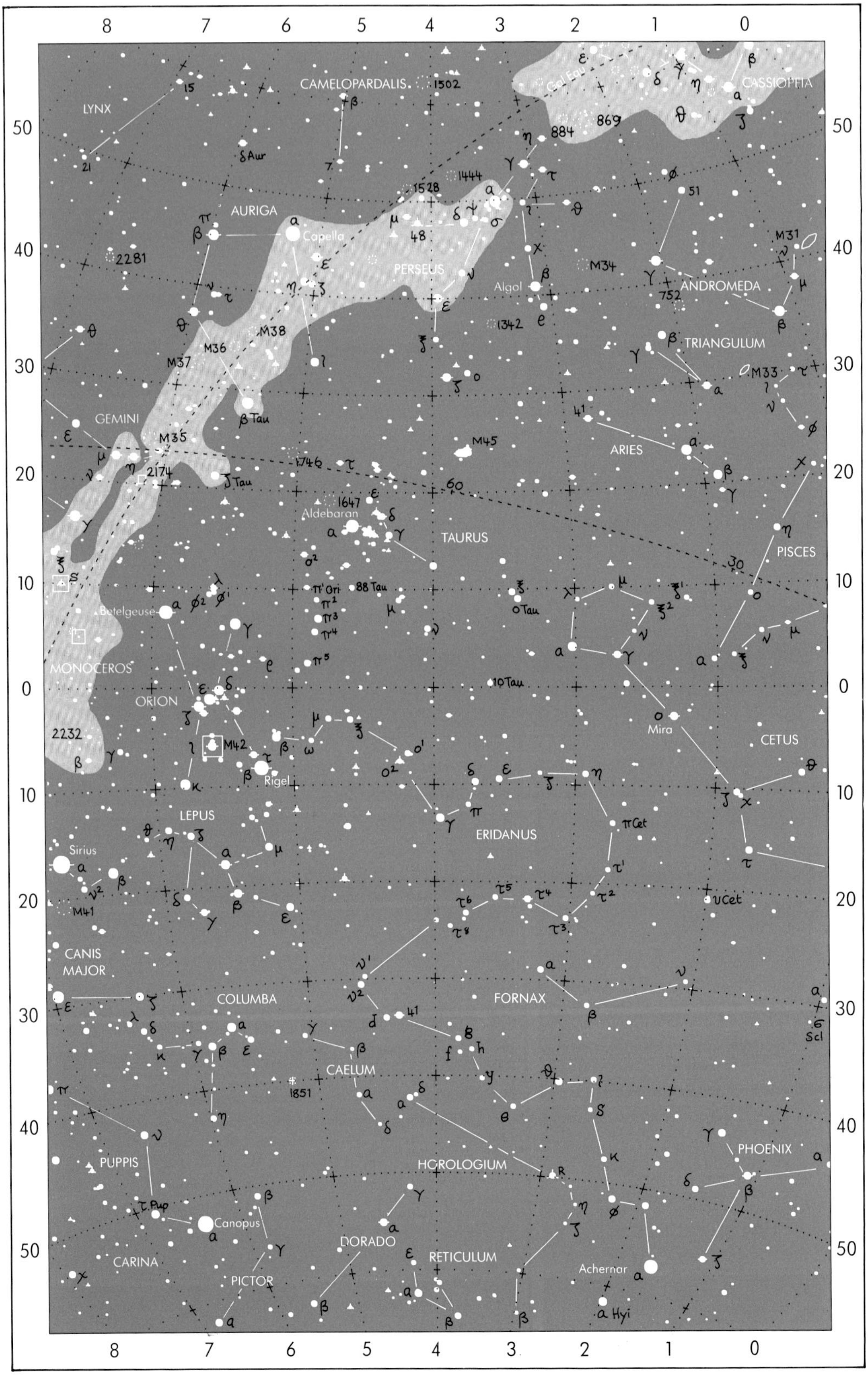
8 7 6 5 4 3 2 1 0
50
40
30
20
10
0
10
20
30
40
50
LYNX
CAMELOPARDALIS
CASSIOPEIA
AURIGA
Capella
PERSEUS
Algol
ANDROMEDA
M31
M33
TRIANGULUM
GEMINI
M35
M36
M37
M38
M34
M45
ARIES
TAURUS
Aldebaran
PISCES
Betelgeuse
MONOCEROS
ORION
M42
Rigel
Mira
CETUS
LEPUS
ERIDANUS
Sirius
M41
CANIS MAJOR
COLUMBA
FORNAX
CAELUM
HOROLOGIUM
PHOENIX
PUPPIS
Canopus
DORADO
RETICULUM
Achernar
CARINA
PICTOR

STAR CHART – DECEMBER

Perseus

The conspicuous inverted Y-shape of Perseus, straddling the pearly luminescence of the Milky Way, is unmistakable. Its brightest star, Algenib, Algenib is a giant star whose light set off on its journey towards us almost six centuries ago. Its true luminosity is more than 4,000 times that of the Sun. Algenib is a white star, although some observers claim to have detected a yellowish tinge.

Algol – the winking demon

Perhaps the most famous star in Perseus is Algol, the name for which is derived from the Arabic, *al ra's al ghul*, meaning 'the Demon's Head'. Legend identifies Algol as the head of Medusa. Algol is one of a class of objects known as eclipsing binaries, and is seen to vary in brightness over a well determined period. This was first measured accurately by the English astronomer John Goodricke in 1782. Goodricke made many observations of Algol and discovered that it faded markedly every two days, 20 hours and 49 minutes. He put forward the suggestion that Algol was in fact a binary star with two components orbiting each other.

One component is actually very much darker and fainter than the other. The plane of their orbits is almost exactly lined up with our position in space and because of this the darker body regularly passes in front of its brighter companion, producing a fall in the overall magnitude of Algol from 2.1 to 3.4. The entire eclipse phase lasts around 10 hours. Algol is 100 light years away..

The Sword Handle or Double Cluster

The Sword Handle or Double Cluster, situated roughly midway between Perseus and Cassiopeia is one of the most visually stunning objects in the night sky. It comprises the two open clusters NGC 869 and NGC 884, the pair being visible to the naked eye as a faint misty patch of light. Binoculars bring out a large number of individual stars. NGC 884, lying between 7,000 and 8,000 light years away, is a little farther than its companion. Each of the two clusters has a diameter of the order of 70 light years, and the total light output from each is equal to around 100,000 times that of the Sun. Both are fairly young objects, NGC 869 being just over six million years old, as compared to the 11.5 million years of its companion.

The Sword Handle lies in the richest region of the Milky Way. There are several clusters near the Sword Handle. Lying at a distance of around 5,000 light years, NGC 744 has a magnitude of 7.9 and contains around 20 stars. NGC 957 is a little brighter at magnitude 7.6 and plays host to around 30 stars. Each of these stellar groupings can be picked up in binoculars as misty patches of light, although care may be needed because you will be trying to spot them against the backdrop of the Milky Way. Trumpler 2, located just to the north of 11 Persei, is also within the grasp of binoculars. Tr2 has a magnitude of 5.9. Telescopes will be required to resolve individual members of this trio of open clusters.

Try also to pick out the bright cluster M34 NGC 1039, situated near Algol and forming a neat triangle with Pi and 12 Persei. At magnitude 5.2, M34 can actually be seen with the naked eye, although an initial search with binoculars is recommended. M34 contains some 60 stars and has a diameter of 18 light years.

Open star clusters, NGC 869 and 884

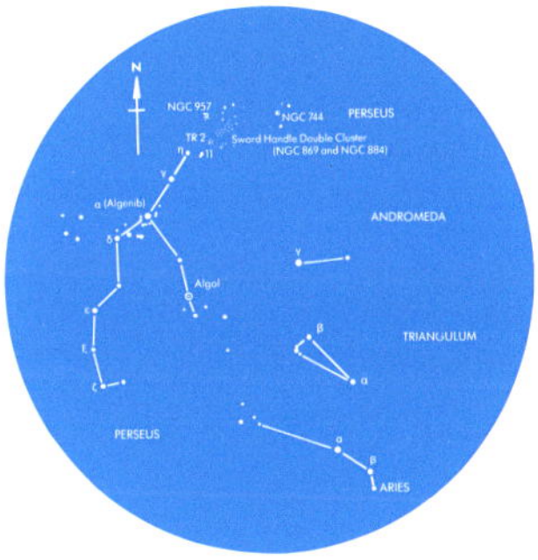

Finder chart for area around Sword Handle or Double Cluster.

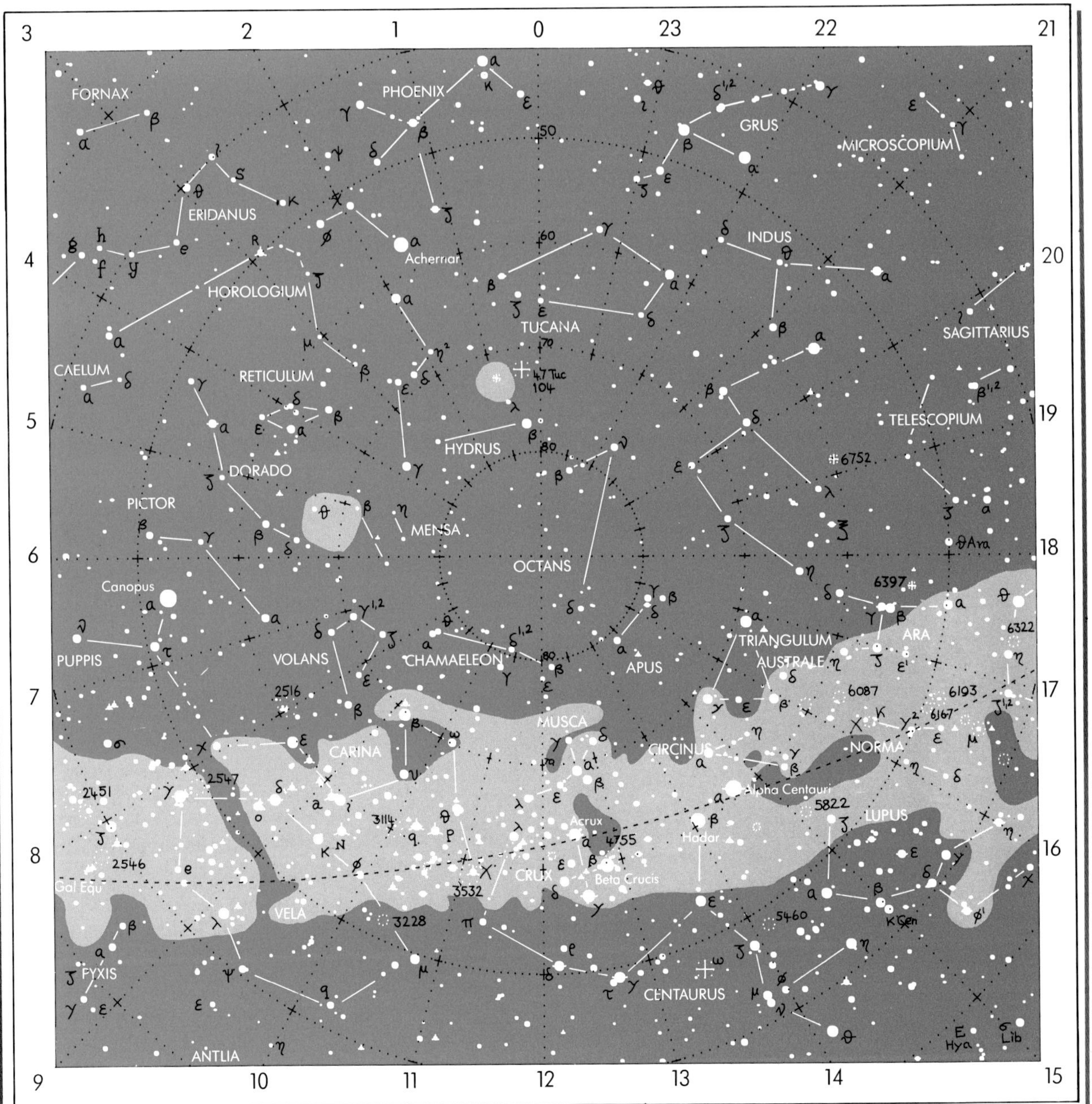
FORNAX
PHOENIX
GRUS
MICROSCOPIUM
ERIDANUS
INDUS
Acherrnar
HOROLOGIUM
TUCANA
SAGITTARIUS
CAELUM
RETICULUM
47 Tuc
104
TELESCOPIUM
HYDRUS
6752
DORADO
PICTOR
MENSA
OCTANS
Canopus
6397
ARA
6322
PUPPIS
VOLANS
CHAMAELEON
APUS
TRIANGULUM AUSTRALE
2516
6087
6193
6167
MUSCA
CARINA
CIRCINUS
NORMA
2547
2451
Alpha Centauri
5822
LUPUS
3114
Acrux
4755
Hadar
2546
CRUX
Beta Crucis
Gal Equ
3532
VELA
3228
5460
PYXIS
CENTAURUS
ANTLIA
Hya
Lib
3
2
1
0
23
22
21
4
5
6
7
8
9
10
11
12
13
14
15
16
17
18
19
20

KEY

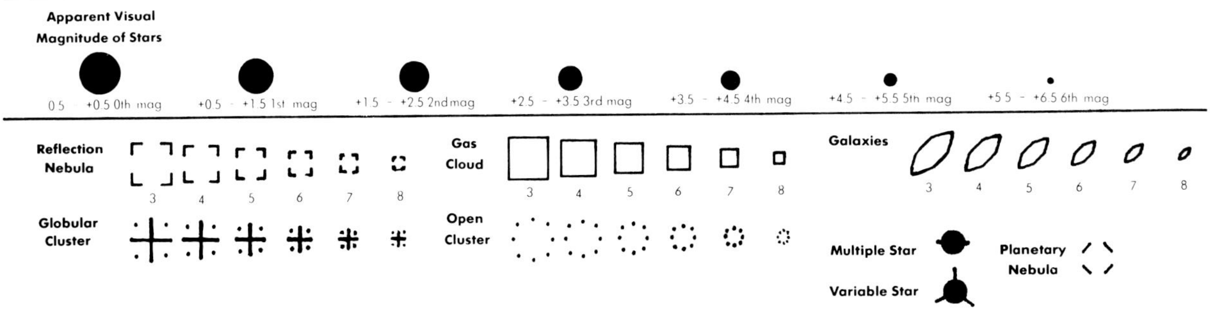
Apparent Visual Magnitude of Stars
0.5 - +0.5 0th mag
+0.5 - +1.5 1st mag
+1.5 - +2.5 2nd mag
+2.5 - +3.5 3rd mag
+3.5 - +4.5 4th mag
+4.5 - +5.5 5th mag
+5.5 - +6.5 6th mag
Reflection Nebula
Gas Cloud
Galaxies
Globular Cluster
Open Cluster
Multiple Star
Planetary Nebula
Variable Star
3 4 5 6 7 8

STAR CHART – SOUTH CIRCUMPOLAR STARS

Polar region

For observers in the northern hemisphere, the position of the north celestial pole is marked by the reasonably bright star Polaris, the Pole Star. However, there is no conspicuous star indicating the position in the sky of the south celestial pole (SCP), the nearest naked-eye star being Sigma Octantis, magnitude 5.46. Seen here is a 90-second exposure taken on 1,600 ISO film, which shows the stars around the SCP as points of light. The small quadrilateral of stars seen just below and to the right of centre consists of Delta, Pi1, Pi2, Rho and Omega Octantis. From here, Sigma Octantis can be located and the position of the SCP plotted. The other photograph is a five-minute exposure of the star trails that are centred on the SCP. The stars in each photograph can be cross-referenced quite easily.

Crux

The photograph shows the area of sky around Crux together with the two pointers Alpha and Beta Centauri (to the left of the picture). The Coal Sack dark nebula is.an unmistakable area of sky apparently devoid of stars, seen to the immediate lower left of Crux and the bright Jewel Box (NGC 4,755) open star cluster is visible as a bright point just to the lower left of Beta Crucis.

The brightest star in Crux is Alpha Crucis, or Acrux, and is the 14th brightest star in the sky. It is also one of the finest double stars in the heavens, with components of magnitudes 1.4 and 1.9 situated 4.4" apart. Both stars can be seen in a 75mm (3-inch) telescope. A third star, of magnitude 4.9, is located 90.1" away.

Forming a small triangle with Iota and Beta Crucis, the Jewel Box open cluster is a fine sight for small to medium-sized telescopes. NGC 4,755 is considered by many to be one of the finest objects of its kind in the sky. Most of the stars within the cluster are bluish-white, although a fine colour contrast is provided by the orange-red Kappa Crucis.

Small Magellanic Cloud

This photograph of the Small Magellanic Cloud (SMC) in Tucana also includes the bright globular clusters NGC 104 to the west (upper right) and NGC 362, seen a little way to the north (upper left). Also known as 47 Tucanae, NGC 104 is one of the best globulars in the sky and is well populated with stars. Binoculars of magnification 10x or over will resolve some of outlying members. NGC 362 is somewhat harder to resolve, telescopes of 75mm (3-inch) aperture being required to bring out individual stars.

These two globular clusters are actually associated with our own galaxy, not the SMC, and simply lie in the same line of sight as seen from Earth. The SMC is situated at a distance of around 200,000 light years; NGC 104 and NGC 362 are foreground objects, situated just 15,000 and 30,000 light years away respectively. However, the SMC does contain numerous open star clusters, some of which are evident in this picture.

Southern Cross Milky Way area

Apus and the South celestial pole trailed

Apus and the South celestial pole

The Small Magellanic Cloud in Tucana

GLOSSARY

ABSOLUTE MAGNITUDE The apparent magnitude a STAR would have if it were to be viewed from a distance of 10 PARSECS (32.6 LIGHT YEARS)

ALT-AZIMUTH MOUNTING A type of mount that allows the telescope to be moved in two axes; vertically (ALTitude) and horizontally (AZIMUTH)

APERTURE The clear (unobstructed) diameter of the mirror or objective in a telescope or binoculars

APHELION The point in its ORBIT around the SUN at which an object is furthest from the SUN

APOGEE The point in its ORBIT around the Earth at which an object is furthest from the Earth

APPARENT MAGNITUDE The apparent visual brightness of a STAR or other celestial object

ASHEN LIGHT A dim glow sometimes seen on the dark side of Venus when it is visible as a thin crescent. The cause is not fully understood

ASTEROID Another name for MINOR PLANET

AURORA Glows seen over the polar regions which occur when energised particles from the SUN react with particles in the Earth's upper atmosphere

AUTUMNAL EQUINOX The point at which the apparent path of the SUN, moving from north to south, crosses the CELESTIAL EQUATOR

BINARY STAR A system of two STARS orbiting each other around their common centre of gravity

BLACK HOLE A region of space around a very small and extremely massive collapsed STAR within which the gravitational field is so intense that not even light can escape

BOLOMETRIC MAGNITUDE A measure of the total energy at all wavelengths received from a STAR

CELESTIAL EQUATOR A projection of the Earth's equator onto the CELESTIAL SPHERE, equidistant from the CELESTIAL POLES and dividing the CELESTIAL SPHERE into two hemispheres

CELESTIAL POLES The points on the CELESTIAL SPHERE directly above the north and south terrestrial poles around which the CELESTIAL SPHERE appears to rotate

CELESTIAL SPHERE The imaginary sphere of STARS surrounding the Earth

CIRCUMPOLAR STARS A STAR which never sets from a given latitude

COMET An object comprised of a mixture of gas, dust and ice and which travels around the SUN in an ORBIT that is usually very eccentric

CONJUNCTION The position at which two objects are lined up with each other (or nearly so) as seen from Earth. Superior conjunction occurs when a PLANET is at the opposite side of the SUN as seen from Earth and inferior conjunction when a PLANET lies between the SUN and Earth

CONSTELLATION One of a total of 88 arbitrary groupings of STARS on the CELESTIAL EQUATOR

DECLINATION The angular distance between a celestial object and the CELESTIAL EQUATOR

DOUBLE STAR Two STARS which appear to be close to each other in the sky. BINARY STARS are physically related while OPTICAL DOUBLES simply lie in the same line of sight as seen from Earth

ECLIPSE The obscuration of one celestial object by another, such as the SUN by the MOON during a solar eclipse

ECLIPTIC The apparent path of the SUN through the sky. The ecliptic passes through a band of CONSTELLATIONS called the Zodiac

ELLIPSE The closed, oval-shaped form obtained by cutting through a cone at an angle to the main axis of the cone. The orbits of the PLANETS around the SUN are all elliptical

EPHEMERIDES Tables showing the predicted positions of celestial objects such as COMETS or PLANETS

EQUATORIAL MOUNT A type of mount that allows a star or other celestial object to be followed across the sky by adjustment in one axis only

EQUINOX The AUTUMNAL and VERNAL equinoxes are the two points at which the ECLIPTIC crosses the CELESTIAL EQUATOR

FIREBALL A very bright METEOR or SHOOTING STAR

GALACTIC CLUSTER Another name for an OPEN CLUSTER

GALAXY A vast collection of STARS, gas and dust measuring many LIGHT YEARS across

GEGENSCHEIN A very faint and elusive glow seen directly opposite the SUN in the sky

GLOBULAR CLUSTER Large, almost spherical collections of old STARS

HERTZSPRUNG-RUSSELL DIAGRAM A diagram in which STARS are plotted according to their spectral types/temperatures and ABSOLUTE MAGNITUDES/luminosities

HUBBLE CLASSIFICATION A system, devised by Edwin Hubble, in which GALAXIES are classified according to their shape

INFERIOR PLANET A planet that travels around the SUN inside the ORBIT of the Earth

LIGHT YEAR The distance which a ray of light would travel in a year, equal to approximately 10,000,000,000,000km (6,000,000,000,000 miles) . This is a standard unit of length used by astronomers

LIMB The edge of the visible disc of an object such as the MOON or a PLANET

LOCAL GROUP A cluster of GALAXIES of which our own is a member

MAGNITUDE See **ABSOLUTE MAGNITUDE, APPARENT MAGNITUDE** and **BOLOMETRIC MAGNITUDE**

MERIDIAN An imaginary line crossing the CELESTIAL SPHERE and which passes through both CELESTIAL POLES and the ZENITH

METEOR A streak of light in the sky seen as the result of the destruction through atmospheric friction of a METEOROID in the Earth's atmosphere

METEORITE A METEOROID which is sufficiently large to at least partially survive the fall through Earth's atmosphere

METEOROID A term applied to particles of interplanetary meteoritic debris

MILKY WAY The faint band of light crossing the sky which is the result of the combined light from the thousands of stars that lie along the main plane of our GALAXY

MINOR PLANET One of a large number of small planetary bodies which orbit the SUN largely between the ORBITS of Mars and Jupiter

MOON The Earth's only natural SATELLITE

NADIR The point on the CELESTIAL SPHERE directly opposite the ZENITH

NEBULA An interstellar cloud of gas and dust

NEUTRON STAR The remnant of a massive STAR which has exploded as a SUPERNOVA

NOVA A STAR which suddenly flares up to many times its original brightness before fading again

OBJECTIVE The main lens or lenses of a telescope or binoculars

OCCULTATION The temporary covering up of one celestial object, such as a STAR, by another, such as the MOON

OPEN CLUSTER A loose and irregularly shaped collection of STARS

OPPOSITION The point in its ORBIT at which a SUPERIOR PLANET is directly opposite the SUN in the sky

ORBIT The closed path of one object around another

PARALLAX The apparent shift of a nearby object against a more distant background when viewed from two points

PARSEC The distance at which a STAR would have a PARALLAX of one second of arc, equal to 3.26 LIGHT YEARS

PENUMBRA The lighter part of a sunspot. Also the area of partial shadow around the main cone of shadow cast by the MOON during a solar ECLIPSE or the Earth during a lunar ECLIPSE

PERIGEE The point in its ORBIT around the Earth at which an object is closest to the Sun

PRECESSION The shift of the CELESTIAL POLE and EQUINOXES caused largely by the gravitational influence of the SUN and MOON on the Earth's equatorial bulge

PRIME MERIDIAN The MERIDIAN that passes through the VERNAL EQUINOX

PULSAR A rapidly-spinning NEUTRON STAR which gives off regular bursts of radiation

QUASAR Extremely remote and highly luminous objects, now believed to be the cores of active GALAXIES

RIGHT ASCENSION The angular distance, measured eastwards, of an object from the VERNAL EQUINOX. Right ascension is expressed in hours, minutes and seconds

SATELLITE A small object orbiting a larger one

SHOOTING STAR The popular name for a METEOR

SIDEREAL PERIOD The time taken for an object to complete one ORBIT around another

SOLAR SYSTEM The collective description given to the system dominated by the SUN and including the PLANETS, MINOR PLANETS, COMETS, planetary SATELLITES and interplanetary debris that travel in ORBITS around the SUN

SOLAR WIND The constant stream of energised particles emitted by the SUN

SOLSTICE The positions in the sky at which the SUN is at its maximum angular distance (DECLINATION) from the CELESTIAL EQUATOR

SPECTROSCOPE An instrument used to split the light from a STAR into its different wavelengths or colours

SPECTROSCOPIC BINARY A BINARY STAR whose components are so close to each other that they cannot be resolved visually and can only be studied through SPECTROSCOPY

SPECTROSCOPY The study of the spectra of astronomical objects

STAR A self-luminous object that shines through the release of energy produced by nuclear reactions at its core

SUPERIOR PLANET A PLANET that travels around the SUN outside the ORBIT of the Earth

SUPERNOVA A huge stellar explosion involving the destruction of a massive STAR and resulting in a sudden and tremendous brightening

SYNODIC PERIOD The interval between successive OPPOSITIONS of a PLANET or SATELLITE

TERMINATOR The division between the light and dark hemispheres of a PLANET or SATELLITE

TRANSIT The passage of an object across the observer's MERIDIAN or of one object across the face of another

UMBRA The darker part of a sunspot. Also the main cone of shadow cast by the MOON during a solar ECLIPSE or the Earth during a lunar ECLIPSE

VARIABLE STAR STARS whose brightness varies, these effects being due either to changes taking place within the STAR itself or the periodic obscuration of one member of a BINARY STAR by another. These systems are called eclipsing binaries

VERNAL EQUINOX The point at which the apparent path of the SUN, moving from south to north, crosses the CELESTIAL EQUATOR

ZENITH The point in the sky directly above the observer

ZODIACAL BAND A faint band of light sometimes seen extending along the ECLIPTIC and joining the ZODIACAL LIGHT and GEGENSCHEIN and due to the scattering of sunlight by interplanetary particles

ZODIACAL LIGHT A faint cone of light sometimes seen reaching up from the horizon, caused by the scattering of sunlight by interplanetary particles

CATALOGUE OF ASTRONOMICAL OBJECTS

THE MESSIER CATALOGUE

MN	NGC	RA hr min	Decl. ° ′	Constellation	Type of object	Popular name
1	1952	05 34.5	+22 01	Taurus	Supernova remnant	Crab Nebula
2	7089	21 33.5	-00 49	Aquarius	Globular cluster	
3	5272	13 42.2	+28 23	Canes Venatici	Globular cluster	
4	6121	16 23.6	-26 32	Scorpius	Globular cluster	
5	5904	15 18.6	+02 05	Serpens	Globular cluster	
6	6405	17 40.1	-32 13	Scorpius	Open cluster	Butterfly Cluster
7	6475	17 53.9	-34 49	Scorpius	Open cluster	
8	6523	18 03.8	-24 23	Sagittarius	Nebula	Lagoon Nebula
9	6333	17 19.2	-18 31	Ophiuchus	Globular cluster	
10	6254	16 57.1	-04 06	Ophiuchus	Globular cluster	
11	6705	18 51.1	-06 16	Scutum	Open cluster	Wild Duck Cluster
12	6218	16 47.2	-01 57	Ophiuchus	Globular cluster	
13	6205	16 41.7	+36 28	Hercules	Globular cluster	Great Hercules Cluster
14	6402	17 37.6	-03 15	Ophiuchus	Globular cluster	
15	7078	21 30.0	+12 10	Pegasus	Globular cluster	
16	6611	18 18.8	-13 47	Serpens	Nebula and associated cluster	Eagle Nebula
17	6618	18 20.8	-16 11	Sagittarius	Nebula	Omega or Horseshoe Nebula
18	6613	18 19.9	-17 08	Sagittarius	Open cluster	
19	6273	17 02.6	-26 16	Ophiuchus	Globular cluster	
20	6514	18 02.6	-23 02	Sagittarius	Nebula	Trifid Nebula
21	6531	18 04.6	-22 30	Sagittarius	Open cluster	
22	6656	18 36.4	-23 54	Sagittarius	Globular cluster	
23	6494	17 56.8	-19 01	Sagittarius	Open cluster	
24	6603	18 18.4	-18 25	Sagittarius	Star-cloud in Milky Way	
25	4725	18 31.6	-19 15	Sagittarius	Open cluster	
26	6694	18 45.2	-09 24	Scutum	Open cluster	
27	6853	19 59.6	+22 43	Vulpecula	Planetary nebula	Dumbbell Nebula
28	6626	18 24.5	-24 52	Sagittarius	Globular cluster	
29	6913	20 23.9	+38 32	Cygnus	Open cluster	
30	7099	21 40.4	-23 11	Capricornus	Globular cluster	
31	224	00 42.7	+41 16	Andromeda	Spiral galaxy	Andromeda Galaxy
32	221	00 42.7	+40 52	Andromeda	Elliptical galaxy (companion to M31)	
33	598	01 33.9	+30 39	Triangulum	Spiral galaxy	Triangulum Spiral
34	1039	02 42.0	+42 47	Perseus	Open cluster	
35	2168	06 08.9	+24 20	Gemini	Open cluster	
36	1960	05 36.1	+34 08	Auriga	Open cluster	
37	2099	05 52.4	+32 33	Auriga	Open cluster	
38	1912	05 28.7	+35 50	Auriga	Open cluster	
39	7092	21 32.2	+48 26	Cygnus	Open cluster	
40	—	12 22.4	+58 05	Ursa Major	Double star Winnecke 4; mags 9.0/9.6; sep. 50″	
41	2287	06 47.0	-20 44	Canis Major	Open cluster	
42	1976	05 35.4	-05 27	Orion	Nebula	Great Orion Nebula
43	1982	05 35.6	-05 16	Orion	Nebula	Part of M42
44	2632	08 40.1	+19 59	Cancer	Open cluster	Praesepe
45	—	03 47.0	+24 07	Taurus	Open cluster	Pleiades
46	2437	07 41.8	-14 49	Puppis	Open cluster	
47	2422	07 36.6	-14 30	Puppis	Open cluster	
48	2548	08 13.8	-05 48	Hydra	Open cluster	
49	4472	12 29.8	+08 00	Virgo	Elliptical galaxy	
50	2323	07 03.2	-08 20	Monoceros	Open cluster	
51	5194	13 29.9	+47 12	Canes Venatici	Spiral galaxy	Whirlpool Galaxy
52	7654	23 24.2	+61 35	Cassiopeia	Open cluster	
53	5024	13 12.9	+18 10	Coma Berenices	Globular cluster	
54	6715	18 55.1	-30 29	Sagittarius	Globular cluster	
55	6809	19 40.0	-30.58	Sagittarius	Globular cluster	

56	6779	19 16.6	+30 11	Lyra	Globular cluster	
57	6720	18 53.6	+33 02	Lyra	Planetary nebula	Ring Nebula
58	4579	12 37.7	+11 49	Virgo	Spiral galaxy	
59	4621	12 42.0	+11 39	Virgo	Elliptical galaxy	
60	4649	12 43.7	+11 33	Virgo	Elliptical galaxy	
61	4303	12 21.9	+04 28	Virgo	Spiral galaxy	
62	6266	17 01.2	-30 07	Ophiuchus	Globular cluster	
63	5055	13 15.8	+42 02	Canes Venatici	Spiral galaxy	
64	4826	12 56.7	+21 41	Coma Berenices	Spiral galaxy	Black Eye Galaxy
65	3623	11 18.9	+13 05	Leo	Spiral galaxy	
66	3627	11 20.2	+12 59	Leo	Spiral galaxy	
67	2682	08 50.4	+11 49	Cancer	Open cluster	
68	4590	12 39.5	-26 45	Hydra	Globular cluster	
69	6637	18 31.4	-32 21	Sagittarius	Globular cluster	
70	6681	18 43.2	-32.18	Sagittarius	Globular cluster	
71	6838	19 53.8	+18 47	Sagitta	Globular cluster	
72	6981	20 53.5	-12 32	Aquarius	Globular cluster	
73	6994	20 58.9	-12 38	Aquarius	Asterism of four faint stars	
74	628	01 36.7	+15.47	Pisces	Spiral galaxy	
75	6864	20 06.1	-21 55	Sagittarius	Globular galaxy	
76	650	01 42.4	+51 34	Perseus	Planetary nebula	Little Dumbbell
77	1068	02 42.7	-00 01	Cetus	Spiral galaxy	
78	2068	05 46.7	+00 03	Orion	Nebula	
79	1904	05 24.5	-24 33	Lepus	Globular cluster	
80	6093	16 17.0	-22 59	Scorpius	Globular cluster	
81	3031	09 55.6	+69 04	Ursa Major	Spiral galaxy	
82	3034	09 55.8	+69 41	Ursa Major	Irregular galaxy	
83	5236	13 37.0	-29 52	Hydra	Spiral galaxy	
84	4374	12 25.1	+12 53	Virgo	Spiral galaxy	
85	4382	12 25.4	+18 11	Coma Berenices	Spiral galaxy	
86	4406	12 26.2	+12 57	Virgo	Elliptical galaxy	
87	4486	12 30.8	+12 24	Virgo	Elliptical galaxy	
88	4501	12 32.0	+14 25	Coma Berenices	Spiral galaxy	
89	4552	12 35.7	+12 33	Virgo	Elliptical galaxy	
90	4569	12 36.8	+13 10	Virgo	Spiral galaxy	
91	4548	12 35.4	+14 30	Coma Berenices	Spiral galaxy	
92	6341	17 17.1	+43 08	Hercules	Globular cluster	
93	2447	07 44.6	-23 52	Puppis	Open cluster	
94	4736	12 50.9	+41 07	Canes Venatici	Spiral galaxy	
95	3351	10 44.0	+11 42	Leo	Barred spiral galaxy	
96	3368	10 46.8	+11 49	Leo	Spiral galaxy	
97	3587	11 14.8	+55 01	Ursa Major	Planetary nebula	Owl Nebula
98	4192	12 13.8	+14 54	Coma Berenices	Spiral galaxy	
99	4254	12 18.8	+ 14 25	Coma Berenices	Spiral galaxy	
100	4321	12 22.9	+15 49	Coma Berenices	Spiral galaxy	
101	5457	14 03.2	+54 21	Ursa Major	Spiral galaxy	Pinwheel Galaxy
102					Duplicated observation of M101	
103	581	01 33.2	+60 42	Cassiopeia	Open cluster	
104	4594	12 40.0	-11 37	Virgo	Spiral galaxy	Sombrero Hat Galaxy
105	3379	10 47.8	+12 35	Leo	Elliptical galaxy	
106	4258	12 19.0	+47 18	Ursa Major	Spiral galaxy	
107	6171	16 32.5	-13 03	Ophiuchus	Globular cluster	
108	3556	11 11.5	+55 40	Ursa Major	Spiral galaxy	
109	3992	11 57.6	+53 23	Ursa Major	Spiral galaxy	
110	205	00 40.4	+41 41	Andromeda	Elliptical galaxy (companion to M31)	

The last object in Messier's original catalogue was M103: the remaining objects were all added in more recent times. M104 was included by Camille Flammarion in 1921 after he discovered a note about the object in Messier's original observing notes. Then came M105, M106 and M107, these additions having been suggested by Helen Sawyer Hogg. M108 and M109 were added by Owen Gingerich, after which Kenneth Glyn Johns rounded off the Catalogue with M110, an object that was actually observed by Messier in 1773 and included on his drawing of M31 published in 1807.

TELESCOPE DOUBLES

Stars	RA hr min	Dec ° ′	Mags	Sepn. ″	PA °	Remarks
Beta^{1} Tucanae	00 31.5	−62 58	4.5/ 4.0	2.2	149	
Beta^{2} Tucanae	00 31.5	−62 58	4.9/ 5.7			Binary 44.43 years
Eta Cassiopeiae	00 49.1	+57 49	3.5/ 7.2	12.0	310	Binary 480 years; great contrast
Beta Phoenicis	01 06.1	−46 43	4.0/ 4.2	1.4	346	
Zeta Piscium	01 13.7	+07 35	4.2/ 5.3	23.6	063	Yellow and orange
Gamma Arietis	01 53.5	+19 18	4.8/ 4.8	7.8	000	Matched pair of white stars; easy
Alpha Piscium	02 02.0	+02 46	4.2/ 5.1	1.9	279	Binary 933 years
Gamma Andromedae	02 03.9	+42 20	3.0/ 5.0	9.4	064	Yellow and blue
Alpha Ursae Minoris	02 31.8	+89 16	2.0/ 9.0	18.4	218	Yellowish and blue-white
Gamma Ceti	02 43.3	+03 14	3.7/ 6.4	2.8	294	Pale yellow and bluish; difficult
Eta Persei	02 50.7	+55 54	3.9/ 8.6	28.3	300	Yellowish-white and blue; nice field
Sigma 331 Persei	03 00.9	+52 51	5.5/ 6.5	12.1	085	Gold and orangish
32 Eridani	03 54.3	−02 57	5.0/ 6.0	6.8	347	Gold and greenish blue
1 Camelopardalis	04 32.0	+53 55	5.0/ 6.0	10.3	308	White and bluish
Beta Orionis	05 14.5	−08 12	0.1/ 6.8	9.5	202	Rigel; blue and white; difficult
118 Tauri	05 29.3	+25 09	6.0/ 6.5	4.8	204	White and red
Lambda Orionis	05 35.1	+09 56	4.0/ 6.0	4.4	043	White and orangish
Theta^{1} Orionis	05 35.3	−05 23	5.4/ 6.3	9.0	032	The Trapezium; four components;
			v(6.7/ 7.7)			very pretty
			v(8.0/ 8.7)			
Iota Orionis	05 35.4	−05 55	2.8/ 6.9	11.3	141	White and blue
Sigma Orionis	05 38.7	−02 36	3.9/ 6.5	42.0	061	Two main components 170 years;
			7.5	12.9	084	Triple; orangish, blue and white
Gamma Leporis	05 44.5	−22 27	3.6/ 6.2	96.3	350	Yellowish and blue
Beta Monocerotis	06 28.8	−07 02	4.7/ 5.2	7.3	132	All yellowish;
			6.1	10.0	124	nice triple
12 Lyncis	06 46.2	+59 27	5.4/ 6.0	8.5	308	Binary 699 years; bluish white and orange red
Gamma^{2} Volantis	07 08.8	−70 30	4.0/ 5.9	13.6	300	Slow binary; superb sight
Delta Geminorum	07 20.1	+21 59	3.5/ 8.2			Binary 1,200 years
19 Lyncis	07 22.9	+55 17	5.6/ 6.5	14.8	315	Bluish white and orange
Sigma Puppis	07 29.2	−43 18	3.3/ 9.4	22.3	074	
Alpha Geminorum	07 34.6	+31 53	1.9/ 2.9	2.7	085	Castor; binary 511(?) years
			8.8	72.5	164	
Zeta Pyxidis	08 39.7	−29 34	4.9/ 9.1	52.4	061	
Iota^{1} Cancri	08 46.7	+28 46	4.2/ 6.6	30.5	307	Orange and blue; nice contrast
Gamma Leois	10 20.0	+19 51	2.5/ 3.5	4.3	122	Algieba; binary 619 years
54 Leonis	10 55.6	+24 45	4.5/ 6.3	6.5	110	Greenish white and blue
Alpha Crucis	12 26.6	−63 06	1.4/ 1.9	4.4	115	Acrux
			4.9	90.1	202	
Delta Corvi	12 29.9	−16 31	3.0/ 9.2	24.2	214	Yellow and reddish purple
24 Comae Berenicis	12 35.1	+18 23	5.2/ 6.7	20.3	271	Orange and blue-white
Gamma Virginis	12 41.7	−01 27	3.5/ 3.5			A rich binary 171.4 years; both whitish
Alpha Canum Venaticorum	12 56.0	+38 19	2.9/ 5.5	19.4	229	Cor Caroll; both yellowish white
Theta Virginis	13 09.9	−05 32	4.4/ 9.4	7.1	343	Yellow and red
Zeta Ursae Majoris	13 23.9	+54 56	2.3/ 4.0	14.4	152	Mizar; white and greenish white
Kappa Boötis	14 13.5	+51 47	4.6/ 4.6	13.4	236	White and blue
Alpha Centauri	14 39.6	−60 50	0.0/ 1.2			Binary 79.9 years Proxima Centauri (mag 10.7) nearby
Pi Boötis	14 40.7	+16 25	4.9/ 5.8	5.6	108	Blue and orange
Alpha Circini	14 42.5	−64 59	3.2/ 8.6	15.7	232	
Epsilon Boötis	14 45.0	+27 04	2.5/ 4.9	2.8	339	Izar; yellow and blue-green
Xi Boötis	14 51.4	+19 06	4.7/ 7.0	7.2	332	Binary 151.5 years; yellow and reddish purple
Delta Boötis	15 15.5	+33 19	3.5/ 8.7	104.9	079	
Delta Serpentis	15 34.8	+10 32	4.2/ 5.2	4.4	177	Binary 3,168 years; both white
Zeta Coronae Borealis	15 39.4	+36 38	5.1/ 6.0	6.3	305	Blue-white and greenish
Beta Scorpii	16 05.4	−19 48	2.6/ 4.9	13.6	021	Primary has a 10th-mag. companion
Nu Scorpii	16 12.0	−19 28	4.3/ 6.8	0.9	003	Binary 45.7 years
			6.4	41.1	337	
Sigma Coronae Borealis	16 14.7	+33 52	5.6/ 6.6	7.0	234	Binary 1,000 years
Sigma Scorpii	16 21.2	−25 36	2.9/ 8.5	20.0	273	
Alpha Scorpii	16 29.4	−26 26	1.2/ 5.4	2.9	275	Antares; binary 878 years; red and green

Zeta Herculis	16 41.3	+31 36	2.9/ 5.5			Binary 34.5 years
Mu Draconis	17 05.3	+54 28	5.7/ 5.7			Binary 482 years; both white
Alpha Herculis	17 14.6	+14 23	var/ 5.4	4.7	107	Rasalgethi; binary 3,600 years
36 Ophiuchi	17 15.3	-26 36	5.1/ 5.1	4.7	150	Binary 548.7 years
Psi Draconis	17 41.9	+72 09	4.9/ 6.1	30.3	015	Yellow and purple
41 Draconis	18 00.2	+80 00	5.7/ 6.1	19.3	232	
95 Herculis	18 01.5	+21 36	5.0/ 5.1	6.3	258	Green and red
100 Herculis	18 07.8	+26 06	5.9/ 5.9	14.2	183	
Lambda Coronae Australis	18 43.8	−38 19	5.1/ 9.7	29.2	214	
Epsilon^1 Lyrae	18 44.3	+39 40	5.0/ 6.1	2.6	357	Famous 'double-double'; separation
Epsilon ^{2} Lyrae			5.2/ 5.5	2.3	094	207.7'between 1 and 2; Epsilon^1 period
						1,165 years; Episilon^2 period 585 years
Zeta^2 Lyrae	18 44.8	+37 36	4.3/ 5.9	43.7	150	Topaz and green
Beta Lyrae	18 50.1	+33 22	var/ 8.6	45.7	149	
Psi Cygni	19 55.6	+52 26	4.9/ 7.4	3.2	178	
Alpha^1 Capricorni	20 17.6	−12 30	4.2/13.7	44.3	182	
			9.2	45.4	221	
Alpha^2 Capricorni	20 18.1	−12 33	3.6/11.0	6.6	172	
			9.3	154.6	156	
			11.3	1.2	240	
Gamma Delphini	20 46.7	+16 07	4.0/ 5.0	10.1	268	Yellow and pale green
Beta Cephei	21 28.7	+70 34	3.2/ 7.9	13.3	249	White and blue
Xi Cephei	22 03.8	+64 38	4.4/ 6.5	7.7	277	Binary 3,800 years; both blue
Zeta Aquarii	22 28.8	−00 01	4.3/ 4.5			Binary 856 years; both white
Beta Piscis Austrini	22 31.5	−32 21	4.4/ 7.9	30.3	172	Yellowish white and bluish
107 Aquarii	23 46.0	−18 41	5.7/ 6.7	6.6	136	White and blue

VARIABLE STARS

Star	RA hr mn	Dec. °	Mag. range	Period (days)	Type
S Sculptoris	00 15.4	−32 03	5.5 -13.6	365.3	Mira
R Andromedae	00 24.0	+38 35	5.8 -14.9	409.3	Mira
Gamma Cassiopeiae	00 56.7	+60.43	1.6 - 3.0	—	Gamma Cassiopeiae
Zeta Phoenicis	01 08.4	−55 15	3.9 - 4.4	1.67	Algol
S Cassiopeiae	01 19.7	+72 37	7.9 -16.1	612.43	Mira
Omicron Ceti	02 19.3	−02 59	2.0 -10.1	331.96	Mira
R Trianguli	02 37.0	+34 16	5.4 -12.6	266.48	Mira
Beta Persei	03 08.2	+40 57	2.1 - 3.4	2.87	Algol
Lambda Tauri	04 00.7	+12 29	3.3 - 3.8	3.95	Algol
VW Hydri	04 09.1	−71 18	8.4 -14.4	100	Dwarf nova
R Leporis	04 59.6	−14 48	5.5 -11.7	432.13	Mira
Epsilon Aurigae	05 02.0	+43 49	2.9 - 3.8	9892	Eclipsing
Beta Doradus	05 33.6	−62 29	3.5 - 4.1	9.84	Cepheid
Alpha Orionis	05 55.2	+07 24	0.1 - 0.9	2110	Semiregular
U Orionis	05 55.8	+20 10	4.8 -12.6	372.4	Mira
Eta Geminorum	06 14.9	+22 30	3.2 - 3.9	233	Semiregular
S Monocerotis	06 41.0	+09 54	4.6 - 4.7	—	Irregular
Zeta Geminorum	07 04.1	+20 34	3.7 - 4.2	10.15	Cepheid
R Geminorum	07 07.4	+22 42	6.0 -14.0	369.8	Mira
R Canis Majoris	07 19.5	−16 24	5.7 - 6.3	1.14	Algol
X Cancri	08 55.4	+17 14	5.6 - 7.5	195.0	Semiregular
R Carinae	09 32.2	−62 47	3.9 -10.5	308.7	Mira
ZZ Carinae	09 45.2	−62 30	3.3 - 4.2	35.54	Cepheid
R Leonis	09 47.6	+11 26	4.4 -11.3	312.4	Mira
S Carinae	10 09.4	−61 33	4.5 - 9.9	149.5	Mira
U Antliae	10 35.2	−39 34	5.7 - 6.8	—	Irregular
U Hydrae	10 37.6	−13 23	4.8 - 5.8	450.0	Semiregular
Eta Carinae	10 45.1	−59 41	−0.8 - 7.9	—	S Doradus
X Centauri	11 49.2	−41 45	7.0 -13.8	315.1	Mira
S Centauri	12 24.6	−49 26	6.0 - 7.0	65.0	Semiregular
SS Virginis	12 25.3	+00 48	6.0 - 9.6	354.7	Mira
R Virginis	12 38.5	+06 59	6.0 -12.1	145.6	Mira
R Hydrae	13 29.7	−23 17	3.0 -11.0	389.6	Mira
T Centauri	13 41.8	−33 36	5.5 - 9.0	60.0	Semiregular

R Centauri	14 16.6	−59.55	5.3 -11.8	546.2	Mira
W Boötis	14 43.4	+26 32	4.7 - 5.4	450.0	Semiregular
Delta Librae	15 01.0	−08 31	4.9 - 5.9	2.33	Algol
R Coronae Borealis	15 48.6	+28 09	5.7 -14.8	—	R Coronae
R Serpentis	15 50.7	+15 08	5.2 -14.4	356.4	Mira
R Arae	16 39.7	−57 00	6.0 - 6.9	4.43	Algol
Alpha Herculis	17 14.6	+14 23	3.0 - 4.0	—	Semiregular
RS Ophiuchi	17 50.2	−06 43	5.3 -12.3	—	Recurrent nova
X Ophiuchi	18 38.3	+08 50	5.9 - 9.2	334.4	Mira
R Scuti	18 47.5	−05 42	4.45- 8.2	140.0	RV Tauri
Beta Lyrae	18 50.1	+33 22	3.3 - 4.3	12.94	Beta Lyrae
R Lyrae	18 55.3	+43 57	3.9 - 5.0	46.0	Semiregular
Kappa Pavonis	18 56.9	−67 14	3.9 - 4.7	9.1	W Virginis
R Aquilae	19 06.4	+08 14	5.5 -12.0	284.2	Mira
RY Sagittarii	19 16.5	−33 31	6.0 -15.0	—	R Coronae
RR Lyrae	19 25.5	+42 47	7.1 - 8.1	0.57	RR Lyrae
Chi Cygni	19 50.6	+32 55	3.3 -14.2	406.9	Mira
Eta Aquilae	19 52.5	−01 00	3.5 - 4.4	7.18	Cepheid
RR Sagittarii	19 55.9	−29 11	5.9 -14.0	334.6	Mira
U Cygni	20 19.6	+47 54	5.6 -12.1	462.4	Mira
EU Delphini	20 37.9	+18 16	5.8 - 6.9	59.5	Semiregular
W Cygni	21 36.0	+45 22	5.0 - 7.6	126.0	Semiregular
SS Cygni	21 42.7	+43 35	8.2 -12.4	50.0	Dwarf nova
Mu Cephei	21 43.5	+58 47	3.4 - 5.1	730.0	Semiregular
S Gruis	22 26.1	−48 26	6.0 -15.0	401.4	Mira
Delta Cephei	22 29.2	+58 25	3.5 - 4.4	5.37	Cepheid
Beta Pegasi	23 03.8	+ 28 05	2.3 - 2.8	—	Irregular
R Cassiopeiae	23 58.4	+51 24	4.7 -13.5	430.4	Mira

NAKED-EYE DOUBLE STARS

Stars	Mags	Sepn. ″	Remarks
Theta^1 and Theta^2 Tauri	3.5/4.0	337	In Hyades
Alcor and Mizar	4.0/2.1	708	In the Plough 'Handle'
Epsilon^1 and Epsilon^2 Lyrae	4.5/4.5	208	Famous 'Double-Double'; very difficult (see below)
Alpha^1 and Alpha^2 Capricorni	3.6/4.2	376	Easy; both components double again (see below)

BINOCULAR DOUBLES

Stars	RA hr min	Dec ° ′	Mags	Sepn. ″	PA °	Remarks
Beta^1 and Beta^2 Tucanae	00 31.5	−62 58	4.4/4.5	27.1	170	Lovely sight; both components double (see below)
Delta Orionis	05 32.0	−00 18	2.2/6.7	52.8	359	Very difficult
Theta^2 Orionis	05 35.4	−05 25	5.2/6.5	52.5	92	White pair
20 Geminorum	06 32.3	+17 47	6.0/6.9	20.0	210	Very difficult
Gamma Velorum	08 09.5	−47 20	1.9/4.2	41.2	220	Difficult
Tau Leonis	11 27.9	+02 51	4.1/8.0	91.1	176	Difficult
Nu Scorpii	16 12.0	−19 28	4.0/6.4	41.1	337	Difficult; primary double
16 and 17 Draconis			5.0/5.0	90.3		Very easy
Nu Draconis	17 32.2	+55 11	4.6/4.6	61.9	312	Easy; both white
Zeta Lyrae	18 44.8	+37 36	4.2/5.5	43.7	150	Topaz and green
Theta Serpentis	18 56.2	+04 12	4.5/5.0	22.3	104	Very difficult; both yellowish-white
Beta Cygni	19 30.7	+27 58	3.0/5.3	34.4	54	Yellow and blue
Omicron^1 and ^{2} and 32 Cygni			3.8/4.0/4.8			Pretty trio in a nice field
61 Cygni	21 06.9	+38 45	5.3/5.9	28.4	148	Both yellowish-orange
Delta Cephei	22 29.2	+58 25	var/6.3	40.7	191	Orange and blue

INDEX

ACKNOWLEDGEMENTS

Quarto and the author would like to thank the following for their help with this publication and for permission to reproduce copyright material. *Abbreviations used: SPL= Science Photo Library: JPL= Jet Propulsion Library*
p2 JPL; p6 Robin Scagell; p7 Anglo-Australian Telescope Board; p8 Dr Jean Lorre/SPL; p10 NASA/SPL; p11 Dr Carey Fuller/SPL; p12 (top) NASA/SPL, (bottom) FOTOKHRONIKA/TASS; p13 (top left) NASA/SPL, (top right) NASA/SPL; p15 NASA/SPL; p17 John Sanford/SPL; p18 (top) NASA/SPL, (centre) NASA/SPL, (bottom) Dr Jean Lorre/SPL; p19 (top) NASA/SPL, (bottom) Dr Jean Lorre/SPL; p20 Royal Astronomical Society; p21 (top) Royal Astronomical Society, (bottom) Yerkes Observatory; p22 (top) NASA/JPL/SPL, (bottom) NASA/SPL; p23 NASA/SPL; p24 NASA/SPL; p25 NASA/SPL; p26 (top) NASA, (bottom) NASA/SPL; p27 (top) Lick Observatory/SPL, (bottom) NASA/SPL; p28 (centre) H&R Lines/Millom/SPL, (bottom) photo ESA; p29 photo ESA; p30 SPL; p31 John Sanford/SPL; p34 (top) Simon Fraser/SPL, (bottom) Jack Finch/SPL; p35 John Sanford/SPL; p36 Robin Scagell; p37 (left) Ronald Royer/SPL, (right) Chris Floyd; p38 (left) Anglo-Australian Telescope Board, (right) Chris Floyd; p39 John Sandford/SPL; p40 (bottom) Robin Scagell/SPL, (top) Starlink/Rutherford Appleton Lab/SPL; p41 Chris Floyd; p42 Doug Johnson/SPL; p43 Physics Dept, Imperial College/SPL; p45 (top) Royal Astronomical Society Library, (bottom) John Sandford/SPL; p46 Yerkes Observatory; p49 (left) John Sanford/SPL, (right) Robin Scagell; p50 Robin Scagell; p52 Anglo-Australian Telescope Board; p53 Brian Jones; p54 Anglo-Australian Telescope Board; p55 (top) European Southern Observatory/Brian Jones, (bottom) Anglo-Australian Telescope Board; p57 Roland Royer/SPL; p58 Harvard College Observatory/SPL; p59 (top) Dr Steve Gull/SPL, (bottom) Starlink/Rutherford Appleton Lab/SPL; p60 Fred Espenak/SPL; p61 (top) Royal Greenwich Observatory/SPL, (bottom) Royal Observatory, Edinburgh/SPL; p62 AT&T Archives; p63 Jodrell Bank; p84 Robin Scagell; p85 Robin Scagell; p88/89 Richard Baum; p90/91 D.L. Graham; p96 D.L. Graham; p98 John Sanford/SPL; p99 Bernard Abrams; p100 John Sandford/SPL; p101 John Sandford/SPL, Bernard Abrams; p103 Robin Scagell; p110 Royer/SPL; p111 Fred Espenak /SPL; p114 Robin Scagell; p116 Bernard Abrams; p117 Chris Floyd, Robin Scagell; p118 Brian Jones; p119 Variable Star Section; p121 US Naval Observatory/SPL; p125 John Fletcher; p127 Brian Jones, Derek Aspinall; p129 Bernard Abrams; p131 David Graham, Chris Floyd; p133 Chris Floyd, U.S. Naval Observatory/SPL; p135 Chris Floyd, Bernard Abrams; p137 Chris Floyd; p139 Robin Sagell; p141 Derek Aspinall, Chris Floyd; p143 Chris Floyd; p145 Rev Ronald Royer/SPL, John Fletcher; p144 Chris Floyd.
Every effort has been made to trace and acknowledge all copyright holders. Quarto would like to apologise if any omissions have been made.